Don Jordan is a writer and filmmaker who has won, among other awards, two Blue Ribbons at the New York Film and Television ~~. He has worked widely in television current affairs, ~~entaries and drama. He co-wrote and co-produced the award-~~ing feature film, *Love is the Devil*, about the painter Francis Bacon.

Michael Walsh is a writer and filmmaker. After twelve years as a reporter/presenter on the ITV series *World in Action*, he worked on many other programmes, most recently a documentary on the Holocaust. His programmes have won six national and international awards.

Together they have written three books, including *White Cargo*, acclaimed by Nobel Laureate Toni Morrison as 'an extraordinary book'

Also by Don Jordan and Michael Walsh:

Van Hoogstraten: Blood and Retribution

White Cargo: The Forgotten History of
Britain's White Slaves in America

THE KING'S REVENGE

Charles II and
the Greatest Manhunt
in British History

DON JORDAN
AND MICHAEL WALSH

ABACUS

First published in Great Britain in 2012 by Little, Brown
This paperback edition published in 2013 by Abacus

A CIP catalogue record for this book
is available from the British Library.

ISBN 978-0-349-12376-9

Typeset in Electra by M Rules
Printed and bound in Great Britain by
Clays Ltd, St Ives plc

Papers used by Little, Brown are from well-managed forests
and other responsible sources.

MIX
Paper from
responsible sources
FSC
www.fsc.org   FSC® C104740

Abacus
An imprint of
Little, Brown Book Group
100 Victoria Embankment
London EC4Y 0DY

An Hachette UK Company
www.hachette.co.uk

www.littlebrown.co.uk

To Dian and to Eithne

CONTENTS

THE KING'S REVENGE

PREFACE

The fate of the men who dared to sit in judgment upon King Charles I has intrigued us ever since we began work on our previous book, *White Cargo*. During our research we came across a curious folk tale from New England which made us wonder if we had spotted the tip of a more significant story. This is how we came to write *The King's Revenge*.

The folk tale, dating from the early English settlements in Massachusetts, was of the Angel of Hadley. The story goes that the remote pioneer village of Hadley was attacked by an overwhelming force of Algonquin warriors and faced certain annihilation. When all seemed lost, a mysterious figure appeared with flowing white hair and beard, brandishing a sword. Exhibiting considerable military prowess, the stranger marshalled the townsfolk into an effective fighting force. The enemy was repelled and the town saved. As soon as the battle was over, the stranger disappeared as quickly as he had come. Afterwards, the God-fearing people of Hadley put their rescue down to an avenging angel sent by God.

Today, there is debate about whether the attack took place or not. But what interested us was that there existed a real-life candidate for the angel – a former Cromwellian general by the name of William Goffe, who had sat as a judge in the court that sentenced King Charles I to death. Following Charles II's ascension to the throne, the general became a wanted man and fled to Massachusetts. British troops were dispatched to find him and bring him back to face trial for treason. Unknown to the people of Hadley, their Puritan pastor hid the runaway in the attic of his house for many years. If the attack really occurred, then the former Civil War officer would have been the ideal candidate to lead the townsfolk in battle.

This story led us to wonder about all sixty-nine men who had determined the execution of King Charles I. How many, like the soldier in Massachusetts, had fled? Where did they run to and were they pursued? How many stayed in England to state their case and face the probability of death? How many were executed? How many were imprisoned? These were among the questions thrown up by the tale of the avenging angel. We decided to follow our lead and research the fate of the men who became known simply as the regicides. We discovered that their stories had never been gathered together into one coherent whole.

Several months after the execution of Charles I in 1649, his eldest son, Charles, the Prince of Wales, wrote from exile in Holland, vowing vengeance on those blamed for his father's death: '... we shall therein by all ways and means possible endeavour to pursue and bring to their due punishment those bloody traitors who were either actors or contrivers of that unparalleled and inhuman murder'.

Of course, the prince had no means by which to carry out his threat. He lived on the charity of the ruling families of Europe and, as continental states gradually came to terms with republican England, was increasingly isolated. This all changed in the summer of 1660 when Charles was invited to return and take up the throne. Catapulted into power, he could at last do something about those who had brought about his father's death.

The story of the ensuing retribution is essentially that of an unrelenting manhunt for everyone who had signed Charles I's death warrant, plus a few more whom Charles II wanted rid of.

To tell the story required our starting with the actions that led to the hunt, the trial and execution of the king. It also required the creation of a narrative that encompasses a series of individual biographies. Of necessity, these biographies must play second fiddle to the narrative. Hence they cannot all be given the depth of attention they might each merit on their own. It is the greater story that we are after here and we have had to make judgments with which others might disagree. Those who wish to discover more on any one person will find the general bibliography at the end of the book a useful starting point.

Today we know a great deal about the frivolous side of Charles II but we know less about his more ruthless side, which saw him callously send his political enemies to the scaffold. Fresh insights into his character may still be found. Contemporary parliamentary records reveal a new role for Charles: that of the interrogator. In late 1660, just a few months after ascending to the throne, the king went to the Tower and interrogated prisoners accused of treason. According to reports, the notoriously lazy monarch was a dab hand at drawing out confessions. Fortunately for the modern researcher and writer, the seventeenth century saw the explosion of the written and printed word: official records of all types, contemporary memoirs, newspapers, propaganda sheets, personal diaries and letters, plays and poems. All these and more flowed from pens and presses. We are grateful to have been able to access these precious documents, chiefly at the British Library and the Public Record Office.

Thanks to this desire to record events, we have a greater idea of the struggle some men faced: a struggle with their consciences and their impulse for self-preservation. For example, at the last Parliament to be held before the return of Charles II, Thomas Scot effectively signed his own death warrant by declaring he was proud they had killed Charles I. By contrast, Thomas Fairfax, who commanded the New Model Army in its defeat of the royalist forces, provided a white horse for Charles II to ride at his coronation. Fairfax was not alone in changing sides. For most this was a simple matter of survival. Many of our most important characters did not, however, change their allegiance. They are interesting precisely because they stood up for their beliefs.

Perhaps most exhilaratingly of all, seventeenth-century records bring to life a world of espionage. From papers held at the Public

Record Office at Kew, spymaster Sir George Downing – 'that perfidious rogue', as Samuel Pepys described him – is revealed to us in all his brilliant treachery. We see him plan with ruthless efficiency to go to the Continent and kidnap his former friends and bring them back to be executed for treason. We see a honeytrap set by Aphra Behn, the Mata Hari of her day, successfully turn a republican exile into a spy for the House of Stuart.

Some characters are interesting simply because they were *there* – and wrote down what they saw and thought. Hence the larger-than-life legal grandee Bulstrode Whitelocke who wrote in his memoirs that he evaded trial for his participation in the republic's affairs by bribing, among others, Edward Hyde, a former fellow parliamentarian and friend. Hyde was by then Charles II's Lord Chancellor and much given to moralising and lecturing the king about his mistresses, but not above extracting a small fortune from a former ally in need. Hyde's more punctilious side allowed him to write a brilliant history of those turbulent years.

The surviving documentation of the time also reveals the unsavoury side of statecraft and the law. One account of the court that was set up to judge the alleged regicides reveals that it was fixed, sending men to their deaths on specious charges and insufficient evidence. In a fit of hubris, the king's counsel John Kelying wrote a legal memoir in which he recalled how judges and the prosecutors got together beforehand to rig the rules in order to meet their own ends.

In dealing with our large cast, we have had to be wary of the sometimes misleading nature of the accounts. For example, Lucy Hutchinson's famous memoir of her husband, Colonel John Hutchinson, one of the men who signed Charles I's death warrant, needs to be approached with caution. It gives a sanitised version of how her husband evaded the death penalty after the restoration. Edmund Ludlow's published memoirs were thought to be entirely by his own hand until his original manuscript, titled A *Voyce from the Watchtower*, was discovered at Warwick Castle in 1970. Thanks to the detective work of Dr Blair Worden, we now know this was a large part of Ludlow's original manuscript and that the memoirs as previously published were a radically rewritten version by a different hand in order to present Ludlow as more of a late-seventeenth-century Whig and less of the religious radical he was in real life.

Sometimes historical characters are fascinating because of their opacity. By far the most impenetrable character was George Monck, a professional soldier who first plied his trade for the House of Stuart. He later became one of Cromwell's most trusted commanders. After Cromwell's death, his career took a further twist: he helped to crush all parliamentary and army opposition in order to pave the way for the return of Charles II. It is hardly surprising that opinions differ on Monck's motives. The reader will see we have reached our own conclusions.

Today, the House of Stuart is remembered chiefly for its sexual scandal, a wonderful art collection and the formation of the Royal Society. Its Puritan adversaries are remembered almost solely as king killers and for Irish atrocities. They have been described as dangerous fanatics or, at best, foolhardy men who carried out a heinous deed. This is a shame, for among them were remarkable men. They played a critical role in British history, formulating forward-looking social, political and legal ideas that still hold good today, yet they have few monuments and, in the case of those who were executed, no graves. The remarkable struggle between Charles II and his recalcitrant subjects led to the longest-running manhunt in British history – a story worthy of a new and wider audience.

I

THE WATCHTOWER

The middle-aged man who climbed the hill to the church above the little town on the shores of Lake Geneva had a heft and strut that marked him out as an old soldier. He carried a sword and wore a breastplate under his cloak. A casual observer might have marvelled at the vanity of a man trying to recapture the martial glories of his youth, but the truth was that the old soldier feared for his life.

A plot to assassinate him had been thwarted only by the vigilance of his landlord, who on his way to church early one Sunday had spotted two 'ruffian like fellows, desperados with long cloaks and carbines under them'.[1] He returned home and told his tenant he thought the men were up to no good. Taking a chance, the old soldier crept out to catch a surreptitious glimpse of the rogues. What he saw confirmed his landlord's fears. After that, he went to church well armed.

Though he generally shunned company, to anyone who asked he introduced himself as Edmund Phillips, an Englishman who had chosen to travel and live abroad for a while. In reality he was a fugitive with a price on his head, unable to return home on pain of death, branded a traitor and compelled to live in exile under an assumed name.

His real name was Edmund Ludlow. Born into minor gentry in Wiltshire, he was a veteran of the British Civil Wars. Before his enforced exile he had been a high-flyer: scholar of Trinity College, Oxford, attorney at the Inner Temple, Member of Parliament, Lieutenant-General of Cavalry, Commander-in-Chief of the Commonwealth Army in Ireland, High Sheriff of Wiltshire and member of the Commonwealth's Council of State (the Cabinet).

A portrait of him in later life shows a square sort of fellow with a large face and a determined yet small mouth above a large chin. He wears a full wig, a lace ruff and full armour befitting his status as a lieutenant-general.[2] But the old soldier's real claim to fame – or infamy – was that he had royal blood on his hands. He was a regicide, a king-killer, one of sixty-nine judges who tried Charles I for treason and sentenced him to death by beheading.

The sixty-nine men who found Charles guilty of treason were a varied lot. What they shared was the belief that Charles had a view of monarchy at odds with the spirit of the age, pursuing autocratic decision-making and promoting religious policies that stifled freedom of conscience. Most of the sixty-nine were members of the House of Commons – or, rather, remnants of Parliament after royalist sympathisers had been ejected in a military *coup d'état* in late 1648. The aim of this had been to create a Parliament composed purely of radically minded men who would agree to put the king on trial for treason for having waged war against his people. Senior officers of the New Model Army (the Parliament's victorious military force) including its creator, Oliver Cromwell, also sat as judges. The rest of the bench was made up of radical lawyers and wealthy merchants serving as aldermen, elected councillors, of London. To begin with, Parliament appointed 153 commissioners to try the king. The trial was so contentious that half refused to sit. Those who did voted unanimously to have the king executed for high treason.*

---

* For a full list of the regicides see Appendix 1.

By killing a king and establishing a republic, the king's judges not only changed the course of English history but altered their own futures beyond their imagining. Following eleven years of experiments in government unparalleled in British history, the son of the executed king returned to England to rule as Charles II. He had left England fourteen years before when, at the age of sixteen, he fled into exile at the tail end of the Civil War.

Charles II grew up in warfare and came of age in a foreign country, without a father. He joined his mother's court in exile at St Germain near Paris, provided for by her French royal relatives. In the seventeenth century the age of sixteen was regarded as adulthood, though thanks to growing up in war-torn England, Charles could at times be socially awkward. To the eyes of the refined French royal court, he was even *gauche*, though not completely a lost cause. One of his mother's grand relatives described him as 'Swarthy, with fine black eyes and a wide, ugly mouth ... his head was noble, his hair black, his complexion brown, his person passably agreeable.'[3]

Charles reached maturity as an impecunious prince without a state, flitting between the courts of Europe, selling his silver plate and keeping his demons at bay with a growing passion for sex that would propel him to take on a succession of mistresses in ensuing years. When the throne was suddenly and unexpectedly awarded to him, he seized the opportunity to make up for lost time with an instinctual thirst for luxury and excess – and an understandable desire for revenge upon those who had put him through hell by killing his father.

The end of fourteen years of exile for Charles marked the beginning of a life of exile for many of his father's enemies, including Edmund Ludlow. Prime movers behind the revolution – 'the good old cause' as they called it – including Oliver Cromwell and his son-in-law Henry Ireton, only evaded retribution by dying before the accession of the new king. Ludlow watched as parliamentarians, lawyers, members of the oldest families in England, were imprisoned and charged with treason.

Ludlow realised he had become a wanted man. Sooner or later, officers of the Tower would come to arrest him. He moved to the home of friends he could trust. When he learned the two Houses of Parliament were debating who should be placed on lists for trial and execution, he quietly left the city, travelling up-river at night towards Richmond. To match his new renegade status he changed his habits and his appearance. The former government minister grew a beard and flitted in and out of London on foot, joining the robbers, prostitutes, homeless and other unfortunates who kept their watch on the city by night. Ludlow knew it was risky to frequent the city but he was anxious to keep in touch with events and in contact with his family and those who could help him.

To decide upon his future, Ludlow risked convening a meeting of close friends and relatives at a house in Westminster. 'A friend and kinsman' advised him that he should 'withdraw out of England ... assuring if I stayed I was a dead man'. Ludlow was told he would only have to go abroad for a short while and that 'he supposed within three or four months the hate and rage would be over'.[4]

Ludlow hoped that some form of the pre-restoration Parliament might be re-established, but 'not believing that it was yet a tyme to expect deliverance, I resolved to hasten my departure.'[5] His wife and friends arranged notes of credit to be sent ahead to France, and guides and accomplices to get him out of the city and across the Channel to Dieppe.

On the appointed night, his wife and some other relations arrived at his safe house with a coach. They crossed London Bridge and made through Southwark to the church of St George the Martyr. Here a guide was waiting with two horses to take the fugitive statesman to the coast.

'I tooke my leave of my deare relations, my poore wife and another friend accompanying me,' wrote Ludlow.[6] His old life was over for good. He and his guide rode through the night along the least frequented roads to Lewes, where a merchant loyal to the parliamentary cause was expecting him. For three days he 'lay as privately as I could' until word came that a ship was ready at the coast. Stormy weather delayed the boat's departure and Ludlow was almost apprehended when searches were carried out among ships waiting to leave. Fortunately, he was hidden on a craft which the agents thought not worth searching as it lay aground on a sandbank.

The next day he got away to Dieppe and afterwards made his way to Paris, then Lyons, and ultimately towards Geneva, all the while trying to evade the royalist spies who watched out for him through Europe. Only when he arrived at Geneva – 'Calvin's City' – did he feel safe. Finally, he moved to a small, out-of-the-way town on the shores of Lake Geneva.

Years before, Charles II and Ludlow had faced one another in battle, though neither realised it at the time. It was on 23 October 1642, at the first pitched battle of the Civil War at Edgehill in Warwickshire. Twelve-year-old Charles, then Prince of Wales, was present with his father, Charles I, and his younger brother, James. Edmund Ludlow was twenty-five and a member of the life guard of the parliamentary army's commander-in-chief, the 3rd Earl of Essex, Robert Devereux. The earl bore a famous name – that of Elizabeth I's one-time favourite. Unlike his flamboyant and headstrong father, the 3rd Earl was a dour fellow, a cuckold and a laughing-stock at court.

Both sides expected the action at Edgehill to be the deciding action of the war. The king, confident of victory, had brought his sons along to watch. Up to this time, the princes had lived in pampered comfort. As heir to the throne, Charles had his own court at Richmond quite separate from the establishments of his parents at Whitehall. Since the age of eight he had been in the care of a series of aristocratic lords who acted as his governors. The first had been the unutterably grand Earl of Newcastle, who had little or no interest in looking after someone else's boy, prince or otherwise. Newcastle was a cultured man and a fine horseman whose idea of instructing the prince seems to have consisted of a series of didactic letters interspersed with short visits for a spot of archery or hunting.

In the earliest letter that has come down to us, the prince writes to his governor, 'I ride every day, and am ready to follow any other directions from you. Make haste to return to him that loves you.'[7] According to contemporary reports, Newcastle taught the prince to 'ride leaping horses and such as would overthrow others'.[8]

On more academic matters, the earl wrote perceptive letters of advice. 'What you read, I would have it history that so you might compare the dead with the living; for the same humours is now as was then, there is no alteration but in names.'[9] The earl's dry wit may have rubbed off on the boy, for the letter contains something of the cynicism with which the adult Charles was later to view his fellow creatures.

In 1641, having spent £40,000 of his own money running the prince's court, the earl decided the honour of being governor to the prince was one he could no longer shoulder. The dubious honour was handed on to the equally grand Marquis of Hertford, a bookish man with no interest in outdoor pursuits and none whatever in passing on his considerable wealth of knowledge. Like Newcastle, he carried out his task largely by remote control and lasted two years in the job. The prince thus had an easy-going upbringing, with a personal tutor and various ladies of the court for company and a few friends of his own age such as the sons of the Duke of Buckingham. It was a life with a little culture, a little academic effort, a little learning of field pursuits and a great deal of pleasure.

Charles was growing up to be a confident if moody boy who was, like his father, an accomplished horseman. When war broke out, his education took a practical turn with first-hand observation of the many sides of humanity under stress – the weaknesses, the prevarications, the bravery, self-interest, shrewdness and more.

For the battle at Edgehill, the young prince was given the purely honorary command of a cavalry regiment. The king's physician, William Harvey (famous for having discovered the circulation of blood), was put in charge of young Charles and his brother. As the fight progressed, Harvey forgot about his charges, who were placed at a field medical station. When the parliamentary forces attacked the right flank of the royalist army, the Prince of Wales took his command seriously and tried to lead a charge, shouting 'I fear them not!' He was prevented from heading into battle by members of the royal party who grabbed his horse's reins. When the parliamentary forces seized an advantage and pushed through the flank of the royalist army, Charles and his brother were in great danger of being captured. Once more, quick action directed the princes away from the fighting and prevented a disaster.

As for Ludlow and his fellow life guards, they made something of a hash of their first military action. By the end of the day, thanks to tactical blunders on both sides, the battle was inconclusive. War would drag on for six more years. The heir to the throne would find himself experiencing a great deal very quickly, though after his spirited action at Edgehill, in future he was kept well away from the scene of combat.

In early 1645, Charles I made his eldest son commander-in-chief of all royalist forces in the West Country. This meant that he would now be separated from his father. He was just turning fifteen. The campaign in the west was in turmoil but the king hoped the nominal title of command would help his son grow to manhood. This it most certainly did, in more ways than one.

In the spring, the prince and his council moved to the royalist stronghold of Bridgwater in Somerset. Here, Charles was reunited with his former governess, the beautiful and pushy Christabella Wyndham. According to a contemporary account, Charles was 'diverted by her folly and petulancy'. Even when the company surrounding the prince was most numerous, Christabella would 'run the length of the room and kiss him'.[10] There were rumours the beautiful ex-governess introduced the prince to the joys of sex. The fun and games did not last long; the war was running against the royal cause. On Christmas Day the prince received a letter from his father telling him to leave England and not delay one hour.[11] The prince lingered until he could disobey no longer and sailed from

Land's End to the Scilly Isles on the night tide of 2 March 1646. From there, he went to Jersey and then to Paris to be reunited with his mother. He would never see his father again.

As for Ludlow, within two years of riding out at Edgehill, he was promoted to major. By the time he was thirty-two, he had helped organise the trial of the king, signed his death warrant and become a member of the government of a new republic. Two years later he was an effective commander-in-chief in Ireland. As a firm believer in political reform and religious freedom, Ludlow's rite-of-passage carried him through from young squire to active republican. By the age of forty-three he was a pariah and exile with a price on his head. In a period of two decades, Ludlow experienced and did more than most men could expect to see or achieve in several lifetimes – and yet at the time of his enforced flight abroad he still had thirty-two years ahead of him.

In Switzerland, he sat down to write a history of all that had occurred between taking up arms in 1642 and the end of his religious and republican dreams. When Ludlow and his fellow life guards joined up, most thought the war would last a few months at most. Two years later it was bogged down in stalemate. On the parliamentary side, the aristocratic commanders did not wish to inflict an outright victory over the king, thinking the conflict would quickly be resolved in a negotiated settlement. Essex had been appointed supreme commander by Parliament to exercise its cause on the battlefield while also preserving the life of the king.[12] Ludlow watched as the war progressed and the old aristocratic generals were replaced by the 'middling sort of men', Cromwell's appointees to run the New Model Army that would ultimately crush the royalist forces. He saw how the main protagonists who had entered the war on the parliamentary side were replaced by a generation of more radical figures who no longer adhered to the old system of royal favour and inherited influence.

In the evenings by Lake Geneva, after a day's labour at his history, Ludlow's mind would be crowded with the ghosts of the dead and the memories of the living. Among the ghosts that visited most was that of John Cook, the brilliant young lawyer who wrote the prosecution case against Charles I. When brought to the Tower, Cook had requested that his life should be taken so that Ludlow's should be spared. What a man that was – no truer friend or colleague could any man have had. Shortly after Ludlow had made his escape, Cook was executed for treason.

When he did not dwell upon the terrible fate of his friend John Cook, Ludlow thought of the fate of many others, including his fellow exile, John Lisle, recently murdered in a Swiss churchyard barely twenty miles from Ludlow's own hideaway. The old soldier was in little doubt that the same assassins plotted to come for him, too.

And what of the ghost of Oliver Cromwell, that brilliant man who, in the eyes of Ludlow and others, betrayed the Commonwealth by becoming a king in all but name? Hated though the memory of Cromwell was, the face that leered most malevolently in Ludlow's imagination was that of George Monck, the parliamentary general who had become a turncoat and secretly plotted to install Charles II as king.

Fifteen years later, the republic was only a broken dream. General Monck, who had started out as an impoverished soldier for hire, was living in luxury with a dukedom and a fortune from a grateful king. Ludlow, who had lost everything, lived quietly with his wife Elizabeth, who had managed to join him in exile. She was his only comfort as he spent his days writing his memories of the great events he had taken part in. On his desk lay a brace of exquisite pistols, a present from a fellow exile who would later die for his convictions. The pistols were a talisman, a call to arms, to join a new army of revolutionaries and overthrow Charles II. But Ludlow was no longer the young firebrand who had handled weapons and directed men on the battlefield. He was nearing sixty and the fire had gone out in him.

From his fortified house, Ludlow could see the light shift on the waters of Lake Geneva. It held no charms for him. He longed for the fields of England. He dipped his pen in ink and tried to conjure up the earthly paradise that England should have been, the paradise he thought he could help create. The light across the lake looked alien and unwelcoming. There was no beauty in this scene; God had turned against him. He entitled his work A *Voyce from the Watchtower*, the words taken from the book of Isaiah:

> My Lord, I stand continually upon the watchtower ... And behold there cometh a chariot of men ... And he answered and said, Babylon is fallen, is fallen.[13]

In the evening light, the mountains turned ultramarine and sapphire, their images reflected in the still waters of the lake. Ludlow wrote of his flight from England and journey to Switzerland. His description of the city of Paris said as much for his view of life as for the French capital:

> I saw the King's stable of horses, which, though not extraordinarily furnished, gave me more pleasure than I should have received by seeing their master, who thinks fit to treat them better than his miserable people. But I loathed to see such numbers of idle drones, who in ridiculous habits, wherein they place a great part of their religion, are to be seen in every part, eating the bread of the credulous multitude, and leaving them to be distinguished from the inhabitants of other countries by thin cheeks, canvas clothing, and wooden shoes.[14]

In these words the old soldier spelled out his creed: his hatred of inequality, of priests and poverty – the Puritan credo wrapped up in words that might have been written by any young Englishman on his grand tour. As for mention of his nemesis, Charles, Ludlow could not bear to write the name, preferring to use terms like 'usurper' and 'enemy of the people'.

As the shadows lengthened across the lake, Ludlow tried not to think of the shadowy figures moving across Europe and North America, searching for him and his fellow regicides – men who had dared to sit in judgment on a king.

2

'THAT MAN OF BLOOD'

January 1647–January 1649

On the gloomy afternoon of 30 November 1648, two hundred foot soldiers and forty cavalry disembarked on the Isle of Wight after a choppy sea crossing from the mainland. With darkness falling, they set off in driving rain for the town of Newport, lying about four miles up the River Medina. On arrival, they set up a ring of road blocks around the town, cutting it off from the outside world and sealing in its most illustrious inhabitant – Charles Stuart, king of England, Scotland and Ireland. The soldiers had orders to take the king to Hurst Castle on the mainland.

The arrival of the detachment took everyone by surprise, including the town's military commander, who had not been informed. One thought reverberated through the town: that the persistent rumours that the king would be assassinated were true – and that he would be killed that very night. This was not the only time such fears had circulated around the king. Fear of assassination was what had driven him to the Isle of Wight in the first place.

When the first Civil War had ended following major parliamentary victories at Marston Moor and then at Naseby, the king decided that rather than surrender to the New Model Army, he would give himself up to the Scots. He hoped to make a deal whereby he would lead a Scottish invasion of England to regain his throne. The Scots and the king could only agree to differ and in January 1647, they handed him over to the English Parliament. Charles then lived under informal house arrest at Holmby House, an enormous Renaissance palace in Northamptonshire. He was guarded by troops answerable to the Presbyterian faction in Parliament, which was hovering on the verge of a deal with the king. In June, fearing that Parliament was about to allow the king to move back into Whitehall Palace and take up the trappings of power once more, the army decided to take the king into its own custody. A detachment of five hundred troopers was sent to Holmby House. They were led by a keen young officer, Cornet George Joyce, a political radical who had been in Cromwell's own regiment. The source of his orders is unclear, though he claimed that his authority came from Cromwell. When the king asked for his authority, Joyce indicated the five hundred Ironsides, or cavalry, massed behind him.

Later in the summer, the army moved the king to the palace of Hampton Court in Surrey. Here, Charles lived in opulent captivity, attended by a full retinue of servants and courtiers and surrounded by part of his famed art collection. Among his most precious masterpieces was the great series of nine paintings by Andrea Mantegna, *The Triumphs of Caesar*, depicting the fruits of military success. For a king who had lost control of his kingdom, the series was a mocking rebuke. In this gilded cage echoing with failure, Charles continued to reject all efforts to reach a negotiated settlement either with Parliament or the army. Cromwell and his fellow generals, Henry Ireton and Sir Thomas Fairfax, all came and left without agreement. The army had suggested a detailed settlement. Written by Ireton and another parliamentary general, John Lambert, this proposed a constitutional monarchy with reduced powers for the king. Charles rejected it outright. His *modus operandi* was one of non-cooperation, banking on his adversaries squabbling and burning themselves out, after which his powers would hopefully be restored.[1]

In the autumn, rumours spread that various revolutionary or radical elements – army agitators and Levellers* – planned to murder the king. When the stories reached Hampton Court, Charles took them seriously. On the evening of 11 November, his jailer, Colonel Edward Whalley (a cousin of Oliver Cromwell), went to check on his prisoner to find he had vanished, having escaped down the back stairs, leaving behind only his cloak. Under cover of darkness, Charles and several courtiers took a boat down the Thames.

In exasperation, the influential religious radical Colonel Thomas Harrison called for the king to be prosecuted for treason, in the process famously referring to him as a 'man of blood'.[2] Two days later, Charles resurfaced on the Isle of Wight. He believed the island's garrison commander, Colonel Robert Hammond (another of Cromwell's cousins), was wavering in his allegiance and might come over to the royal side. Although conflicted, Hammond thought it best to take the king into captivity once more and locked him up in Carisbrooke Castle. The one positive aspect of this arrangement for Charles was that Hammond felt he had to answer to the will of Parliament, which was better disposed towards the king's restoration without root-and-branch reform than many in the army.

At Carisbrooke, Charles retained a retinue of servants and courtiers and was allowed regular contact with the outside world. He was, after all, still the king, even if he was not allowed to rule. He used his time and relative freedom to do clandestine deals and plot with the Scots for them to send an army to invade England. Politics and the restoration of his throne were not the only matters on his mind. He had not seen his queen, Henrietta Maria, for four years and he was lonely. For comfort, he took up with Jane Whorwood, the stepdaughter of a courtier. In code, he wrote to her suggesting how she could come to him secretly and how he wished for a 'swiving' (crude slang for sexual intercourse).[3]

---

* A radical movement that wanted sweeping electoral and constitutional reform along with equal rights for all men.

The king's plotting bore fruit. In the spring, there were royalist uprisings around England and South Wales. Much more seriously, in July 1648 the Scots invaded and the second Civil War was under way. Gradually, the English uprisings were put down. In August, Cromwell defeated the Scottish army in a brilliant victory at Preston. Up to this point, Cromwell, Ireton and the other army leaders had continued to be monarchists, believing in a settlement which allowed the king to rule the country while increased powers were granted to Parliament and wider freedom to worship was permitted. Now, hearts had been hardened. Wild rumours circulated that Charles was about to be killed. Theories abounded, including one that he would be shot as the leader of an enemy force (i.e. the Scottish army), another that he would be tried in a kangaroo court, and yet another that he would be assassinated.

These rumours marked a significant change in the views of the king's opponents: many influential figures in the army and a few in Parliament were beginning to consider whether constitutional monarchy was any longer the only way forward – at least if it included Charles Stuart as its representative. Experience had changed Henry Ireton from a conservative thinker to a much more radical one. Where once he had believed in evolution, he now saw the necessity for a complete break with the past.

Edmund Ludlow was another of those convinced that the future lay in a clean break with the past. Ludlow rode from London to Colchester, where the supreme commander of the New Model Army, General Sir Thomas Fairfax, was engaged in besieging one of the last royalist strongholds. Fairfax came from one of Yorkshire's oldest families, which had supported Parliament's side since the beginning of the war. He was a brave and capable soldier who had – as is so often the case in time of war – been promoted to senior rank at a very young age. The transition from warfare to the subtler arts of negotiation and deal-making was proving difficult for Fairfax's traditional mind.

Like the majority of people in the land, Fairfax envisaged a return to something like the old order, with a few constitutional changes to make the king more of an instrument of Parliament. His worry was what part the army should play in reaching a settlement. Ludlow was in no doubt. He wanted the army to move to forestall the majority in Parliament who now seemed bent on reinstating the king without any real concessions. Ludlow informed Fairfax that the agreement which was 'being pressed with more heat than ever' would 'render all our victories useless thereby'.[4] He pressed Fairfax for the army to take action but found him 'irresolute'.

A few weeks later, Parliament selected fifteen commissioners to begin a new round of negotiations with the king later known as the Newport negotiations. The eminent lawyer and politician Bulstrode Whitelocke was rightly sceptical about the talks, saying he was glad not to have been chosen, 'all the previous treaties wherein I was a commissioner having proved so ineffectual'.[5] His misgivings were prophetic.

The king was moved to a private house in Newport, a more fitting venue for talks than Carisbrooke's Norman keep. When negotiations opened on 19 September, Charles reverted to form, dragging his feet and agreeing to little. The role of the bishops was a major stumbling block. Charles emphasised that the bishops were – like himself – divinely appointed and so could not be swept away. For Puritan nego-tiators like the republican Sir Harry Vane, a persistent critic of the Stuarts' rule, the bishops were a key element in the king's arbitrary power over his subjects and a symbol of religious intolerance. The two sides circled around this impediment for weeks but made little progress.

After many weeks of negotiation, the king made several conces-sions, agreeing that certain powers could pass to Parliament – as long as the arrangement was open to revision after a specific number of years. He also agreed that Presbyterianism would become the offi-cial state religion. The Church would no longer be run by bishops but by elected elders. This was not what religious dissenters wished to hear, for, unlike the Presbyterians, they were wary of the crown's arbitrary powers; neither were the temporary shifts in power sufficient to placate those like Ireton and Cromwell who sought more permanent constitutional reform. It became clear that Charles was not negotiating in good faith; he continued to talk secretly with the Scots and he also entertained plans to escape to France.

On 18 October, Henry Ireton's regiment sent a petition to the House of Commons demanding that those responsible for the second Civil War should be brought to justice. After much heart-searching, Oliver Cromwell had finally come round to the same position. The petition stipulated that 'the same fault may have the same punishment in the person of the king or lord, as in the person of the poorest commoner'.[6] Bulstrode Whitelocke recalled afterwards that it was the 'beginning of the design upon the king's person, but not discerned till afterwards'.[7]

To add to the controversy, Parliament ignored the army petition and agreed that once negotiations ended, Charles would be allowed to live in London, with his property and income restored. It looked as if Parliament was getting ready to restore the king to the throne no matter what. Inside the army, debate raged on how to proceed. While hardliners felt that all negotiation with the king was now fruitless, others believed there was still the chance of a deal.* It was decided to move Charles to Windsor Castle, a step nearer London. To begin with, he would be brought back across the Solent to Hampshire. A trusted, battle-hardened colonel named Isaac Ewer was given the task.

---

* There is some controversy over the intentions behind the decision to put the king on trial. Sean Kelsey has argued (in *The Historical Journal*, vol. 45, 2002, and the *Law and History Review*, vol. 22, 2994, and elsewhere), that 'the king's trial was contrived as a final bid for peaceful settlement and not as a prelude to king-killing'. This view is strongly refuted by Clive Holmes (*The Historical Journal*, vol. 53, 2010), who says of Kelsey's argument: 'It relies on an uncritical approach to the evidence' and 'misunderstands the significance of ... the army's November Remonstrance, the act of establishing the High Court of Justice, and the charge against the king'. We tend to side with Holmes' interpretation of the purpose of the trial as being to bring to public justice 'this man against whom the Lord hath witnessed', as Cromwell had it.

The process that led to the king being snatched from Newport had begun only two weeks before in St Albans. Army radicals had demanded a meeting of the Army General Council, to which General Fairfax unenthusiastically agreed. Meeting in the ancient abbey on 16 November, the council discussed sending another petition to Parliament, setting out why the army was against the king's reinstatement. The prime mover of the petition was Ireton, with Fairfax much opposed. The petition began by recalling the words of Cicero: '*Salus populi suprema lex esto*' – 'let the good (or safety) of the people be the supreme law'.[8] Before the century was out, John Locke, the Whig philosopher, would use this phrase as a key tenet of his treatise on constitutional government. In the middle of the seventeenth century, however, it was a contentious proposition, striking at the very heart of the idea of the divine authority of a king.

After much discussion, Fairfax was reluctantly won over. The army council agreed to back Ireton's proposal that all negotiations should be broken off and the king brought to trial. Fairfax agreed the manifesto could go out under his name.[9] It was presented to Parliament on 20 November. Fatefully, Parliament ignored it and continued with the Newport proposals.

Cromwell, who was still travelling south from Scotland with his army, wrote to Fairfax, saying that 'all the regiments' in his army were against the treaty at Newport: 'My Lord, I find a very great sense in the officers of the regiments of the suffering and ruin of this poor kingdom, and in them all a very great zeal to have impartial justice done upon offenders; and I must confess, I do in all, from my heart, concur with them.'[10]

By now Cromwell had reached a shattering conclusion – that the views of the people were only truly represented by the army, by virtue of its composition of thousands of soldiers who had fought two wars in which a hundred thousand had died. According to Cromwell, these soldiers now wanted 'justice done upon offenders' – which could only mean upon the king. A revolution was growing and Parliament remained largely oblivious. The majority of MPs were fixated on the discussions in Newport, while the flow of history was turning towards the army in St Albans, its political supporters in Westminster, and the steady, southern march of Oliver Cromwell.

With no positive response from Parliament, Fairfax ordered the army to leave St Albans and move to Windsor on 25 November – sending out the signal that while the army was officially the tool of Parliament, it had in fact become an autonomous force that could, if necessary, impose its will on Parliament.

That day, Cromwell wrote to his cousin Robert Hammond, the garrison commander of Carisbrooke. He argued that the people's victories over the king's forces meant that God was with them rather than with Charles: 'My dear friend, let us look into providences; surely they mean somewhat. They hang so together; have been so consistent, so clear and unclouded.' Furthermore, if Cicero's argument were followed, then the people counted for more than a king. Cromwell concluded by calling the Treaty of Newport a 'ruining, hypocritical agreement'.[11]

Events began to move towards a climax. Ireton, Ludlow and their allies held a secret meeting. They decided that if Parliament restored an unrepentant king to the throne, all dissenting MPs should call publicly upon the army to come to their aid to restore public trust in Parliament. This declaration would prepare the ground for a military coup against both Parliament and king.

At the end of November, Colonel Hammond received orders to move the king from Newport to Hurst Castle on the mainland. Hammond, a stickler for form, refused, saying he could only do so on orders from Parliament. Fairfax quickly wrote to Cromwell, telling him to get to London immediately. Perhaps he thought his best general, like the king, was deliberately dragging his feet – waiting to see what would happen.

Parliament then received another petition, this time from Henry Ireton's regiment, stating that the king could no longer be considered to be above ordinary mortals and bore responsibility for the second Civil War. Parliament ignored it. When the parliamentary negotiating team left the island, Colonel Hammond received orders calling him away from his command on a spurious mission. Before the day was done, the army council had given orders for the military occupation of London.

Three days later, as the rain beat down on Newport, Colonel Ewer took a detachment of his Roundheads (Cromwellian footsoldiers wore their hair in rounded basin cuts) and marched through the town to the house of Sir William Hopkins, where the king was billeted. With their musket fuses lit and smoking in the lantern light, the Roundheads entered the house. Searching for the king, they moved from room to room, permeating the interior with the unmistakable whiff of saltpetre, the smell of the battlefield and death. The king's companions feared the worst.

When the soldiers opened the door to the king's private room, Charles was seated by the fire. He turned to face his visitors with a calm expression. Though he remained impassive, the king knew that the soldiers' unannounced arrival late at night could only mean they were acting on the orders of the army and not of Parliament. It could even mean they were acting not solely on Fairfax's orders but on those of sterner men like Henry Ireton.[12]

Fearing for the king's life, courtiers demanded that a messenger be sent to Carisbrooke Castle to find out whether there was indeed a plot to kill the king. Meanwhile, they hatched a plan to smuggle Charles to safety. The Duke of Richmond dressed up in a military cloak and demonstrated that he could walk straight past the guards at the door unchallenged. The king refused to attempt an escape. He was heartened by news from Carisbrooke that there seemed to be no plot to do away with him that night. He finished a letter to the queen, and went to bed.[13]

In the morning, Charles was put in a coach and transported to the coast, where he was ferried across the Solent to Hurst Castle. News that the king had been taken by the army caused outrage in

Parliament but its members could do little more than formally complain to Fairfax.

There was little cheer for Charles during his first night at Hurst Castle. The Tudor fort was built on a blighted spit sticking out into the Solent and surrounded by a shingle beach exposed to the westerly winds blowing in from the Atlantic. Charles no longer had his retinue of courtiers and friends about him for advice and solace. He was allowed only a few servants and one or two companions chosen by Parliament, including Sir Thomas Herbert, who acted as his groom.

The day after the king arrived at Hurst Castle, the army marched into London. In its vanguard was a regiment commanded by a man well known in the city, Colonel Thomas Pride, who had run a successful brewery in London before the wars. When war broke out, he joined the parliamentary forces and rose to the rank of lieutenant-colonel, returning to his adopted city at the head of an occupying army.

Meanwhile, Parliament debated whether the king's concessions in Newport were grounds for a settlement. Sir Harry Vane, one of the Newport negotiators, reported that 'the justice of our cause was not asserted, nor our rights secured for the future'. Others felt there was the basis of an agreement: Edmund Ludlow was disgusted that some Members of Parliament argued the king's case, 'as if they had been employed by him'. Late that evening, Parliament adjourned without a decision.

On Tuesday 5 December, 129 Members of Parliament voted for the treaty and 83 against. Radicals, including Edmund Ludlow, went into secret consultations with their allies in the army. Henry Ireton was present, but Oliver Cromwell was still marching south with his regiments, possibly taking it slowly to see which way events would turn out. He did not have long to wait: the plotters decided on nothing less than a military *coup d'état* – the army would exclude from Parliament all MPs who favoured the terms of the Newport talks. There would be no waiting for Cromwell and his famous powers of persuasion. The deed would be done in the morning. It was the beginning of a revolution.

There is room for debate over who first proposed such a course, but there is little doubt that the man who gave the order for the first act of the revolution was Henry Ireton. In the face of Fairfax's continuing lack of resolve, Ireton was the de facto head of the army in London. He knew he had to select a steadfast officer to carry out the purge of the pro-Newport MPs. Colonel Pride had not only been a brewer before the war, he had also been a part-time soldier in the London militia. Who better, reasoned Ireton, to ensure there was no popular uprising against their action? Pride was a many-sided man, who in peacetime crusaded against corruption and courted unpopularity by campaigning against bear baiting and cock fighting. But he would go down in history for directing the events that took place the next day, 6 December 1648, which became known as Pride's Purge.

The following morning, Sir Bulstrode Whitelocke and his fellow Commissioner of the Great Seal, Sir Thomas Widdrington, arrived in their legal finery for service in one of the courts held within the warren of buildings that contained Parliament. They were surprised to find lines of troops drawn up in the yards. Two regiments had taken over the buildings and their surroundings. The distinguished lawyers were even more surprised to be stopped and vetted at the door. It was what Sir Bulstrode had feared: an army coup. Deciding to brazen it out, the two grandees explained they were on business at the Court of Chancery and were allowed to enter.

Once inside, Widdrington and Whitelocke were advised by a clerk that despite the army coup developing around them, they should take their seats in the Commons. No sooner had they done so than a clerk came up and told them not to sit. The two great office bearers rose in confusion. Whitelocke was then invited to talk to the Lords. As he went down the corridor towards the Lords' chamber, he came across Colonel Pride, who was directing his men to arrest various members of the Commons and prevent others from entering. To his astonishment, Pride broke off from directing the coup to let

Whitelocke through. On his way back from the Lords, he was even more amazed when Pride 'saluted him civilly'. In a strangely understated judgment on so momentous an event, Whitelocke noted it was 'sad to see such things'.[14]

By the end of the day, Whitelocke was one of about two hundred members left in what became known as the 'Rump' of the Parliament. Colonel Pride's men arrested 45 MPs and excluded 186 who they thought would not support the trial of the king, or who had voted to support the Newport treaty. The next day, another fifty MPs were excluded and three arrested.

Realising the king's situation was worsening by the day, close followers once again plotted his escape. Horses were hired on which Charles could flee while taking his daily exercise on the beach beside Hurst Castle and a ship was chartered to wait at anchor off the coast. The Duke of Lennox urged Charles to seize the moment but the king answered that he had given his word and would not break it.[15] On 15 December, the army council decided to move Charles to Windsor. Shortly after, Thomas Harrison arrived to tell Ewer the news. Harrison did not meet the king, who remained ignorant of his visit.

In London, discussions were under way about how to proceed against the king. Cromwell favoured a trial but he was unsure how it could be done. The established laws of the land seemed to be an obstacle to putting the king on trial. If the king was set above all other men by God, how could other men try the king? Wrestling with this headache, on 18 December he called his friend and confidant Colonel Richard Deane – that 'bold and excellent officer'[16] – to a meeting with Sir Bulstrode Whitelocke and Sir Thomas Widdrington. We don't know what advice the lawyers gave, but we can deduce by subsequent events that it was not what Cromwell and Deane had hoped for.

Despite this setback, the army began to move the king to Windsor. The journey would take several days on horseback. The detachment of troops together with their prisoner and his depleted entourage set off for Winchester, where they spent the night before heading across the Downs to Alresford. People gathered along the roadside and shouted, 'God preserve Your Majesty.'

On the road out of the market town of Alton, the travellers came upon a troop of cavalry lined up along the side of the road. The appearance of the handsome and finely dressed commanding officer impressed the king. According to Sir Thomas Herbert, the officer was 'gallantly mounted and armed; a velvet Montero was on his head'. He wore a new buff coat with 'a crimson silk scarf about his waist, richly fringed'.[17] The king asked Herbert the identity of this paragon of fashion. The answer chilled him to the bone. Of all the Roundheads and Cromwellians Charles knew, or knew of, this was the one he least wished to meet. This was the man who wished to see him dead in order that Christ could rule on earth in his place; this was the person who had called him 'that man of blood'. It was the dandy Puritan himself, Colonel Thomas Harrison.

And so it was that two of the most fanatical, headstrong and stubborn characters of the seventeenth century met one another. Harrison's extreme religious opinions were matched in rigidity by Charles's view of himself as a king appointed by God to rule with absolute powers.* At Fareham that evening, the two men dined together. Given his situation, Charles decided a little flattery would not go amiss. He told Harrison that he could see by his physiognomy he was a valiant man. Having softened up his companion, he then said he had heard that Harrison had plotted to murder him but that now he had met him and seen his noble appearance he knew it could not be so. Harrison graciously replied that he hated all such 'base, obscure undertakings'.[18]

The next day, they headed to Bagshot, where the king was entertained to lunch by Lord and Lady Newburgh. The Newburghs were

---

* Fifth Monarchists believed that there were five historical periods, each ruled by a monarch. The fifth, or last, of these would be the reign of Christ. Hence, Charles I was the fourth and stood in the way.

royalist sympathisers and planned to help Charles escape. Their idea was that the king would complain that his horse had gone lame, whereupon Newburgh would provide him with an especially fast animal and Charles would race off into the distance. After lunch, Harrison spotted that the king's retinue were being offered some fine horses. He immediately pointed out to Charles that his own cavalry horses were of similar fine quality. Realising this was Harrison's way of saying he knew what was afoot, the king put all thought of flight from his mind.

As the troop approached Windsor, Charles passed within three miles of Runnymede, where King John had been forced into signing a document granting liberties to his people four centuries earlier. Charles felt himself made of sterner stuff than John. He would sign no agreement giving away his royal prerogatives. Among the clauses of the Magna Carta was one which Charles approved of very much. This clause stated that every man had the right to be tried by his peers. As the king had no peers, it followed he could not be put on trial. No matter how grave the misdemeanours of a ruling king, no matter how much he made them suffer, he could not be held accountable by his subjects.

This very point had thoughtfully been made by Charles's father. In an instruction manual on monarchy, James I had described the condition of a king: 'The absolute master of the lives and possessions of his subjects; his acts are not open to inquiry or dispute, and no misdeeds can ever justify resistance.'[19]

Charles had taken this to heart. James had also given some good advice: be a wise king, know one's subjects, don't be a tyrant, participate in the council of the land, choose a wife of the same religion, and rule in a Christian manner. Unfortunately for him, Charles ignored almost all of this. Now he was about to pay the price for swimming against the tide of Reformation England.

On the evening of 23 December, Charles completed his journey, passing under the portcullis of Windsor Castle in heavy rain. By now he was resigned to whatever turn events might take; but he was certain that he could not be put on trial, for he believed the laws of England did not allow it. A monarch was appointed by God and no one was above the monarch. This was held to be the case across all European kingdoms and was well understood.

The Rump Parliament had not moved so far with its revolutionary intentions to be stumped by existing laws. It was determined that a way would be found to try the king. On the same day that Charles arrived in Windsor, the Commons appointed a committee of thirty-eight MPs and lawyers to draw up a charge against him. Whitelocke and Widdrington were not among its members. However, when the committee called for them to attend on Christmas Day and again on Boxing Day, Whitelocke decided on what action to take. The affable lawyer was famous for his clear-sightedness. He informed his friend Widdrington that his coach was ready. The two friends made off as fast as Sir Bulstrode's horses could gallop. Their swift departure provided Oliver Cromwell with a clear message regarding their thoughts on any attempt to try the king.[20]

News of his father's impending trial reached the Prince of Wales, who was by then in Holland, the guest of his sister Mary and her husband Prince William of Orange. Charles's younger brother James had already arrived at The Hague, having escaped England disguised as a girl. Despite the Christmas celebrations, this was a generally gloomy time for the members of the Stuart family. The atmosphere was lifted for Charles by his first real love affair. After a family break-up, the teenage beauty Lucy Walter found herself in The Hague where she became the lover of the republican Robert Sidney (younger son of the more famous Algernon). When the eighteen-year-old prince caught sight of her he was immediately captivated. Lucy jumped beds and launched into an affair with the prince that soon led to pregnancy. Despite the power of his first big fling, Charles devoted time to seeking ways to save his father from what increasingly looked like certain doom. Entreaties to the powers in France and in Holland to intervene came to nothing, as would desperate pleadings to Parliament and the army in England.

On the first day of 1649, the much-reduced ranks of the House of Commons decided that the king should be tried by a High Court created expressly for that purpose. The following day, the House of Lords rejected the proposal. The Commons now had to decide how far it should push its authority. After two days, the House declared that it was the supreme authority in the land and could pass laws without consent of either lords or king. On 6 January 1649, the Commons passed an Act setting up a special High Court of Justice to try the king.

At Windsor Castle, King Charles was kept well informed of these preparations. Though schooled since childhood in the art of never letting the regal mask slip, human frailty finally burst through. One of his courtiers wrote:

> His Majesty hath received intelligence from Westminster that the General Council of the Army have resolved to bring him to a speedy tryall. All of which his Majesty doth very ill receive; for (with a sad dejected countenance, and tears trickling down his sacred cheeks) he saith that his conscience begins to dictate sad and dismall apprehensions to his memory and that he much feareth the clouds begin to gather to a head for the eclipsing and eradicating the splendour and glory of his days.[21]

On 13 January a parliamentary committee decided the king should be tried at Westminster Hall, the scene of many other historic trials, including those of William Wallace and the gunpowder plotters.

Charles now knew that his fate would shortly rest in the hands of those he could least wish to hold it: a court consisting of mere subjects who considered themselves his peers.

3

A WICKED DESIGN

8 January–27 January 1649

There was only one building in London big enough to stage the king's trial: Westminster Hall, built at the end of the eleventh century on the orders of William II. Its glorious hammer-beam roof, commissioned by Richard II in the fourteenth century, required no internal supporting columns and provided the hall with the largest uninterrupted interior in England, measuring two hundred and forty feet by nearly seventy. It had been built for great events; Charles's own coronation banquet had been held in it, as had those of many kings before. But then, so had many treason trials.

The question facing the trial's organisers was twofold: how to give it legitimacy and how to make that legitimacy apparent to the people. The answer to the second part seemed relatively easy – the king should be tried in front of a large panel of judges and in the presence of the public, so that justice could be seen to be done. To facilitate this, all public sessions of the trial would be held in Westminster Hall.

The answer to the first part was more difficult. The task of giving the trial lawful authority involved much legal head-scratching. For the people of England, the trial of their king was the latest in a drawn-out series of miseries. The country was broken by war, there was widespread hunger and people lived in fear and uncertainty characterised by the witchcraft trials still held up and down the land.

Not many years had passed since the prosperous early period of Charles's reign, when the country's manufacturing had been growing and its overseas trade thriving. But at the same time, Charles alienated many sections of his people. From 1629 to 1640 he ruled without calling a Parliament and imposed forced loans from the gentry and aristocracy to raise finance. New customs duties were levied, to the anger of the business classes, who were further infuriated by the selling of trade monopolies to the highest bidder and – most explosive of all – the king's expansion of ship money, a tax traditionally paid only by counties on the coast, to cover all counties in England.[1] He then alienated Parliament over the balance of power. If that were not enough, he also alienated large sections of the population by dictating how they should worship.

Once Charles did call a Parliament, in 1640, the struggle became one between a king who longed for a pre-Reformation style of rule based on monarch and Church, and a Parliament that wished to keep the northern European Reformation firmly on track, with fewer powers for the king and more powers and religious freedom for the people. While the king longed for a medieval world of certainty and hierarchy, many of his people were turning in frustration to English political history, the classical world and the Bible for examples of how the powerful could be held to account. A heady brew of new and old ideas swirled around mid-seventeenth-century England. Those who were about to put the king on trial felt that somewhere in all of this, legitimacy could be discovered.

Judges were chosen by the Rump for the High Court of Justice to try the King. The court's composition was designed to represent a cross-section of the non-royalist establishment – parliamentarians, lawyers, senior army officers and wealthy businessmen. As for the actual charge, that would be drawn up once the court was convened.

On 8 January 1649, at two in the afternoon, the High Court of Justice sat for the first time in a preliminary session, without Charles being present. The purpose was to choose court officials and decide how to announce the trial to the people. The meeting took place in the Painted Chamber in the Palace of Westminster. The room was a sorry sight. Once it had been the glory of the Plantagenet kings, its walls brightly painted with coloured images of saints, kings and queens; now the silvery afternoon light played across paintings dulled by four hundred years of soot and neglect.

The session did not start well. Two-thirds of those appointed by Parliament as judges failed to turn up. In all, 53 out of 153 took their places. The quorum had been set at twenty, so discussions went ahead.

Two clerks were appointed. Little is known of one of them, Andrew Broughton. The other, John Phelps, was to play a crucial role, arranging a daily shorthand record to supplement the notes taken by the stenographers. It is from these sources that we have most of what we now know about the conduct of the trial. Phelps was an ambitious young man from Salisbury, educated at Corpus Christi College, Oxford. Having been an assistant to the senior clerk of the House of Commons, he was an ideal choice. Next, the court selected four lawyers to conduct the prosecution. The most senior by far, the Lord Chief Justice, feigned illness and didn't turn up. Another appointee also failed to show up. The two who agreed to participate were well qualified for the historic task. Isaac Dorislaus was an eminent Dutch academic who had been the first professor of ancient history at Cambridge before falling foul of royalist interests and being sacked for lecturing on Tacitus and the difference between legal and tyrannical monarchy.[2] John Cook was a young lawyer who had made a name for himself in Dublin before becoming a reforming barrister in London. Dorislaus and Cook would make legal history by drafting the charges against the king. In essence, they would bring the first charges for war crimes against a head of state.[3]

Unless it was in use for official events, Westminster Hall was open every day as a marketplace for lawyers and booksellers and their clients. On the morning of 9 January, the hall was filled with the usual crowds of barristers, litigants and browsers at bookstalls. They were stopped in their tracks by a shrill trumpet blast. Through the north door entered six trumpeters and two companies of cavalry. At their head was the sergeant-at-arms, Edward Dendy, who declared that a special High Court of Justice was to be convened to try the king.

Dendy then rode to the City, where at the Old Exchange and in Cheapside, he bellowed out the proclamation again. He went on to St Paul's churchyard where he informed the usual throngs of booksellers, idlers and pickpockets of the trial, accompanied this time by no fewer than ten trumpeters.

Following Dendy's exertions, the court sat again on 10 January. Once more, most of the commissioners failed to appear. The most noticeable of the absentees this time was Sir Thomas Fairfax, who had attended the first session. Fairfax had made an extraordinary journey in his thirty-six years, from scion of a Yorkshire landowning family to head of the parliamentary army in two Civil Wars. Having signed the army remonstrance that named Charles as 'the capital and grand author of our troubles' who should be tried for 'treason, blood and mischief',[4] and gone along with the purge of Parliament, when it came to the trial itself he discovered he was too much of a man of the old social order to see his king tried for treason.[5] As his colleagues prepared for the final act, he silently left the stage.

Fairfax was far from the only judge absent from the Painted Chamber on 10 January. Of the possible 153, only 45 were present. Among the other absentees was John Bradshaw, a lawyer, who had yet to show up at all. In spite of this, the court elected him its Lord President and summonsed him to attend. The court was anxious about filling the post; normally it would have been taken by the Lord Chief Justice, Oliver St John, except that he, too, had declined to serve. Of those who did serve as judges, the numbers ebbed and flowed throughout the trial. Some, like Fairfax, appeared only once, while others attended every session.

The court now appointed a committee to consider how the king's trial would be managed. Its membership included names that would feature prominently in another treason trial eleven years in the future – John Lisle, Nicholas Love, Gilbert Millington, Augustine Garland, Harry Marten, Thomas Challoner, Sir John Danvers, Sir Henry Mildmay.

At the next sitting, Bradshaw reluctantly put in an appearance. He asked for time to think about the honour being bestowed. After a further day of deliberation, he agreed to accept. The court appointed more committees to oversee various aspects of the trial; one was notable for being entirely composed of army colonels – among them men who would play a large part in all that was yet to pass: Edmund Ludlow, John Hutchinson, John Carew and Thomas Pride.

In the meantime, the committee that liaised with Dorislaus and Cook over the charges was progressing slowly. A new name was added to its membership – that of Lieutenant-General Oliver Cromwell. Two days later, the committee had 'perfected the charge'. The court ordered that Cook, now promoted to solicitor-general, should 'on behalf of the people of England, exhibit and bring into this court a Charge of High Treason and other High Crimes against Charles Stuart, King of England'.[6]

On the morning of Saturday 20 January, the court looked over the charge one last time. The nub of it was that the king was guilty of tyranny by waging war against his people for his personal advancement rather than the good of his subjects. Due to his actions, tens of thousands of his subjects had died in two wars, the first from 1642 to 1646 and the second in 1648. The charge was inscribed on parchment and signed by Cook. The court then adjourned to Westminster Hall to sit in judgment on the king of England.

At twelve noon, a procession entered the vast, echoing hall to begin the trial that would ultimately establish the supremacy of

Parliament over the crown, increase religious freedom with the Toleration Act of 1650 and lead to the independence of the judiciary in 1652. This was the true revolution that would change the country for ever – not the 'glorious revolution' of 1688, which merely restored some of the innovations brought about in 1649. Although generations of writers have sought to downplay the importance of the event and its participants, the first war crimes trial in history was to provide the basis of the rights and freedoms we take for granted today.

The procession was led by Edward Dendy, bearing the great mace of the House of Commons. An assistant carried the ceremonial sword. Then came the Lord President of the Court, John Bradshaw, in ceremonial robes, accompanied by sixty-six other commissioners, all dressed in black. They were escorted by twenty-one soldiers carrying long-handled ceremonial spears known as partisans. Making up the procession were the various office-bearers of the court, including the two clerks, Broughton and Phelps.

Bradshaw proceeded to a long stage that had been built for the judges and jury. In the middle was his seat, a grandiose crimson velvet chair with a desk before it bearing a velvet cushion. As Bradshaw sat he made quite a sight. He wore his armour under his judicial robes and on his head a ridiculous conical hat covered with beaver skin and lined with steel. It was reported that his wife had made him wear it as she feared he might face an assassin's bullet at any moment. In contemporary engravings, Bradshaw looks like an iron-clad Humpty Dumpty.

Although reluctant, John Bradshaw was bravely doing what he believed was his duty. Bradshaw had been thrust unwillingly into the public glare – the king himself said he had never heard of him, but then the king was more likely to know the names of fifteenth-century Venetian painters than those of his own subjects. The second son of a Cheshire landowner, Bradshaw had prospered as a barrister, making a name for himself by successfully defending John Lilburne, the Leveller and freedom campaigner known as 'Freeborn John'. In an appeal against the charge of publishing unlicensed literature, Bradshaw, aided by John Cook, had made legal history, arguing the defendant's right to silence – later to become a central tenet of British criminal trial procedure.*

Bradshaw sat in pomp, looking out over the medieval vastness of the hall, now reconfigured for the trial. On either side and behind him sat his fellow judges in two long rows. At his right hand sat John Lisle, whose experience as a practising judge would be invaluable on points of procedure. Lisle was also a member of parliament and had chaired the committee that set up the New Model Army. On Bradshaw's left sat William Say, another eminent lawyer, who had acted as the court's president until Bradshaw agreed to the role. At a table covered by a Turkish carpet sat the two clerks. Before them was an empty space in which a wooden dock had been erected, stretching across the width of the hall. In the middle of the dock was a large seat for the accused, leaving plenty of room on either side for guards, attendants and messengers. Behind it was a space for several hundred soldiers. Finally, two-thirds of the hall was open for the public to attend, behind stout iron rails. On either side, high wooden galleries reared up, enabling more people to watch from above.

The scabrous newsman Marchamont Nedham published an unflattering picture of the court, including its president and sergeant-at-arms: 'cloath'd in the scarlet of their rebellious sin, their Garments Roul'd in Blood; Their ermin spotted with Carnation ... The outward face and Vissage of a Court they have in all its proportions, from the Fore-top to the Mouth, from the Beetle-brow'd President, to the foul-mouth'd Cryer.'[7]

---

* In 1646, Bradshaw and Cook persuaded the House of Lords to overturn the 1638 Star Chamber judgment against John Lilburne. In doing so, they argued that a defendant should not be put in the position of incriminating himself by signing an oath to answer all questions truthfully before knowing what charges had been levied against him. In time, this right to silence expanded to cover all charges of a criminal nature. However, since 1994 juries have been allowed to draw inferences from a defendant's refusal to answer questions.

The sword and mace were laid on the table in front of the clerks, the guards took up places on either side of the hall and silence was called so that the Act of Parliament that had brought the court into existence could be read. As Phelps stood to read it, the silence was broken by the roar of crowds of people sweeping in through the doors that had just been opened at the northern end of the hall.

Against this boisterous background, the members of the court were asked to answer to their names and a roll was taken. When each name was called, each man stood to acknowledge his presence. As the name of General Thomas Fairfax was read out, a woman in the public gallery shouted out that he had 'more wit than to be here'.[8]

According to some accounts, this was Lady Alice, Fairfax's wife. Eyewitnesses said that the woman was masked and could not be identified. Armed soldiers swooped and escorted her from the court. The commotion caused by the probable Lady Fairfax cannot have been great, for neither Gilbert Mabbott, who published a record the day after the trial finished, nor John Nalson, who later transcribed and published John Phelps's shorthand records, mentioned it. Edward Hyde, later ennobled by Charles II as Lord Clarendon, put forward the idea that Lady Fairfax's intervention was an expression of her abhorrence of the trial and a public expression of her private advice to her husband not to be persuaded by Cromwell to have any part in it.[9] There may well be some truth in this.

The roll call over, Bradshaw instructed the sergeant-at-arms to send for the prisoner. Dendy left the court to tell Colonel Tomlinson to bring the king in.

After a quarter of an hour, Tomlinson escorted the king into the palace from the house of Sir Robert Cotton beside the Thames, where he was lodged for the duration of the trial. Cotton's house had been confiscated by Charles in 1630 and had then been integrated into the growing royal palace. As Charles walked through the palace, past the Painted Chamber, Cromwell is apocryphally said to have watched from a high window and turned white as he exclaimed, 'He is come, he is come.'

Charles was dressed all in black, including his hat and cloak. The great jewelled Order of the Garter hung on his chest from a blue ribbon and the star of the Garter was pinned to his cloak. He was escorted by thirty-two guards bearing partisans, commanded by Colonel Francis Hacker, a veteran professional soldier.

The king was escorted to a chair covered in crimson velvet, directly facing Bradshaw and his fellow judges. Charles exhibited the same composure that had impressed all who had come into contact with him during his captivity. Pretending indifference to the occasion, he kept his hat on and rose from his chair to turn around and gaze at the rows of soldiers and beyond them the public, still flooding into the hall from the north entrance.

Bradshaw informed the king that the 'Commons of England assembled in Parliament, being deeply sensible of the evils and calamities that had been brought upon this nation' had identified Charles Stuart as the 'principal author of it' and had resolved to bring him to 'trial and judgement'.[10]

John Cook then stepped forward and, standing near the king, began to read his preamble to the charge: 'My Lord, on behalf of the commons of England, and of all the people thereof, I do accuse Charles Stuart, here present, of high treason and high misdemeanours.'

One eminent historian has described Cook as 'launching into the charge with evident enjoyment'.[11] This is impossible, for the transcribed shorthand notes make it clear that the charge was read by one of the court clerks and not by Cook. Despite this, one contemporary does describe Cook as 'glaring' at the prisoner.[12]

As Cook read his preamble, Charles leant forward and tapped him gently on the arm with his silver-topped cane. 'Hold a little,' he said.

The great hall held its breath. The contrast between monarch and lawyer could not have been greater. Charles was now forty-nine years old and had the practised authority of a king. His finely trimmed beard descended to a point echoed at right angles by the points of his waxed moustaches. Though slightly built and only five feet four inches in height, he had always expected and received obeisance. He knew little of the world beyond the royal court. His one moment of youthful high spirits, when he travelled in disguise to Madrid to seek the hand of the daughter of the king of Spain, had ended in farce. His life had often been ill-judged, but he had not chosen his calling. He had none of his father's gifts for diplomacy, and ignored his good advice.[13] By temperament and learning, he was an art connoisseur rather than a ruler.

The man who stood a few feet from him, clutching a scroll on which his charge was written, was a farmer's son from Leicestershire, eight years younger than the king, plain-faced and ruddy-cheeked. But behind the farm-boy looks lurked a clever and daring mind. Cook's roots among the ordinary people propelled him to propose a range of reforms to support the weak against the powerful. Just as Charles was a man out of tune with a changing world, Cook was a man entirely of his time.

His natural intelligence had been recognised early. From Wadham College, Oxford, he went to Gray's Inn to practise law. But once in London, the gauche country boy had found it difficult to gain commissions and earn a living. He moved to Dublin, where he was to thrive under the patronage of Thomas Wentworth, Earl of Strafford. Months before the trial of the king, Cook published a remarkable book making the case for a number of revolutionary ideas including a national health service for the poor, a form of legal aid and the right of the accused to call witnesses.[14]

These dramatic differences apart, sovereign and lawyer had one unusual thing in common – they both regretted the execution of the Earl of Strafford, who had been not only Cook's mentor but Charles's most able advisor. Charles had promised to protect his loyal lieutenant who had contemplated the use of an Irish army against the king's English opponents. When the intrigue came to light, Parliament charged Strafford with treason. It was a proxy attack on the authority of the king himself. To deflect the heat radiating off Strafford onto the crown, Charles signed his friend's death warrant. Cook, for his part, had endeavoured to save him, but to no avail.

'Hold a little.'

Cook did not heed the instruction and continued. 'In the name of the commons of England, the charge may be read unto him.'

Charles tapped again. Cook continued to ignore the gesture. The king then gave Cook's arm a good thump and the silver knob of his cane flew off and landed on the floor with a thump. The knob rolled back and forth on the ancient wooden boards. The king looked down at it. Cook looked at it and then up at the king. Charles motioned to Cook to pick it up. Cook stood still. There was not a movement in the hall. Cromwell, Bradshaw, Ireton, Ludlow, Harrison and all the rest looked on. After an eternity, the king stood and picked up the silver knob.[15] It was taken as an omen.

Then Andrew Broughton began to read the charge: 'That the said Charles Stuart, being admitted King of England, and therein trusted with a limited power to govern by and according to the laws of the land ...'[16]

Charles must have winced at the description of his power as 'limited'. After all, if his power came from God it had no limit.

' ... and by his trust, oath, and office, being obliged to use the power committed to him for the good and benefit of the people, and for the preservation of their rights and liberties ... '

This, of course, was exactly the point being argued by Cook and Dorislaus: that the power of a ruler came not from the divine but from the agreement of the people. This right only continued as long as the people continued to give their consent – and consent came only with good and fair government. The limit could be reached if a tyrant abused his power.

Charles looked around in a distracted manner. Broughton continued:

'... a wicked design to erect and uphold in himself an unlimited and tyrannical power to rule according to his will, and to overthrow the rights and liberties of the people ...'

At this, the king laughed to show his contempt for the court. Broughton kept reading.

'... hath traitorously and maliciously levied war against the present Parliament, and the people therein represented ...'

This direct assault on the king as a bloody tyrant was followed by a list of the battles of the first war in which, according to the charge, the king had caused thousands of his fellow countrymen to die:

'Beverley in the County of York, Brentford in the County of Middlesex, Caversham Bridge in the County of Berkshire ...'

Only two years before, Parliament had considered an amnesty to all parties to the war so that a settlement could be reached. Now the king was portrayed as responsible for all the blood that had been shed.

'... he, the said Charles Stuart, hath caused and procured many thousands of the free people of this nation to be slain ...'

What a difference two years had made.

The charge moved on to claim that Charles Stuart had, by evil means, 'renewed, or caused to be renewed, the said war against the Parliament and good people of this nation in this present year, 1648.'

Finally, Charles was accused of continuing to commission revolt from English, Irish and other foreign 'revolters'. Charles smiled when he heard himself described as a 'tyrant, traitor, murderer, and public enemy of the commonwealth'.[17]

Once the charge was completed, Bradshaw addressed the king: 'Sir, you have now heard your charge read, containing such matters as appears in it. You find that in the close of it is prayed to the court, in the behalf of the commons of England, that you answer your charge. The court expects your answer.'

Charles's habitual stammer was well known; it had afflicted him since childhood. The assembled crowds must have expected a halting, rather pathetic statement of his lack of guilt. Instead, Charles spoke confidently and clearly.

'I would know by what authority, I mean lawful (there are many unlawful authorities in the world, thieves and robbers by the highways) but I would know by what authority I was brought from thence, and carried from place to place (and I know not what), and when I know what lawful authority, I shall answer.'

Bradshaw replied that the authority came from 'the people of England, of which you are elected king, to answer them'.

Charles replied, 'No sir, I deny that.'

This bald rejection of the court placed it in a difficult position. By accepted trial procedure, the prisoner had to plead first before the trial could move forward. Traditionally, English courts had the right to press the accused to plead – literally to press them under an increasing weight until they pleaded either guilty or not guilty. For a king, this was not an option.

Bradshaw realised the predicament and informed the king: 'If you acknowledge not the authority of the court, they must proceed.'

Charles reiterated that he did not recognise the court: 'England was never an elective kingdom, but an hereditary kingdom for near these thousand years; and therefore let me know by what authority I am called hither.'

Bradshaw decided to adjourn the court. As Charles left the hall, there were cries of 'God save the king!' from the public galleries. From the soldiers there were some shouts of 'Justice!'[18] The king was escorted back to Sir Robert Cotton's house.

The following day, a Sunday, both sides had time to reflect on the trial so far. The tussle in which king and Parliament were engaged was an ancient one. The issue of the balance of power between the king and his subjects went back to Magna Carta. For the court, the dilemma was where this left matters in a practical sense. It was decided that Charles should be given another chance to plead.

On Monday morning, 22 January, Charles returned to a packed and rowdy hall. Once again, there were shouts from the public galleries. Bradshaw commanded Colonel Hacker to arrest anyone who disturbed the court.

John Cook took the floor and explained that the king must be given another chance to plead – but now there was a sting in the tail: 'My humble motion,' he said, 'is that the prisoner be directed to make a positive answer, either by way of confession or negation; which if he refuse to do, that the matter of charge may be taken *pro confesso*, and the court may proceed according to justice.'

In other words, a refusal to plead became a confession of guilt. The pressure was on Charles to comply with the court's demand for an answer. The reply that he gave was unexpected and daring. Charles said that if he spoke just for himself he could plead. As it was, his hands were tied as he stood for the freedom and liberty of the people and so had to represent them in law: 'For if power without law make laws, may alter the fundamental laws of the kingdom, I do not know what subject he is in England that can be sure of his life, or any thing that he calls his own.'

It was a good argument – and a shame it was not delivered by a good king, rather than just a brave one. Unfortunately for him, Charles had stonewalled one last time. Bradshaw interrupted him, saying he was not to question the authority of the court but to give a direct answer to the charge.

Charles continued his self-justification, saying that he did 'plead for the liberties of the people of England more than you do'. This statement, coming from a king who had ruled without regard for the liberties granted under Magna Carta, cut no ice. Bradshaw coldly told him he was in contempt of court.

The king continued to argue the case with Bradshaw until the latter grew tired of the confrontation and ordered the sergeant-at-arms to take the prisoner away. Charles continued to profess his support for the 'liberty and freedom of all his subjects'.

An exasperated Bradshaw cut across him: 'How great a friend you have been to the laws and liberties of the people let all of England and the world judge.'

After this petulant exchange, the court adjourned. On his way out of the court, Charles made an extraordinary admission to his guards: that he cared nothing for the blood spilt by anyone but the Earl of Strafford, his close advisor who had been executed for treason eight years before. Given the profuse bloodshed since, this demonstrated to Cook and others that Charles had a heart of stone and was beyond redemption.[19]

That evening, in his temporary jail in Sir Robert Cotton's house, Charles asked Sir Thomas Herbert about the nature of those who made up the court. Herbert told him they were a mixture of parliamentarians, army officers and London merchants. The king replied that he had studied them carefully but had not recognised more than eight faces. We can be sure he at least recognised those of Cromwell, Ireton, Harrison and Vane.

The following day, a Tuesday, the court met in the Painted Chamber. Analysing their predicament, they agreed the king should be given yet another chance to plead. To encourage him, it was decided that Cook should ask the court to proceed speedily to judgment. That, they reasoned, should focus the royal mind. And so they trooped off to Westminster Hall and the king was sent for.

Once Charles was seated, Cook launched into a strenuous argument against any more time-wasting. Bradshaw asked Charles for his final answer – guilty or not guilty?

It was hopeless. Charles announced that he wished to defend the 'ancient laws of the kingdom' and claimed that there was no law that permitted his trial. He was almost right, except that he had not grasped the full nature of what was taking place. The laws of England were being reinterpreted to allow the people to try a tyrant. The absolutist views of the Stuarts were in direct conflict with previous ideas about the order of good government. Almost a hundred years before, a member of Queen Elizabeth's council had described England as a 'commonwealth' with a government made up of monarch, Council of State and Parliament.[20]

Bradshaw wrapped up the public proceedings for another irksome day. The court retired to the Painted Chamber. By now, their resolve had hardened.

On Wednesday, 24 January, the court sat in private in the Painted Chamber to take evidence from witnesses against the king. A procession mainly of ordinary soldiers and civilians reported that they had seen the king raise his standard in declaration of war or had seen him with his army at various battles. One witness described how the king had shown bad faith during the negotiations at Newport by secretly trying to contact the Prince of Wales to raise an army. Evidence continued into the following day.

On Friday morning, the commissioners met in private to discuss the draft sentence. Sixty-two commissioners answered the roll call. Discussions over the exact form of the sentence continued until nightfall. In its final form, the sentence condemned the king as a 'tyrant, traitor, murderer and public enemy to be put to death by the severing of his head from his body'. It was agreed that the court would reassemble in public in Westminster Hall at ten in the morning and read the sentence to the king.

When the court assembled, Charles once again took everyone by surprise. Without waiting for Bradshaw to open the proceedings, he began, 'I desire a word to be heard a little and I hope I shall give no occasion for interruption.'

Bradshaw was taken aback. He was now dressed in red robes which made him look as if he were playing the role of a pope in a bad charade. Mustering his dignity, he told the king he might be heard but first he had to hear the court. It was well known, he said, that the king was charged with treason and other high crimes in the name of the people of England. At this, a woman in one of the public galleries shouted out, 'It is a lie – not half the people.'[21] Colonel Daniel Axtell, commander of the halberdiers guarding the king, reacted swiftly, ordering his men to direct their guns at the woman. He shouted, 'What whore is that who disturbs the court?' It was later claimed that this was Lady Fairfax once more. Although this is likely, there is no real evidence. The galleries were searched but the woman had disappeared. Order restored, the court continued. Bradshaw informed the king that the court would hear anything he had to say in his defence. Charles replied that he wished to speak in the Painted Chamber before both the House of Commons and the House of Lords. At this, one of the commissioners, John Downes, spoke out. In all the hearings, he was the only commissioner to break the rule agreed from the outset that no one but the Lord President should speak. Rising from his seat, he asked, 'Have we hearts of stone? Are we men?'[22]

Cromwell, who was sitting in the row in front of Downes, turned round and swiftly rebuked him. 'Art thou mad?' he asked. Bradshaw ordered an adjournment. The king was escorted back to Sir Robert Cotton's house. The sixty-seven commissioners present filed out of the hall and through to the Court of Wards, situated just beyond the south door.

Phelps appears to have made no record of what occurred in the Court of Wards. Most likely, Downes was stoutly put down by Cromwell so that the court could regain its united face and go back into the great hall to pronounce sentence.

Half an hour later, the judges filed in and the king was called. Once Charles was seated, Bradshaw told him that the court was resolved to proceed to judgment. In response Charles asked that they consider delaying – 'a little delay of a day or two further may give peace, whereas an hasty judgment may bring on that trouble and perpetual inconveniency for the kingdom' – so that he might be heard in the Painted Chamber before the Commons and the Lords.

Bradshaw tersely answered that if the king had no more to say the court would proceed to judgment. To this, Charles replied, 'I have nothing more to say.'

Broughton rose, unrolled a parchment and began: 'He, the said Charles Stuart, as a tyrant, traitor, murderer, and a public enemy, shall be put to death by the severing of his head from his body.'

Charles listened in dignified silence while the sentence was read out. When it was finished, Bradshaw said, 'The sentence read and now published is the act, sentence, judgment and resolution of the whole court.'

At this, on a prearranged signal, the whole body of judges rose as one to show their unanimous agreement with the sentence. After they had sat down, the king spoke very quietly:

'Will you hear me a word, sir?'

Bradshaw replied, 'Sir, you are not to be heard after the sentence.'

For the first time, Charles reacted with passion and cried, 'No, sir!'

Then Bradshaw said, 'No, sir, by your favour, sir. Guard, withdraw your prisoner!'

By refusing to allow the king to speak after the sentence was read, Bradshaw was correctly, but brutally, applying the rules of the time. In seventeenth-century England, last words were reserved for the scaffold.[23] Hacker ordered his men to form a guard around Charles to take him away. Charles again said, 'I may speak after the sentence. By your favour, sir, I may speak after the sentence ever.'

As the guards clustered around him, Charles became clearly distressed. He shouted, 'By your favour, the sentence, sir ... I say sir, I do ... I am not suffered for to speak: expect what justice other people will have!'

In this pitiful manner, the trial ended. Charles was escorted from the hall. Soldiers lining the stairs and corridors shouted 'Justice! Justice!' and jeered at him. Some soldiers blew smoke from their pipes in his face. Others spat on him. Regaining his composure, Charles said, 'Poor souls, for a piece of money they would so for their commanders.'

He was led to Sir Robert Cotton's house and then to Whitehall Palace to await his execution. The following day, the public galleries, the commissioners' benches and the king's velvet chair were taken away. The booksellers and lawyers reclaimed their places, stalls were set up and people gossiped where history had just been made. The court received notice that the king wished to see his children, the Duke of Gloucester and Lady Elizabeth, and Dr Juxon, the Bishop of London. In its final decision, the court granted the king's wishes.

When the trial ended, a committee of the court met in the Painted Chamber to agree on arrangements for the execution. A warrant was drawn up, instructing three colonels – Hercules Huncks, Robert Phayre and Francis Hacker – to organise the king's death by 'the severinge [sic] of his head from his body'.

According to parliamentary records, the death warrant was ready to sign on Monday, 29 January, though there is good evidence that it was in fact ready by the evening of the final day of the trial two days before and that as many as twenty-nine commissioners signed it then.[24] Out of the sixty-seven commissioners present on the sentencing, fifty-seven went on to sign the warrant by the end of Monday. Two commissioners who were not present at the court's final sitting also signed the warrant: Thomas Challoner and Richard Ingoldsby. A famous story is told that Cromwell and the republican Harry Marten daubed ink on one another's faces while signing. Though their signatures are so far apart on the warrant that they may not have signed at the same time, there is a good source for this colourful tale.[25]

The ten commissioners present at the final day of the trial who did not sign were all regular participants in the work and sittings of the court, with the exception of Colonel Tomlinson, whose duties as officer in charge of the king's person throughout the trial precluded his participation except when the king was present. A. W. McIntosh has suggested the absence of signatures should not be taken as signifying any diminution of purpose. However, Nicholas Love, who helped draft the sentence, was later to claim, self-servingly, that he had wished for more discussion before actually moving to the delivery of the sentence.[26]

Over the years, there has been a great deal of speculation about the manner in which some signatures were obtained. While it is undoubtedly true that Cromwell drummed up signatories, there is no evidence to support the contention that some commissioners were forced to sign. Neither is there any evidence that some signatures were forged.

The warrant itself shows us that the first to sign was the president of the court, John Bradshaw. He was followed by Thomas, Lord Grey of Groby, the MP for Leicester. Grey was given prominence because he was the only peer to sit as a commissioner. His signature immediately precedes that of Oliver Cromwell. As the signatures mounted on the parchment, they became increasingly bunched up, until there was space for barely three or four more – perhaps the reason more commissioners did not sign, nor were asked to sign.

The warrant stipulated that the execution was to take place in Whitehall between ten o'clock in the morning and five o'clock in the afternoon, so that it could be carried out in daylight. The date was set for Tuesday, 30 January 1649 – the following day.

4

EXECUTION

29 January–7 February 1649

Throughout the freezing night the carpenters worked hard to finish the scaffold ready for use in the morning. The noise echoed around Whitehall and across the frozen Thames to the hovels on the far shore. It penetrated the locked and guarded room in St James's Palace and woke the man for whom the structure was being built. Sitting up, he pulled back the heavy curtains surrounding his bed. Cold air rushed around his face. By the light of the large candle left burning through the night he read the dial of the little silver clock hanging on the bedpost. It was just after five o'clock on the morning of 30 January 1649. Charles Stuart, appointed by God as king of England, Scotland and Ireland, counted his last hours on earth.

St James's Palace had been built by Henry VIII on the site of a hospital dedicated to the patron saint of lepers. Most of Charles's children were born in the palace. Now he was to be led from it to his death. A court whose authority he had refused to recognise had sentenced him to be executed for crimes against the people. As Charles got out of bed, his servant, Sir Thomas Herbert, woke from his mattress where he had been sleeping beside the king's bed. For more than two years while the king was in custody, Herbert had served as Charles's gentleman of the bedchamber. During that time he had, though a parliamentarian himself, grown fond of the king, whose good humour in the face of adversity had impressed many who came into contact with him.

With Herbert's help, Charles began to dress meticulously. In his memoirs, Herbert would famously tell how the king insisted on wearing two white shirts, so he would not shiver in the freezing air upon the scaffold and give the impression he was afraid.[1] Herbert groomed Charles's hair fastidiously and trimmed his beard. Though he had been appointed by Parliament, a diplomatic career had equipped him with the social graces necessary to serve a king. He had been present the day before while the king heartbreakingly took leave of his two youngest children. The scene that followed was said to have reduced Cromwell to tears.

At the outbreak of war, Princess Elizabeth and Henry, Duke of Gloucester, had been taken into custody by Parliament. They spent the following years in the care of various families, including those of the Earl of Pembroke and the Duke of Northumbria. At the time of their father's execution, Elizabeth was thirteen and Henry eight. The king had not seen them for eighteen months. He told Elizabeth she was no longer to think of her eldest brother, Charles, merely as her sibling, but as her sovereign. Then he said, 'Sweetheart, you'll forget this.'[2] Elizabeth burst into tears and swore she would not forget, and that she would write down what her father told her – and so she did:

He told me he was glad I was come, and although he had not time to say much ... he told me, he had forgiven all his Enemies, and hoped God would forgive them also; and commanded us, and all the rest of my Brothers and Sisters to forgive them: he bid me tell my Mother, That his thoughts never had strayed from her, and that his love should be the same to the last ...

Charles also had serious matters to discuss with young Henry:

he took the Duke of Gloucester upon his knee, said, Sweetheart, now they will cut off thy Fathers head; (upon which
words the child looked very steadfastly on him.) Mark child,
what I say, they will cut off my head, and perhaps make thee a
King: But mark what I say, you must not be a King so long as
your Brother Charles and James do live; For they will cut off
your Brothers heads, (when they can catch them) and cut off
thy head too at the last ... At which the child, sighing, said, 'I
will be torn in pieces first'. At these words, coming so unexpectedly from so young a child, rejoiced my father exceedingly.
    And desired me not to grieve for him, for he should die a
Martyr ...

In The Hague, the Prince of Wales was frantically trying to bring
pressure to have the execution abandoned. He wrote personally to
Fairfax, pleading for mercy for his father. He also asked the States-
General (the Dutch Parliament) for help. As a result, two Dutch
ambassadors came and made direct representations to Parliament. At
the prince's request, the French ambassador also made a plea for
mercy on behalf of Queen Henrietta Maria. Despite all this activity,
the prince would later be criticised for not having travelled across
Europe to solicit help directly from the crowned heads of as many
states as possible. But the prince had done what he thought he
should, though what he did was to no avail.

When daybreak came, the outlines of the frozen city were etched
in frost. Europe was descending to the lowest trough of what was to
become known as the Little Ice Age. The officer in charge of the
king's guard, Colonel Tomlinson, came to check on his prisoner.
Through the barred windows the pallid morning light barely illumi-
nated the room. Tomlinson saw that the king was ready. He was
dressed in black, apart from the white lace of his shirts. As at his trial,
he wore only two decorations: the Order of the Garter on his cloak

and also on a ribbon around his neck. Against his funereal clothing, their symbolic brilliance made it clear that he saw himself as England's martyr.

Less than a mile away across St James's Park, muffled masses were already making their way towards Whitehall Palace to witness the execution. From Charing Cross they pressed under the palace's massive red-brick Tudor gate towers and gathered around the scaffold erected against the Palladian façade of the royal Banqueting House. At ten o'clock a company of halberdiers commanded by Colonel Francis Hacker arrived at the palace to take Charles on his final journey. At this point, Colonel Tomlinson relinquished his role as the king's jailer; Charles was now in the care of Colonel Hacker.

The procession left the palace for the short journey to Whitehall. Their route took them through St James's Park. Unlike today, the park was enclosed and forbidden to the public. When Charles was a boy, it had been a zoo, set up by his father. There had been camels and even an elephant. In the lake, crocodiles had lurked. Now the lake was frozen over. All the animals had long since gone. A regiment of infantry now lined the route. The royal procession made a grand, if melancholy, sight. It was led by Colonel Hacker. The king was flanked by Bishop Juxon and Colonel Tomlinson, while immediately before and behind him walked his gentlemen-in-waiting, escorted by a company of halberdiers. Bright regimental banners fluttered incongruously against the skeletal trees. Drummers beat a rhythm like a dying heart.

When the entourage arrived at Whitehall Palace it became clear there was a hitch in the arrangements: death was not to be so swift. The king was placed under guard in the ornate cabinet-chamber which in happier times had been an anteroom to his bedroom. There was a fire burning in the grate and on the walls hung some of the finest paintings from Charles's peerless art collection, which included masterpieces by Rembrandt, Caravaggio and his favourite, Titian. There were portraits of Charles, among them those by the incomparable wizard Anthony Van Dyck, who had done more than anyone to give Charles the appearance of a divine king.

Among Van Dyck's portraits, the famous triple-head is interesting in the present context. It was produced to be sent to Italy so that the finest sculptor of the age, Gian Lorenzo Bernini, could carve a bust of the king. When he saw the painting, Bernini said the sitter was the saddest person he had ever seen and must surely die a violent death. Not only did the sculptor's prophecy come true but his marble bust also had a violent end, perishing in the accidental fire that destroyed Whitehall Palace in 1698.

While Charles lingered among his paintings, Parliament had urgent business. Legal minds had discovered a problem. It had dawned on them that with the king's death there was nothing to stop the Prince of Wales inheriting the throne. So, as the doomed king toasted his all too mortal toes by the fire, the judges hurried to pass a law stating there could be no successor. They made it illegal for anyone to declare the prince as king.

There was an even more pressing problem: the appointment of an executioner. Given the nature of the prisoner, the executioner could not be called for until the morning when the sentence was to be carried out. At the order of Colonel Hewson, troops went to the house of the public executioner, Richard Brandon, and found him at home; but his assistant Ralph Jones could not be found. So a very reluctant Brandon was taken alone under arrest with what equipment he could carry, and someone still had to be found to fill in for the headsman's assistant. It was to remain a matter of conjecture whether Brandon, who brought the axe, was the man who wielded it.

Poised between life and death, the king prayed with Bishop Juxon. He pledged to God his forgiveness of those who were determined to obliterate the House of Stuart. It was one thing for a condemned king to forgive; as would soon become apparent, however, it was quite another for his heirs or followers to do the same.

While Oliver Cromwell and his closest companions patented the formula to make their revolution stick, another last-ditch drama was being played out around the condemned monarch. General Fairfax received a letter delivered by a courier from the Prince of Wales. When the general opened the envelope, he found two items. One was a piece of parchment, blank except for the prince's signature and seal. The other was a letter explaining the meaning of the blank sheet: in return for his father's life, the prince explained, the general could write his own terms, which he, as the heir to the throne, would see were obeyed. These were the heartfelt pleadings of a son to his enemies intent on executing his father,

> deposing him from the royal dignity given him by God alone, who invested his person with it by a succession undisputed, or even of taking his life; the mere thought of which seems so horrible and incredible that it has moved us to address these presents to you, who now have power, for the last time, either to testify your fidelity, by reinstating your lawful king, and to restore peace to the kingdom – an honour never before given to so small a number as you – or be the authors of misery unprecedented in this country . . .[3]

The Prince of Wales was nothing if not thorough in his pleading. But the army had had enough of trying to do deals with the House of Stuart.

For his part, Charles felt his downfall was due not to misrule but to a bad deed regarding Strafford. The betrayal had gnawed at him ever since. Sitting as a prisoner in his own bedroom, he resolved to say something about it on the scaffold.

There was another hold-up. A day or two before, Cromwell had found it a slow job to obtain sufficient signatories to the king's death warrant. Now he was having difficulty getting signatures on the order for the executioner to carry out the sentence. The death warrant instructed three officers – Colonels Hacker, Huncks and Phayre (who was Herbert's son-in-law) – to ensure that sentence was carried

out. Now Huncks and Phayre refused to sign the order. In exasperation, Cromwell signed it himself and passed it to Hacker, who also
signed.

Shortly before two o'clock, the military guard came to take
Charles to the scaffold, escorting their prisoner through the maze of
corridors linking parts of the old palace, constructed piecemeal over
several centuries. At this point, Colonel Tomlinson had no further
part in the proceedings but the king asked him to accompany him to
the scaffold, to which Tomlinson agreed.[4] A staircase led them into
the imposing Holbein Gatehouse, built by Henry VIII to straddle
Whitehall so that he could reach his cockpits and tilt-yard without
having to enter the street. Now Charles and his escorts took the same
route to cross Whitehall unseen by the crowds swarming below.

In a throng of soldiers, parliamentarians and hangers-on, Charles
emerged into the echoing volume of Inigo Jones's Banqueting
House, with its celebrated ceiling painted by Peter Paul Rubens.
The ceiling was a glorious affirmation of the divine right of the
House of Stuart to rule. Above the doomed king's head his father
ascended gloriously into heaven, stepping from earth onto the wing
of an eagle clutching a thunderbolt in its talons. Charles was up
there too, depicted as an infant with the Roman goddess Minerva
holding a crown above his head, indicating his divinely ordained
succession.

The great chamber had played host to many royal revelries and
masques, attended by the court or by foreign ambassadors. After
many years of war, the great chamber's windows were still boarded
up, obscuring its extravagance in a funereal gloom. One window
was open, its frame ripped out to allow a temporary flight of steps to
lead up and out to the scaffold built against the outer wall. Before
climbing the stairs, Charles said goodbye to Tomlinson, who had
been his jailer since he was taken to Windsor. As a memento,
Charles gave Tomlinson a gold toothpick in a case.[5]

At two o'clock, the king emerged from the Banqueting House.
The huge crowd surged forward but was pushed back by lines of

cavalry and infantry. Across the square, Oliver Cromwell looked on from a window in the palace. Staring around him, Charles realised that a circle of troops kept the crowd too far back for them to hear his speech. This was a blow: his last words – those he had wished to speak in Westminster Hall following his sentence – would have to be addressed to the group standing on the scaffold. Among them were Colonel Hacker, Bishop Juxon, some soldiers and the heavily disguised executioner and his assistant, wearing masks and false beards, like pantomime villains but for their very lethal axe.

Following established protocol, the condemned man addressed the crowd as best he could. He began by protesting that he had not waged war on Parliament and so was innocent: it was Parliament which had waged war upon him. He declared that his death was God's judgment and, alluding to the Strafford affair, said that one unjust sentence was being punished by another. He finished by proclaiming that he was going from a corruptible to an incorruptible crown, adding wistfully, 'Where no disturbance can be, no disturbance in the world.' For a monarch whose reign had encompassed more disorder than any since the Wars of the Roses it was a reasonable sentiment. For a man with one eye on the block and the other on posterity, it was a well-judged speech – the words of a martyr.

Approaching the execution block, Charles realised it was so low that to place his head upon it he would have to lie flat on his belly. He asked if it could be raised up so he could at least have the dignity of kneeling, but was told it could not. It seems this was not some final, mean-spirited humiliation of the king. The executioner had brought a small block he could easily carry.

The king instructed the executioner not to strike until he saw him signal by thrusting his hands forward. The headsman consented. Charles lay down and placed his head on the block. As the executioner stooped to move a wayward wisp of hair sticking out from under the king's cap at the nape of his neck, the king nervously asked a second time if he understood to wait for the signal. This was no small matter. Charles wanted to make sure the blade did not fall until he had composed himself. A severed head with staring eyes would be a bad image for a martyr. Certain that the headsman understood his instruction, Charles lay down and placed his head on the block. After a brief prayer, he thrust out his hands. When the executioner's assistant held up the severed head for the crowd to see, Charles's eyes were modestly closed and the expression the very look of a royal martyr.

Instead of shouting the traditional words, 'Behold the head of a traitor!' the assistant threw the head down with such force that the right cheek was bruised. Among the vast crowd, many groaned, while others cheered. Some rushed forward to dip handkerchiefs in the blood running off the block, either as mementoes or as talismans. Soldiers, it was said, dipped their swords in the royal blood.

Immediately after the execution there arose much speculation (which has continued to the present day) as to the identity of the executioners. It is likely that the main executioner was the 'common hangman', Richard Brandon. The king's head was expertly severed by a heavy blow that sliced cleanly through the neck's fourth vertebra.

Brandon did not survive long after the king's execution. Five months later, on 20 June 1649, following Brandon's death, an anonymous tract appeared claiming to be his confession.[6] The tract claimed that it came to be written after Brandon confessed all to 'a young man of his acquaintance'. According to the published confession, Brandon was paid £30 for the job – and told his wife it was 'the deerest money that ever he earn'd in his life, for it would cost him his life'. Brandon soon lapsed into a fever and 'lay raging and swearing, and still pointing at one thing or another, which he conceived to appear visible before him'. The tract also quoted 'a neighbour' who said that Brandon had told him that at the very moment he was about to strike the blow to execute the king, a great pain struck him in his neck that had continued ever since; and that he had been so troubled by the fact that the king would not give him forgiveness for what he was about to do that he had never slept quietly since. Of course, it may be that the tract was entirely made up in order to cash in on the death of the notorious hangman, or designed to muddy the waters and divert suspicion from other candidates for the role.

Within two days of the execution, royalist pamphlets were circulating, describing the unjust killing of the king. Word of Charles's death began to filter through to the Continent. At first, no one knew whether to believe the stories or not. Queen Henrietta was in Paris with two of their children waiting fearfully for word. Two hundred miles to the north in The Hague, the Prince of Wales and his brother and sister also waited. Rumours were circulating in both cities, but neither queen nor prince would have firm news about events in London for several days.

The news finally reached The Hague and the Royal Palace on 4 February. William of Orange broke the sad news to his wife of her father's death by execution. Mary was too shaken to undertake the task of breaking the news to her brothers. The burden therefore fell to a senior member of the small Stuart retinue, Dr Stephen Goffe, an ardent royalist who as a chaplain to Charles I had carried secret messages for the king after he had been taken into captivity. When the situation became too dangerous for the clerical agent he had taken a boat for the Continent and was now chaplain to the Prince of Wales. Goffe's family had split over the question of king or Parliament. Stephen's brother William was a colonel in the parliamentary army and would later become revered in America as an upholder of liberty.

Goffe steeled himself for the task. As the oldest member of the household and a chaplain to two generations of the royal family, it was his duty. Entering the prince's chamber, he got to the heart of the matter at once by addressing the eighteen-year-old prince as 'Your Majesty'. Grasping the significance, Charles burst into tears and fled from the room. The prince's reaction, according to his advisor Edward Hyde, was of understandable shock: 'The barbarous stroke so surprised him that he was in all the confusion imaginable and all about him were almost bereft of their understanding.'[7]

Charles was now a penniless king without a kingdom. Nine weeks later, his first son was born to his mistress Lucy Walter, the first of many children born out of wedlock as the prince sought to obliterate the world in sex and personal pleasure. On the surface, Charles still seemed as frivolous and charming as ever, but to those who knew him something seemed to harden inside him after his father's death.

By the time news reached Holland of the execution, the king had not yet been buried. Thomas Herbert recorded that immediately after Charles's death, he met Fairfax in the Long Gallery of Westminster Palace. Herbert was surprised when Fairfax asked him how things went with the king. Next, Herbert met Oliver Cromwell, also coming along the Long Gallery. Cromwell was much more to the point and told Herbert that he would have 'orders for the King's burial speedily'.[8] The interesting point here is that when the axe fell, both men were supposedly in a prayer meeting together, yet one appeared aware of exactly what had happened on the scaffold and the other did not. Since all of London knew that Charles had been executed, it is most unlikely that the supreme army commander did not. One may suppose that Fairfax was in some form of denial, or else he had shut himself away so that he might genuinely not know the precise time of the execution, thereby distancing himself from the business. An alternative explanation is that Fairfax may have believed that an appeal he had made earlier in the day for a postponement of the sentence had been successful. His future actions, however, would reveal much more about the commander-in-chief's changes of mind.

Odd though this seemed at the time – and still does today – the king left no specific instructions for his burial. Despite this, those close to him had begun planning his funeral some time before his execution. When his head and body were carried indoors from the scaffold, everything was ready to embalm the corpse and place it in a wooden coffin. A thin lead casing was formed around the coffin to seal it and it was wrapped in a dark velvet covering.[9]

The king's close allies, including Bishop Juxon, decided he should be buried in Westminster Abbey, a traditional burial place of England's kings and queens. They wished him to be placed in the chapel of Henry VII, from whom he was descended, and where his father and brother were buried, along with Edward VI, Mary Queen of Scots and Queen Elizabeth. Thomas Herbert applied to the new governing council for permission for burial in the abbey. Unsurprisingly, it was denied, the reason given that it would be 'inconvenient'. Having a newly martyred king buried right in the centre of the nation's spiritual power was the last thing the republicans wanted.

Herbert and Juxon decided the best way forward was to apply for permission to bury the king at Windsor Castle. Charles had been fond of the castle and also held the Chapel of St George in high regard. The crypt of the chapel housed the remains of several kings: Henry VI, Henry VIII and Edward IV, who had rebuilt the chapel in English Perpendicular splendour. This time, their application was successful. On 6 February, Parliament authorised Herbert to bury the king at Windsor.

The following day, six horses covered in black pulled a black hearse from the courtyard of St James's Palace and headed for Windsor. Four carriages followed, carrying Herbert and the bishop, along with various retainers who had served the king since he was taken into army captivity. Upon arrival, the coffin was first taken to the Dean's House and then laid in Charles's old bedroom while Herbert and the rest of them went to look at the chapel. They decided the best resting place was the vault in which Edward IV was interred on the north side of the choir.

As with almost everything relating to the king's final days, even the choice of a resting place for his corpse would not be straightforward. While Herbert and his companions were inspecting the vault, a group of royalist nobles came in, among them the Duke of Richmond, the Earl of Southampton and the Earl of Lindsey. This group insisted upon viewing all the options for themselves. While this was going on, one of them beat with his staff on the paving stones, which rang with a hollow sound. According to Herbert, the paving was removed and earth dug up to reveal a vault that ran under the choir. The nobles descended and discovered that the vault contained two coffins, one of which was 'very large of antique form, the other little'.[10] These coffins, they surmised, surely contained the bodies of Henry VIII and his third wife, Jane Seymour, who was known to be buried beside her husband (this was confirmed by research 160 years later).[11] The nobles agreed that the vault was the place to bury the king.

Charles's coffin was carried from his bedroom down to St George's Hall, where it was placed for a time under a black velvet pall. A small entourage gathered to carry the king to the chapel under a clear blue sky. No sooner had they left the hall than snow began to fall, turning the pall white. As the bishop opened his copy of the Book of Common Prayer to read from it the order for the burial of the dead, there was another crisis. The governor of the castle, Colonel Whitchcott, intervened, saying the Book of Common Prayer was no longer allowed. And so Charles Stuart went to his grave without even the words he would have wished for to be read over his body. Thomas Herbert recorded that the total cost of the funeral was £229 5s, of which £130 was paid to pall bearers and others he described as 'seventeen gentlemen and other inferior servants for mourning'.[12]

And so England entered a new era without a king – except, of course, that there was one, of sorts. Across the water in Holland, the followers of Charles, Prince of Wales, declared him king. All he had to do was find a kingdom. The problem facing him was that while he had little material support, those who had brought his father to the scaffold had one of the finest armies ever seen. So how was he to find his way back, if at all?

5

PROPAGANDA AND ASSASSINATION

January 1649–October 1651

On the day Charles Stuart was executed, pamphlets appeared on the streets of London proclaiming the Prince of Wales as Charles II. A few copies of a small book also passed furtively from hand to hand. Four days later, street hawkers were selling it on the streets.[1] The book carried no publisher's marks or printer's name but was purported to have been written by Charles I himself. Its message was that the king had died the death of a holy martyr. The book played a major role in bolstering royalist resistance, turning shock and dismay to outrage and the desire for revenge against Cromwell and all the other representatives of the new republic.[2]

As soon as the new government appreciated the incendiary nature of the publication, they moved to ban it. But it was too late – it quickly appeared on the Continent, spreading the cult of the martyr king. It became the biggest selling book of the century.[3]

The book was titled in Greek, *Eikon Basilike* ('The King's Image'). It contained a series of short essays in which Charles justified his actions during the last decade of his reign. Each essay was followed by a prayer. The king's enemies were never blamed for his misfortunes – they were not even mentioned by name. Instead, the king asked God for forgiveness and instructed his eldest son to be forgiving also. Naturally, the Prince of Wales and his supporters were in no mood for forgiveness.

Eikon Basilike was a propaganda coup. So many editions were rushed out that the zinc plate carrying the frontispiece of Charles the Martyr had to be re-engraved eight times.[4] There was no doubt that public opinion, already swaying in the aftermath of his execution, was beguiled by the notion of a martyred king. For the men who put Charles on trial and set up the republic, *Eikon Basilike* smacked of the Counter-Reformation. It was a Puritan's nightmare.

Arguments persist about the exact authorship of *Eikon Basilike*. It appears that Charles began the book some time in 1647 or 1648, as a justification of his actions leading up to and throughout the Civil Wars. When it became clear he would be tried and possibly executed, the work was completed either by Charles or another hand. Likely candidates as ghost writers include the Bishop of Worcester, John Gauden, former royal chaplain Jeremy Taylor, and Dr William Juxon, the Bishop of London.[5] Whoever had a hand in its creation, its power has been well put by Andrew Lacey: 'This little book, perhaps more than anything else, not only fixed the image of the martyr in the public mind, but also demonstrated the power of conservative, royalist and Anglican patterns of thought and allegiance which survived the republic and emerged triumphant in 1660.'[6]

Charles the victim became more attractive than Charles the monarch had ever been. What regal power and robes could not give him, humility and suffering could. In a modest house in High Holborn near Lincoln's Inn Fields, a forty-one-year-old writer read the book with growing alarm. This was John Milton, the greatest poet of the age, and a participant in radical political circles. Milton saw right away that an upsurge of sentiment in favour of hereditary monarchy could stop social and religious reforms in their tracks. A counter-blast was urgently needed – and Milton would write it. Though he was outwardly meek – he had been taunted at Oxford for appearing somewhat feminine – inside was a will of iron.

He rushed to finish his work, *The Tenure of Kings and Magistrates*. Right from the beginning, he took on the cult of the divine right of kings in the bluntest of words: 'No man who knows ought can be so stupid to deny that all men were naturally born free.'[7]

As a student at Cambridge, Milton had intended to become an Anglican priest, but turned away from it, feeling the Church was taking a rigid and doctrinaire path. He also came to the conclusion that monarchy as practised by the Stuarts was authoritarian and allied himself with the anti-monarchist cause. He began work on a treatise justifying the theoretical trial and sentencing of a tyrant or unjust ruler. This became *The Tenure of Kings*. Milton maintained that a king's right to rule did not come from God but from the people. Therefore, the people had the right to remove a king.[8]

What Milton set out was a theoretical basis for getting rid of hereditary monarchy. From earliest times, he said, people had needed to work together or suffer the 'destruction of them all'. To prevent organisational chaos, they had chosen one person above the rest 'for the eminence of his wisdom and integrity'. This person was called a king. The king was not the people's lord and master but their representative, and so could not be selected by inheritance.

To ensure the king would not abuse his powers, laws were invented, including a contract between the king and the people. If the king forgot his duty to the people, the people could break their contract with the king. To put a limit on the king's power, the people decided to create parliaments, for 'the Parliament was set as a bridle to the King'.[9]

Finally, Milton turned his cold eye on Charles himself:

what hath a native king to plead ... why he after seven years warring and destroying of his best subjects overcome and yielded prisoner, should think to [e]scape unquestionable as a thing divine, in respect of whom so many thousand Christians destroy'd should lie unaccounted for, polluting with their slaughtered carcasses all the land over and crying for vengeance against the living that should have righted them?

Was Milton present at the king's trial? We don't know; but he was making the arguments that were not made publicly during the trial. Because Charles refused to recognise the court, John Cook had been unable to deliver his prepared justifications for the trial. Though the trial has often been criticised, Milton's arguments reveal the actions of the Rump Parliament and the king's judges in a clearer light, as indeed did Cook's own arguments when they were published shortly after the trial.

Milton's contention that kings could be deposed was extremely controversial at the time. The king's authority was seen as the bedrock of a peaceful and ordered society – Charles had argued as much during his trial. Other powerful minds agreed: the philosopher and social theorist Thomas Hobbes for one. When Hobbes saw how the country was hurtling into civil war in 1641 he quickly reworked and strengthened a treatise he was writing on government and had it circulated.[10] Contrary to Milton, Hobbes maintained that once the people passed power to a ruler, it should stay there. His reasoning was that if a ruler could be deposed, society might collapse into anarchy at any time.[11] As he was famously to write, life would be 'nasty, brutish and short'.[12] Hobbes's concerns proved only too real – the social breakdown he feared came to pass in civil war. But while Hobbes was a timid man, inherently scared of conflict, others embraced it, seeing it as the only way to resolve the power struggle between king and Parliament. Interestingly, during the Prince of Wales's early exile in Paris, Hobbes had briefly been his tutor, specifically engaged to teach him mathematics. It would not have hurt either party that they shared a belief in absolute monarchy.

At The Hague in early 1649, the young Prince of Wales suddenly became a significant figure in European politics. While dealing with his grief, he also had to decide how to win back his father's crown. It would become apparent to Charles that most continental powers would wait to see which way the wind was blowing. This meant that the immediate choice of countries from which to try to launch an invasion was limited to Ireland and Scotland. Due to the Stuarts' two-hundred-year association with the latter, it seemed the better option. The prospective king would try his luck there. As for England, he would hope that widespread shock at the overthrow of the country's ancient certainties would prepare the ground for a triumphant homecoming.

Since the beginning of the Civil Wars, propaganda had played a major part in the fate of the Stuarts. The war of words had begun during the early 1640s when newspapers blossomed in England. The conflict brought about a huge surge in the production of pamphlets extolling the virtues of the opposing sides and lambasting the vices of their enemies.

The sparkling royalist news sheet *Mercurius Aulicus* (Court Mercury) was a good example. It made its first appearance in Oxford at the beginning of 1643, disseminating news about King Charles's war effort. But its genius lay in satirising the opposition. This was a breakthrough in contemporary journalism. Before *Mercurius* appeared, news sheets had restricted themselves to publishing the news in a more or less factual manner. Now, they let go of reality and lampooned the enemy.[13] *Mercurius* was printed in Oxford and smuggled into London to undermine parliamentary support at a penny a time.[14]

News sheets played an important role in the propaganda war on both sides. The parliamentary paper *Mercurius Britannicus* scored a propaganda coup when it published Charles's private papers, captured at the Battle of Naseby in 1645. These revealed the king's plans to bring foreign mercenaries and an Irish (i.e. Catholic) army to fight against Parliament.

One of the oddest pieces of parliamentary propaganda was a tract by Francis Cheynell, a Presbyterian radical. Cheynell conjured up an imaginary horror state ruled by Charles II – surely a preposterous eventuality![15] Between 1647 and 1650, some fifty different titles were published, both royalist and parliamentary, with more than five hundred actual editions.[16] Wives were not exempt from satirical attack: Elizabeth Cromwell and Lady Fairfax were portrayed fighting over which of their husbands should be king.

In the face of changing fortunes, royalist propagandists decided to home in on one man – Oliver Cromwell. His military successes had marked him out as the man to watch. His appearance was a gift to these early satirists; his lank hair, rugged features and facial warts were exaggerated to portray him as an uncouth, untrustworthy type. Propaganda made the jump from satire to the advocacy of murder in 1645. An edict appeared that purported to come from the Prince of Wales in exile, calling for some gallant to murder Cromwell. This communication, most likely a forgery, was intercepted by Parliament's intelligence chief, John Thurloe.[17]

In their efforts to render him ever more unattractive, royalist satirists accorded Cromwell the raffish trade of brewer and dubbed him Nol – a diminutive of Oliver. They revelled in the fact that Cromwell's great-grandfather had been a brewer who ran a pub in Putney. Following Pride's Purge, a royalist news sheet lampooned the Rump Parliament as 'Nol's Brew-house', satirising it as a group of brewers under Cromwell's leadership: 'The devil's in the beer-brewers (I think).' Among the central characters only Colonel Pride had been a brewer, but the beery imagery allowed Cromwell's enemies to savage his abilities, his probity and his social qualifications for leadership, all at once.

People with a ready wit were much in demand on both sides during and after the wars. Writers even turned to verse and drama. In 1647, *Craftie Cromwell* appeared, asking sarcastically if posterity would forget 'Nol and his levelling crew':

Shall not his nose dominicall
In verse be celebrated;
Shall famous Harry Marten fall*
And not be nominated?

Mercurius Melancholicus, by John Taylor, known as the Water Poet, concluded that the parliamentarians would surely not be forgotten but remembered for their treachery:

And if my muse give aid
This shall be their memorial
The rogues their king betrayd.[18]

All this knockabout fun stopped with the death of the king. Days later, followers of the Prince of Wales proclaimed him King Charles II. Within weeks, Charles issued a bloodthirsty battle-cry against those who had sat in judgment of his father: 'We are firmly resolved, by the assistance of almighty God, to be severe avengers of the innocent blood of our dear father ... to chase, pursue, kill and destroy as traitors and rebels, and chiefly those bloody traitors who had any hand in our dear father's murder.'[19]

The difference in tone from *Eikon Basilike* could not have been greater. As Jason Peacey has said of Charles's pronouncement, 'Such language of revenge ... seems directly responsible for the reign of terror instigated by exiled royalists upon representatives of the Rump posted to Europe during 1649–50.'[20] In truth, for the bloodshed that followed, there were two agents: one inanimate in the form of *Eikon Basilike*, and the other the extremely animated form of Charles II, who would prove true to his word many years later. In the meantime, his bloody rallying call and his father's posthumous influence together provided a mixture as inflammable as air and petrol.

---

* Henry Marten was a parliamentarian who relished the high life and was much hated by the Cavaliers.

In the weeks and months following the king's execution, English communities in northern European cities became hot with outrage and revenge fever. In Hamburg, feeling ran so high that even those who had seen Charles as a despot were deeply affected. A parliamentary spy reported: 'The king's death is strangely taken here by all sorts of people; we can scarce walk in the streets. Tis scarce credible how bitterly the vulgar and better sorts of people do resent it, though few of them hold him less than a tyrant.'[21]

The man who sent this report, Henry Parker, was secretary to the English Merchant Adventurers in Hamburg. He had been a successful propagandist for the parliamentary side during the Civil Wars and was one of the editors of *The King's Cabinet Revealed*, the selection of Charles's letters sensationally published after they were captured at the Battle of Naseby.

Parker had arrived in Hamburg at about the same time as a significant royalist agent. Sir John Cochrane was Parker's complete opposite in nature and deed. Whereas the latter was an urbane lawyer with a noted writing style, Cochrane was a Scottish professional soldier whose persuasive technique was that of the thug. He lost no time in setting out to intimidate the English merchants in the hope of turning their support – and ships – away from the revolutionary cause. He showed little sensitivity in selecting his targets and even attempted to have the chaplain to the English congregation shot. Parker described the event in an intelligence briefing:

The rage is such here against the English that the servants of Col. Cochrane laid wait for the English minister, when he was going to the English house to preach, and would have pistolled him; (but) the pistolls not taking fire, the fellows being made with anger drew their Poyniards to stab the minister, who crying out murther, was rescued by the citizens.

Charles was desperate for both men and money and instructed his continental agents to raise cash by whatever means. One scheme involving Cochrane entailed raising money by kidnapping English merchants and holding them to ransom. At the town of Pinneberg, eighteen kilometres from Hamburg, the kidnappers succeeded in luring three merchants on board a ship with the intention of taking them off and demanding £30,000 for their safe return. After seizing their victims, the kidnappers did not act quickly enough and the merchants raised a troop of two hundred musketeers in a successful rescue bid.[22]

By April, Henry Parker had been recalled home, having been an agent in Hamburg since 1646. His replacement was Richard Bradshaw, a relative of John Bradshaw, who had presided over the court that tried the king and was now president of the ruling Council of State. In early May, a plot to kill the younger Bradshaw was uncovered before any harm was done. For fear of being assassinated in the streets, Bradshaw became a virtual prisoner in his home. He complained that the city fathers did little to deal with those hell-bent on doing away with him. Despite his fears, he survived.

In The Hague, tensions were even higher due to the presence of Charles himself. Royalist exiles ranged from hot-headed young Cavaliers, who maintained their allegiance to Charles undimmed, to former royal advisors and civil servants such as Edward Hyde and Sir Edward Nicholas. The cult of Charles I as the martyred king was well established on the Continent. By now, editions of *Eikon Basilike* were circulating in English, Latin, Dutch and German. In a sermon preached before Charles II, Dr Richard Watson spoke of 'the everlasting stupendous monument of a book raised higher than the pyramids of Egypt in the strength of language and well proportioned expression'.

When word reached the city in early 1649 that Sir Isaac Dorislaus, the Dutch lawyer who had played such a central role in drawing up the charges against the king, was being sent as a parliamentary emissary, the blood in many a young royalist's veins reached boiling point. One man in the city could provide direction for all this boiling blood.

The Marquis of Montrose, a Scottish aristocrat and general who had fought bravely for Charles I in Scotland against the Covenanters,* was an exile like the rest – but he was an exile who would never give up. When he heard the news of the king's death, he is said to have fainted. On recovering, 'he vowed to devote himself exclusively to revenge the murder of his beloved master; and, to give solemnity to his vow, and at the same time expression to his grief, he retired to a private chamber, where he spent two days, without permitting a living being to see or speak to him.'[23] Montrose then wrote to Charles's widow that he would revenge the king, whose epitaph he would write 'with blood and wounds'.[24] If any man would know how to choose a target and organise a band of men to attack it, it was Montrose.

The men he selected for the job were no run-of-the-mill heavies who could be hired for a few shillings to do any rough deed. Montrose hand-picked members of the Scottish establishment who had followed him into exile. Sir John Spottiswood had been a gentleman of the bedchamber to James I and was the son of the former Archbishop of St Andrews and Primate of Scotland. Colonel Walter Whitford was the son of the Bishop of Brechin who had backed the reforms instigated by Archbishop Laud. The others were all former Cavaliers.

Dorislaus arrived in his native city in April. Together with Walter Strickland, the long-serving parliamentary ambassador to the Dutch United Provinces, he was to open negotiations for an alliance with London. The Hague was neither safe nor welcoming. It harboured large numbers of well-armed English and Scottish royalists who held a serious grudge against the Dutch academic. The Commonwealth government should have known better than to send him. Dorislaus should have known better than to go.

On 29 April he set up lodgings at an inn called the Witte Zwaan

---

* The Covenanters wanted to exclude the king and the bishops from control of the Church.

(White Swan). Rumours reached Strickland that a gang of assassins was planning to kill the middle-aged scholar. They had been boasting about it around the town. Strickland sent a note to Dorislaus, advising him to move to a private house where he could be better protected.[25] Dorislaus stubbornly stayed put at the inn, though he did postpone a journey across the town to visit Strickland. The following day, 1 May, an attempt was made on his life, but he escaped.

The day after, doing his best to protect his naive colleague, Strickland made the journey across town to visit Dorislaus at his lodgings. That evening, he left Dorislaus about to eat his supper and went home for his own. An hour later, a group of between six and twelve armed men entered the inn. Thanks to effective groundwork, they knew the location of Dorislaus's rooms. As they ran along the corridor with swords and pistols drawn, servants called out 'Murder'. Hearing the shouts, the servants attending Dorislaus rushed to the door and put their weight against it. The doctor looked for another way out, but finding none, decided he should accept his fate. According to his servants, 'he returned to his chair, and folding his arms, leant upon it, with his face towards the door'.[26]

The assassins pushed their way in to find Dorislaus sitting composed and looking them in the eye. His unarmed servants were pushed back and had pistols and swords held to their chests. Walter Whitford ran forwards and slashed Dorislaus across the head with his sword before running him through his body. The rest of the gang then thrust their swords into the dying man's body.[27] As they ran off, they shouted, 'Thus dies one of the king's judges.'

It was a miserable end to the life of a scholar, lawyer and diplomat; one who had been educated at Leiden University, was an expert on ancient Roman history, and had held the first professorship in ancient history at the University of Cambridge. It was a shoddy beginning to Charles's vow of vengeance upon those who had killed his father. There is, of course, no denying that Dorislaus was foolhardy to take up the post in The Hague. As one Venetian diplomat summed it up, 'he had the audacity to betake himself to Holland where the king's son was.'[28] Strickland, though fearing he was the assassins' next target, arranged for his colleague's body to be transported to England, where he was buried in Westminster Abbey after a state funeral.[29] His son and daughters were awarded pensions.

Following the assassination, Whitford escaped across the border into the Spanish-held Netherlands with the help of the Portuguese ambassador, who was in on the plot. He lived on to receive not one but two royal pensions. Spottiswood was less lucky: he was executed following the doomed campaign in Scotland led by Montrose for Charles II the following year. Montrose, left high and dry by Charles, was executed by hanging and quartering. Parts of his body were exhibited on buildings around Scotland.

Charles was already showing the perplexing mix of characteristics that would become more apparent in future years. His wish to further his cause was undermined by his constant desire to retreat into personal pleasure. This flaw was not without its reasons. He had been forced into a humiliating flight from his country to an uncertain future abroad. As a youth he had suffered the indignity of having no autonomy at his mother's cash-strapped court in Paris. Not only did Henrietta need money herself, she refused to give the prince any allowance of his own, thereby reducing him to the status of a dependant. There was worse: he began to hear most unflattering things about his father, very much at odds with the image portrayed in the *Eikon*. Charles, he gathered, had through stubbornness and lack of statecraft been the author of his own misfortunes. Whatever else he did, the prince knew he had to break out and somehow become his own man. In tattered shoes and with no regular income, it was a tall order.

In England, the constant fear of royalist plots led the Council of State to appoint a head of espionage. Thomas Scot's job was to manage the gathering of intelligence both at home and abroad. He took up his post on 1 July. Scot was a stridently independent supporter of the Commonwealth and a hater of all things Presbyterian. Not much is known for certain about his early years; he was said to have been educated at Westminster School and Cambridge, but there is record of neither. He was said to have practised as an attorney but his name does not appear on the rolls of any of the Inns of Court.[30] With his shadowy past, he was perfect material for a double agent, never mind a spymaster. He set about creating a network of spies that would come into its own in the 1650s.

On the propaganda front, Parliament was slower to react. By the autumn, it decided that the claims of *Eikon Basilike* should be officially refuted. John Milton was commissioned to write a response. Of course, Milton had already written a response of his own at the beginning of the year. But now he had a job in the government. In March he had accepted the post of Secretary for Foreign Tongues, an important diplomatic position that made use of his language skills, for he wrote Latin, French and Italian.

His new counter-blast was called *Eikonoklastes* ('The Iconbreaker'). A severe Puritan riposte, stating that Charles and the monarchy were icons that should be broken down so that the rule of God could prevail, it built on the arguments he had made in *The Tenure of Kings*. Monarchy could lead to tyranny, and Episcopalian religion was similarly tainted. To some extent, the arguments were a rehearsal for themes that would be explored in his poetic masterpiece, *Paradise Lost*. In the event, his arguments had little effect. In any propaganda battle, the first salvo is usually the most effective.

In January 1650, the Commonwealth made another bizarre foreign appointment. The academic and political theorist Anthony Ascham was posted as ambassador to Spain. From early in the Civil Wars, Ascham had supported the parliamentary cause. When the royal princes, Henry, Duke of Gloucester and James, Duke of York (the future James II), were taken into Parliament's care in 1646, he was appointed their tutor.

Ascham was the son of a well-to-do alderman from Boston,

Lincolnshire. He was sent by his father to be educated at Eton and King's College, Cambridge, where he excelled and was appointed a fellow. Ascham joined in the philosophical and political arguments regarding power and authority that gained currency throughout the 1640s. He was of the opinion that once power had been wrested away from the king (the historical authority), the population no longer owed allegiance to the crown but to the body that now wielded de facto power – the army.[31] This point of view was looked upon with revulsion by many who considered it likely to lead to anarchy.

Ascham was not supposed to travel alone to Spain. At the time of his posting to Madrid, a preacher named Hugh Peters (or Peter) was designated consul to Andalucía. It was intended that he and Ascham should travel together as far as Madrid. A Cambridge-educated radical preacher, Peters was something of a favourite of Cromwell's. During an interesting career, he had been the minister to the church in Salem, Massachusetts, and had helped set up the English colony in Connecticut. Cromwell favoured men who had been to America. He had once considered going there himself. For some reason, Peters' appointment to Spain was cancelled and he became chaplain to the Council of State. Perhaps he feared going the same way as Isaac Dorislaus, whose name had been turned into street slang by the Leveller leader John Lilburne: to fear being murdered was to fear being 'Dorislaused'.

Ascham's departure for Spain was delayed by illness. Finally, he was well enough to set off and he sailed in the fleet commanded by Admiral Robert Blake. Blake and Ascham shared a common cause: to neutralise a royalist fleet commanded by Prince Rupert, cousin to the Prince of Wales, which was preying on English shipping, capturing merchant ships and taking them into port on the Tagus in Portugal. Ascham's mission was to persuade King Philip IV of Spain to help stop his enemies, the Portuguese, from making their depredations on Commonwealth shipping; Blake's task was to use force to stop the plunder. As things worked out, Blake would have a much more successful mission than Ascham.

In March, Ascham disembarked near Cadiz. After bouts of illness and various administrative delays, he arrived in Madrid on Whit Sunday, the day commemorating the appearance of the Holy Ghost to the apostles. In the meantime, Charles had also dispatched emissaries to the Spanish court. Edward Hyde and Francis Cottington were ordered to drum up urgent financial support from Philip. So severe was Charles's shortage of cash to run his quickening campaign to regain the throne, the ambassadors were instructed that in return for a large loan, they should offer to relax the penal laws against English Catholics in the event of Charles acceding to the throne.

Prior to presenting himself at the royal court, Ascham established himself in rooms at a Madrid inn. Like Dorislaus's choice of lodgings in The Hague, this was a most unwise move. Ascham's secretary, a man called Griffin, was so concerned he took it upon himself to try to arrange a more secure base for his master. The events that followed bore a striking similarity to the murder of Isaac Dorislaus. On the evening of 6 June, Ascham was having his evening meal when a group of seven Englishmen arrived. Leaving a guard on the stairs, the party went up to the rooms where Ascham was dining. The assassins were 'admitted because they were Englishmen. The visitors took off their hats and one of them said, "Gentlemen, I kiss your hands. Pray which is the resident?" Ascham rose from the table and gave a low bow. As he did so, one of the attackers ran forward, grabbed him by the hair and stabbed him in the head with a poniard.' An accomplice stepped forward and stabbed the ambassador four more times.[32] At this point, Ascham's interpreter, a Genoese friar, tried to escape but was run through the stomach and also murdered. Griffin, the secretary, survived to tell the tale.[33]

The assassins were later identified as John Williams (or Gwilliams), a twenty-year-old captain of foot from Monmouthshire; William Exparch, aged twenty-six, from Hampshire; Sir Edward Halsall, aged twenty-three, from Lancashire; William Harnett (or Arnett), a trumpeter, aged nineteen, from Yorkshire; Valentine Progers, aged thirty-three, from Brecknockshire; his brother Henry Progers (who, notably, was a servant to both Hyde and Cottington); and William Sparke.[34] The men who stabbed Ascham were Williams and Sparke.

When the attackers fled from the inn they ran to a nearby church to seek sanctuary – all except Henry Progers, who went to the house of Pietro Basadonna, the Venetian ambassador. The ambassador was in on the plot and sheltered Progers until he could arrange for him to slip away for France. The fact that Progers alone had such an immediate escape plan, and that he was employed by Hyde, points to one thing: he was the ultimate link from Charles's court, through Hyde, to the murder squad.

The city authorities rounded up the rest of the gang at the church. No sooner had they done so than the Catholic hierarchy complained that the ancient right of sanctuary had been breached. The Spanish court was left with a diplomatic dilemma. Philip wrote to the English Parliament expressing regret at the envoy's death. Though Hyde and Cottington distanced themselves from the murder, any chance of a loan had evaporated.

The matter of what to do with the assailants dragged on. After many months of delay on the part of the Spanish, King Philip IV received a letter from John Milton, written in Latin and demanding justice. Philip did not feel inclined to help a disenfranchised prince whose chances of gaining his crown appeared slim; he had Hyde and Cottington expelled. After a while, the Spanish put Ascham's assailants on trial for murder, accusing them during the proceedings of acting on information from the exiled court of Charles II concerning a treaty they believed Ascham was about to sign with Spain.[35] Except for Valentine Progers, the accused were all condemned to death. Ultimately, the only one to be executed was William Sparke, the sole Protestant among them. The rest escaped, perhaps with the help of the clerics who had given them sanctuary.

The death of Anthony Ascham had proved counterproductive for

Charles's cause in Spain. However, this did not mark the end of clandestine murder plots on the Continent to enact revenge for the death of his father.

At home in England, royalist plotters found it difficult to make headway. Royalist gentry and aristocracy suffered greatly under penalties brought in to destroy their financial power base and deter action against the Commonwealth. Unless they swore to take the 'engagement' to be faithful to the Commonwealth, the offices that had previously given them local power were closed to them. A number of former royalists took the engagement – something that Charles II himself had given them permission to do – rather than see their estates sequestered. Widespread sequestration of property, wealth taxes and fines meant that most royalist families preferred to keep their heads down and hope for better days rather than involve themselves directly in intrigue.

A further deterrent to royalist scheming took place in February 1649. Several of the main royalist leaders in the second Civil War were tried for treason before a court described by John Evelyn as the rebels' 'new court of injustice'.[36] The following month, the Duke of Hamilton, the Earl of Holland and Lord Capel were executed.

The brutality had its effect. Senior royalist grandees became reluctant to join a mooted secret committee to restore the crown. The Commonwealth simply had too strong a hold on the country via the army and its intelligence network. The regime's spymaster, Thomas Scot, had informants throughout the land listening for any word of insurrection. Scot's secret service had become adept at intercepting letters, code breaking and the use of 'decoy ducks' or *agents provocateurs* to flush out royalists ready to engage in plots.

By now Charles II had gained some headway in making his own choices and was even putting together plans to encourage uprisings at home. Thanks to the advice and guidance of several senior courtiers who had gathered around him, he began to take a grip on his position and even plan ahead. In September, he landed on the island of Jersey, which was still under royalist control, in the faint hope that his appearance might help foment an insurrection in England. Despite schemes for uprisings around the land, including the Isle of Ely, Cornwall, London, Shropshire and Flintshire in Wales, nothing more came of it and Charles sailed away.

In March 1650, with hopes of backing from major European powers fading, Charles went to Breda and opened new negotiations with the Scots. In return for Charles embracing Presbyterianism, the Scots would invade England to help him gain the throne. This was a contentious and high-risk plan. His father's pact with the Scots only two years before had led to the second Civil War and his trial for treason. Any new involvement of the Scots was anathema to the majority of Charles's followers in England and Presbyterianism was unthinkable to the Anglican aristocracy. The Scots, for their part, were uncertain about the reality of Charles's new enthusiasm for Presbyterianism.

Despite these problems, Charles arrived in Scotland in June to begin his campaign. In London, the Council of State decided to mount a pre-emptive invasion. Fairfax declined to lead the invasion force and, rather than fighting against fellow Presbyterians, resigned his commission. Cromwell was appointed in his place. After much skirmishing, Cromwell decisively defeated the Scots army at Dunbar. Five thousand prisoners were taken south in a notorious march during which many died. More expired of illness and starvation while imprisoned in Durham. The survivors were shipped to the West Indies as slaves.[37]

Following this crushing defeat, Charles remained resolute and positive. Thanks to a new understanding with the Covenanters (which would shortly lead to his being crowned king of Scotland) Charles believed a new and formidable army could be gathered up in Scotland. While recruitment gathered pace north of the border, in England royalists remained largely subdued. Thanks to the efforts of a secret agent close to Charles II named Thomas Coke, activity slowly began to pick up. Coke criss-crossed England, quietly garnering support. He was hampered in his work by Scot's network of agents. There were arrests and some hangings. In the closing days of

1650, Coke's efforts led to a vainglorious uprising of two hundred or so in Norfolk. The participants ran away across open fields pursued by a small company of cavalry troopers.

In January 1651, Charles was crowned king of Scots at Scone, the ancient site of Scottish coronations. He now became the commander of the Scottish army, taking over from the experienced Scottish grandee David Leslie. This would have a profound effect upon the outcome of Charles's campaign to win the English throne.

In March, a plot was uncovered in the north-west of England after a Captain Isaac Birkenhead confessed to being a go-between for the Earl of Derby and the Scots. Under interrogation, he revealed the identity of the secret agent who maintained contact between Charles II and his supporters in England – Thomas Coke. Coke was cornered in a house in the Strand and during interrogation in the Tower decided to co-operate. He revealed conspiracies in Kent, London, Worcestershire, Yorkshire, Gloucestershire and the south-west. As a result, Scot was able to send out forces to mop up a collection of mainly armchair insurrectionists. More importantly, in May, the Scilly Isles surrendered to the Commonwealth.

Against the advice of David Leslie, Charles now decided to launch the invasion of England. With an army of 14,000 men, he marched south from Stirling. Within a week, he had crossed into England and camped at Carlisle. English support was almost completely absent.

Charles saw a way clear to march south down the western side of England. He was falling into a trap. At Worcester, he came up against an army commanded by Oliver Cromwell, with several of the New Model Army's finest officers in attendance. The battle commenced with the parliamentary army staging an audacious crossing of the River Severn by a pontoon bridge. The Scottish army's Highland brigades fought well and drove the parliamentarians back. As the battle swayed one way and then the other, it gradually became clear it was going in favour of the English. Charles left his vantage point on top of the tower of Worcester Cathedral and headed into the fray to rally his troops. He acted valiantly, with little thought for personal safety, leading a counter-attack and, when all seemed lost, attempting to rouse his men one last time. Finally, the Scots had to admit defeat against Cromwell's superior force. Three thousand Scotsmen died. On the parliamentary side, only two hundred were killed. Despite the crushing defeat, Worcester was a remarkable day for Charles. True, he had proved himself hopeless as a military strategist, but he had demonstrated that the impulsive bravery he had exhibited as a boy at Edgehill was no flash in the pan. There was something excellent about Charles that day, something he would not be called upon to find within himself ever again.

But bravery turned quickly to bathos with Charles's ridiculous escape through England; his flight turned royalist mythology into something miraculous. In its way, it *was* miraculous. Like an inanimate parcel, the royal personage was passed from the retreating Scottish army into helping royalist hands, hence to various recusant Catholic families who stuffed him into priest holes and the trunk of the famous oak tree, before being passed on to what remained of the royalist rearguard in the south-west, until he pitched up on the quayside at Shoreham like a sad old package. He left England in disguise as a 'broken merchant' fleeing from his creditors.[38]

Back on the Continent once more, Charles had to face the fact that he might never have the English crown placed on his head. At the age of twenty-one, this was a heavy load to bear. He was not entirely broken, but from now on he would focus his attention as much on pleasures of the flesh as on plotting how to gain the throne. This did not mean that all royalist activity ceased, but with a military attack out of the question for now, royalist resistance in England was channelled into subversion and plots to strike at the heart of the republic and kill Oliver Cromwell.

6

'THE HONOUR OF DYING FOR THE PEOPLE'

April 1653–August 1658

Having come into existence following one *coup d'état*, the Rump Parliament was sent packing in another. On 20 April 1653, Oliver Cromwell chased the sitting Members of Parliament out of the chamber following a protracted failure to reform and organise fresh elections. On 16 December, Cromwell was installed as Lord Protector for life. The concentration of power in his hands caused an explosion of bile. Many republicans and other mainstream supporters felt Cromwell had betrayed 'the Good Old Cause' of liberty and the Commonwealth.* For royalists, he had not only presided over the execution of the king but had now assumed the pomp and power that traditionally went with the throne. Plotters in both camps set out to displace or kill Cromwell.

---

* The term 'the Good Old Cause', took on many meanings but covered, broadly, the republican aspirations of a wide assortment of people. It appears in the writings of such divergent personalities as the militant Puritan Harry Vane and the republican theorist Algernon Sidney, and in the rallying call of General John Lambert in attempting to save the Commonwealth in 1660. It also appeared in many pamphlets of the time.

In the anti-monarchy camp, the political revolutionaries the Levellers were horrified at the destruction of the Commonwealth. Their ground-breaking pamphleteering had been banned by the new republic and now they watched as the republic itself was quashed. Driven underground, they made contact with even more shadowy figures on the royalist side. The fact that those from apparently irreconcilable camps could consider working together was quite an achievement on both sides. It seems royalists were keen to gain allies of any sort in England, while the Levellers felt that after Cromwell's death a resurgence of the monarchy would quickly become anathema and they would step into the ensuing political vacuum.

The Levellers' fear that their egalitarian dreams were slipping away was confirmed when a new national constitution emerged the day before Cromwell was made Lord Protector. According to Edmund Ludlow, whose Leveller sympathies were well known, this came about in a way that might have been worthy of the Levellers themselves: 'in a clandestine manner carried on and huddled up by two or three persons, so more they were not who were let into the secret of it, so that it may justly be called a work of darkness'.[1]

The new constitution disqualified from voting anyone who did not have property worth at least £200. Ludlow, the manor-house hearty turned man of the people, was disgusted. The Levellers' wish for universal male suffrage was crushed. The offending document was called *The Instrument of Government*.[2] Despite the misgivings of radicals, the charter was an historic milestone – it was Britain's only written constitution. By comparison with government under the Stuarts, it marked a great leap forward in ensuring a free Parliament and a wide degree of public representation and fairness.

The Instrument of Government was drawn up chiefly by Major-General John Lambert, the energetic soldier and politician from Yorkshire who was increasingly thought of as a possible successor to Cromwell. Cromwell's new spy chief John Thurloe also advised on the constitution. He was the ultimate back-room civil servant and apparatchik. In the summer of 1653, he replaced Thomas Scot as head of the intelligence service. He would go on to become Cromwell's secretary of state, while carrying on with his duties running intelligence gathering abroad and counter-espionage at home. As Protector, Cromwell would rely on no one more than Thurloe.

In its final form, the *Instrument* gave executive power to the Lord Protector, supported by a Council of State which the Protector did not appoint. This executive power was separated from the legislature, a reformed single-house Parliament to be elected every three years, with the power to pass laws and to levy taxes for a standing army. Religious toleration was permitted, with exceptions for Roman Catholics and those guilty of licentious behaviour – a reference to extreme sects thought to condone immoral sexual activity.

Importantly, the constitution set out for the first time a binding legal framework for the laws and taxes imposed upon the people: 'That the laws shall not be altered, suspended, abrogated, or repealed, nor any new law made, nor any tax, charge, or imposition laid upon the people, but by common consent in Parliament . . . '[3]

Although this was a considerable advance on anything that had gone before, for the radicals, with their wider agenda of social and political change, it was not nearly enough. The fact that executive powers rested with the Protector was anathema.

Unsurprisingly, some of the plots against the Protectorate, and the Protector, had more substance or were better organised than others. Royalist plotters fell into two main camps: those who felt it best to organise and bide their time and those who wished to bring about an uprising immediately.

The Sealed Knot was most definitely in the former category. It was set up by Charles II in 1653 as a secret society of aristocrats expressly to nurture royalist resistance.[4] It reported to Charles through Edward Hyde, who ran a small number of messengers slipping between England and the Continent. Both Hyde and the main members of the Knot were cautious men. On 2 February 1654, one of its members, Edward Villiers, wrote to Hyde in Paris: 'The Sealed Knot still meet with an intention to design somewhat for his service.'[5] In other words, the Knot was discussing insurrection or assassination, but had no actual plans to report. The Knot communicated by letters written in code. These were often intercepted by John Thurloe and the contents deciphered by a new type of specialist – the code-breaker.

There were probably only three founding members of the Sealed Knot. Their appointment came directly from Charles, who wrote in code asking them to 'make another venture in trade'.[6] Lord Belasyse was the second son of Thomas, Lord Fauconberg, and was related to both Fairfax and Lambert. At the outbreak of war, he had fought on the king's side, like his father and brother. In 1644 he was defeated in battle by Fairfax at Bradford and at Selby by Lambert.

John Russell was the third son of the Earl of Bedford. He had fought at Naseby, where he was wounded. While there was no doubting Russell's allegiance to the crown, his elder brother William (who became the 5th Earl) changed sides between Parliament and king with bewildering regularity.

The third of the founding members, Sir Richard Willys, was a professional soldier who had fought on the Continent before returning to join Charles I's campaigns against the Scots and again during the first Civil War. His membership of the Sealed Knot was unexpected because he had once challenged Belasyse to a duel.

There were three other members: alongside Edward Villiers were Lord Loughborough and Sir William Compton, the latter described by Samuel Pepys as 'one of the worthiest men and best officers ... of the best temper, valour, abilities of mind, integrity, birth, fine person and diligence ...'

Despite the excellent Cavalier credentials of its members, the Sealed Knot proved to be so tightly bound that it could move neither against the Protectorate nor the Protector. Hyde said the Knot 'would not engage in any absurd and desperate attempt'.[7]

The truth was that the Sealed Knot was too languid to plot – or at least to do so vigorously. It met irregularly and did very little except vigorously enquire around the estates of old royalist families as to whether they would be prepared to answer the call if and when it came. Charles had inadvertently created a turkey.

It was hardly surprising, then, that in 1654 a secret proclamation appeared in Charles's name, offering £550 a year and a knighthood to anyone who would kill 'a certain base mechanic fellow called Oliver Cromwell'. The purpose was clear: wilder men should take up the challenge.[8] Edward Hyde was later to claim that he and the Earl of Ormond had vetoed such outrageous ventures.

At around the same time as the Knot was formed, another set of plotters came together. Because of the timing, it was often thought the two groups were somehow connected,[9] but the men who met in the Ship Tavern in Old Bailey in the City of London could not have been more different from the genteel members of the Sealed Knot. Their reckless and drunken wrangling brought them to the attention of Thurloe's agents.

Among those plotters arrested in February 1654 was one Roger Coates, who admitted the existence of a plot. Coates was turned by Thurloe and paid £12 for his information, with more promised later. Fanciful pictures were painted of the nature of the plot. There was supposedly a grand council composed of eminent and proven Cavaliers including Lord Loughborough, a member of the Sealed Knot. The grand council existed only in the minds of the conspirators. Loughborough later managed to convince the State Council he had nothing to do with the Ship Tavern group.

However, two names mentioned by the conspirators made Thurloe sit up. The first was that of Roger Whitley, a brother-in-law of Lord Gerard who was a senior figure in the circle of Charles II's cousin, Prince Rupert of the Rhine, a military expert. The second was John Gerard, a cousin of Lord Gerard, also with connections to Prince Rupert. The participation of the Gerards indicated that this conspiracy might possibly have been set up in direct opposition to the Sealed Knot. It could be that Prince Rupert was trying to prove he was better than Hyde.

Thurloe rounded up conspirators but let them go without trial over the following months.[10] No sooner had that plot subsided than a second one arose in its place, also involving the Gerard cousins but this time much more serious.

In Paris, three English soldiers of fortune went to see Roger Whitley and John Gerard with a scheme to kill Cromwell and bring down the Protectorate. Thomas Henshaw and his half-brother, John Wiseman, had fought for foreign princes, while the third, Colonel John Fitzjames, had previously been employed by the Commonwealth. Their scheme was taken to Prince Rupert and Lord Gerard. John Gerard and Henshaw then sailed for England.

As befitted a king in all but name, Cromwell had moved into Whitehall Palace. It was common knowledge that every Saturday morning he left Whitehall to spend the weekend at Hampton Court. The plan was that Cromwell and his mounted escort of thirty men would be surprised in a narrow street, and that in the melee the Lord Protector would be shot down. The ambush was set for 13 May.

On the appointed day, Cromwell changed his plans. He did not ride out of the palace at Whitehall but instead set off by boat to Chelsea, where he alighted and rode the rest of the way. Meanwhile, his would-be assassins waited and waited. When the penny dropped they went home. Undaunted, they planned to make another attempt a few weeks later. This time they intended to shoot Cromwell at prayer in his chapel in Whitehall. On the morning allotted for the operation, several key conspirators were arrested. A well-prepared trawl around the capital resulted in dozens being detained. Henshaw escaped to France but Gerard was arrested and taken to the Tower.

Thurloe's intelligence operation had triumphed. It transpired that the general calibre of those involved in the enterprise was low. Henshaw had failed to gain support among the gentry, while even the

Londoners involved were mostly apprentices, with an odd assortment of co-conspirators including a brewer, a schoolmaster and a blind clergyman.[11]

The government-controlled news sheets went wild: the plot was all that London wished to read about. There were reports in the *Weekly Intelligencer* and *Mercurius Politicus*.[12] Thurloe interrogated the conspirators. Gerard denied all knowledge of the plot. Others were not so reticent. A Leveller named John Wildman, who had colluded with the royalists, confessed. As they made their statements, Thurloe would have marvelled at their naivety:

> The Examination of Nicholas Watson, barber:
> Saith, That upon sunday was seven-night, there came to him one Thomas Barnes ... told him, that there was a design against the lord protector and this present government, and divers gentlemen were engaged in it; and that three or four thousand men were listed already to that purpose; that they intended to make an attempt upon the lord protector's person, either at dinner, or as he went to Hampton-court; and at the same time would surprise the guards at Whitehall, which he said was easy to do ... and for that purpose a new suit was given him, and a belt worth five or six pounds.[13]

Due to the discrepancy between the serious nature of the plot and the rather pathetic nature of many of the plotters, very few were actually charged. However, the authorities continued to round up suspects in what became an intelligence-gathering exercise. Members of the Sealed Knot, including Sir Richard Willys and Edward Villiers, were arrested and held in the Tower. At the conclusion of the security sweep, only three conspirators were arraigned for trial: John Gerard, Peter Vowell and Somerset Fox. The court hearing made sensational headlines for the news sheets and a special account was rushed to the presses to satisfy demand.[14]

The trial took place in the Painted Chamber. The court heard from many of the conspirators how they had plotted to overthrow the government and install Charles as monarch. As the attorney-general, Edward Prideaux, set out the case, there grew an inescapable sense that *agents provocateurs* had been at work. Henshaw, who had fled, was the chief suspect.[15] He had promised his fellow plotters the backing of unrealistic numbers of continental troops: 'Mr. *Hinshaw* declared to his confederates here in *England* what overtures had been with *Charles Stuart* and that Prince *Rupert* had engaged to send ten thousand *Scots*, *English*, and *French*, and the Duke of *York* to come with them to land in *Sussex*, and other places ...'[16] The assertion that Charles's brother James would come with an invasion force was clearly designed to stiffen the resolve of the deluded conspirators.

The reality was very different, as Henshaw himself well knew:

> *John Wharton* was sworn, who said, he keeps a Victualling house in *Black Fryers*, and that a Gentleman, a stranger, came to him, and asked him if hee would serve the King, and fell in discourse about his calling; that he told him he had married a poor widow: And that the Gentleman told him that if the Design went on, he might have money enough, and said that hee would find him better imployment. The Gentlemans name, hee said, was *Hinshaw*.

The verdict was a foregone conclusion. Gerard, Vowell and Fox were executed on 10 July. Several conspirators were 'Barbadosed' – sent off as slaves to an almost certain death in the sugar plantations. According to one of Thurloe's agents the king was well aware of what was planned and had sanctioned it.[17]

The foiling of the Gerard plot had huge consequences. Public sentiment swayed towards Cromwell. The lid was firmly screwed down on dissent and the Sealed Knot all but unravelled. Willys was arrested and, blaming his old enemy Belasyse for betraying him to Thurloe, challenged Belasyse to another duel. Once again, the two men never drew a sword nor fired a pistol. According to Edward Hyde, the dissent that broke out in the Sealed Knot rendered it even less active than before.[18] Perhaps it had been Thurloe's intention to exaggerate the threat in order to destabilise the Knot and win public support for the Protectorate.

With the Sealed Knot infuriatingly inactive, Charles decided to listen to those advocating an immediate uprising. He was now twenty-four years old, three years had passed since he had sailed away from Shoreham, and his life was passing him by. If he was ever to have revenge, ever to gain the throne, something had to be done – and done quickly. A new underground movement in England seemed to present the answer. Unlike the Sealed Knot, the Action Party was designed not to be run by aristocrats, but by a group of well-connected and ambitious gentry.

Chief among these was a veteran of the Civil Wars, Sir John Grenville. He had entered the first Civil War at the age of fourteen in 1642 as a lieutenant in his father's regiment. Following the Battle of Newbury, he became a courtier to the Prince of Wales and one of his closest friends and advisors. After surrendering the Scilly Isles to a parliamentarian fleet in 1651, he elected to live in England, having given his word he would withdraw from active pro-royalist activity.

In late 1654, the Action Party persuaded Charles of the possibility of a successful rising across England. There were rumours that a major parliamentary figure such as Fairfax would defect. This was not so very far-fetched, for Fairfax and Grenville were second cousins and Grenville had been attempting to woo the general into his camp. Fairfax proved infuriatingly hard to entice. The Action Party's plans took a serious knock when its arms supply network was infiltrated by Thurloe's men and various arms dumps were raided. In February 1655, Charles decided it was now or never. To ensure maximum support, a truce between the Sealed Knot and the Action Party was imperative. Charles sent an emissary, Daniel O'Neill, to mediate. He was picked up by agents of the Protectorate as soon as he landed in England and thrown in Dover Castle.

Confusion grew up as to when exactly the uprising was to take place. The same month, a group of Cavaliers turned up for a rendezvous in Salisbury only to discover they were too early. They dispersed, but not before they had alerted the authorities that rebellion was in the air. Several leading royalists were arrested and held for interrogation, weakening the incipient rebellion.

Despite the setbacks, Charles stuck to his plan: leaving Cologne, where he was currently based, he moved to the coastal town of Middelburg in the Netherlands, ready to cross to England once the rising took hold. The date for the uprising was set for 8 March. With hindsight, one can see that Charles must have been receiving very optimistic reports from England.

On the day Charles left Cologne, another key figure in the plan left the city and went to England. This was the quarrelsome Henry Wilmot. For all his faults, Wilmot had pluck – he had accompanied Charles on his flight from Worcester and had sailed with him from Shoreham on board the *Surprise* in 1651. The escape sealed their friendship and Charles made Wilmot the Earl of Rochester the following year.

From the moment Rochester landed at Margate and made for London, hardly anything went right. One of the few occasions for optimism was when Daniel O'Neill escaped from Dover Castle. After that, there was little to cheer. Thurloe's agents discovered arms caches in London and several conspirators were arrested. As a result, defences at the Tower and other strategic points were strengthened. Rochester realised that London could no longer be the focal point of the uprising. He headed north, believing York was ready to declare for the king. He was greatly mistaken; when he and a hundred or so Cavaliers assembled on Marston Moor, the city was unimpressed and kept the gates closed. The conspirators fled. In Cheshire, Nottinghamshire and Northumberland, uprisings also failed.

In the south, the conspiracy took a more serious turn. Rochester had brought with him a soldier of fortune named Sir Joseph

Wagstaffe, known to be brutally effective. Wagstaffe was ordered to team up with Colonel John Penruddock, a Cavalier from Wiltshire, and launch an attack on Winchester, where the assizes were in session.* This plan was modified when the conspirators learned the judges were about to wrap up their hearings in Winchester and head for Salisbury.

In the early hours of 12 March, Penruddock and Wagstaffe led a troop of several hundred men into Salisbury.† They occupied the square, took over stables and entered the jail, releasing prisoners who agreed to join them. The High Sheriff of Wiltshire and the assize judges were taken prisoner from their beds. Wagstaffe was for making an example of them by hanging them in the square, but Penruddock intervened. The rebels erected their standard over the town but then appeared to lose all sense of purpose. Taking the high sheriff along as a hostage, they marched out of Salisbury and through the towns of Blandford, Sherborne and Yeovil, calling upon the people to rise up and accompany them. They met with little enthusiasm.

When word spread of the daring but strangely futile raid on Salisbury, the militias in surrounding towns were called up. Cromwell ordered his brother-in-law, Major-General John Desborough, to crush Penruddock's rebellion. Desborough was one of England's most accomplished military commanders. He immediately instigated military rule in the south-east, linking local militias and army units into a single network. He then set off in pursuit at the head of an army. As he headed further west into Devon, Penruddock must have known the game was up. Without any great strategic plan, he made for Barnstaple, a royalist town.

Penruddock's force stopped at the village of South Molton, nine

---

* The courts of assize were criminal courts in England and Wales held in rotation around designated assize towns until 1972, when they were replaced by the Crown Court.
† Some sources put the strength of Penruddock's force as high as 1500 men, but this seems highly unlikely, particularly in the light of what occurred later at South Molton.

miles to the east of Barnstaple. As the insurgents ate and rested their horses, they were surprised by a troop of cavalry that had made speed from Exeter. In a scrappy fight and chase through the village, most of Penruddock's men broke and fled. Wagstaffe galloped off with them but Penruddock fought until there was no point in continuing and surrendered.

Along with twenty-five other conspirators, Penruddock was charged with treason. A special court was set up in Exeter. Among the judges was the lawyer John Lisle, who was a close supporter of Oliver Cromwell, had helped draw up the sentence against Charles and had acted as a legal advisor to the court. He went on to advise on the Commonwealth constitution and sat on the committee that decided on the membership of the Council of State. The fact that such a heavyweight figure was drafted in showed the significance of the trial. Penruddock argued he could not be guilty of treason as Cromwell had not been appointed Lord Protector by Parliament. This excellent legal point cut no ice with Lisle and his fellow judges. They sentenced Penruddock to death.

Penruddock's wife, Arundel, petitioned Cromwell, asking for clemency for her husband. If he was executed as a traitor all their family wealth would automatically be sequestrated and their seven children would starve. Cromwell had a gentler side when he wished to show it, but on this occasion he was implacable. The stability of the state came before the pleading of a mother for her children.

The sentence on Penruddock was carried out on 16 May. As befitted a gentleman, he was beheaded. One other conspirator was beheaded and seven men of lesser social standing were hanged. In all, seventy or more rebels were shipped off to the West Indies to work in the sugar plantations.[19]

Other rebels were luckier. The Earl of Rochester was arrested in Aylesbury. Demonstrating once more his wonderful ability to escape, he bribed the owner of an inn where he was held in temporary custody, and made his way to Cologne. Wagstaffe also made it out of the country. Dozens of conspirators were captured and condemned to death. Their sentences were commuted to transportation and, like their predecessors, they were 'Barbadosed'.[20]

The Penruddock/Rochester uprising had little chance of succeeding, but it had a great effect upon the manner in which England was governed. The military rule instigated by Desborough in the south-east was rolled out nationwide. Major-generals were appointed in each county to run what was in effect a police state. The activities of all royalist families were severely constricted. There was a precedent for such widespread suppression: the Puritan regime had turned Ireland into an even harsher police state. Just before the Penruddock rising, General Fleetwood, commander-in-chief in Ireland, ordered that any Irish who refused to move to Connaught under a mass migration programme were to be starved by having their crops confiscated. Shortly after this, all Catholics were expelled from Dublin. The dire effects of the Cromwellian colonisation of Ireland in the 1650s require no rehearsal here, for they have been thoroughly examined elsewhere.[21]

The clampdown in England extended beyond Cavaliers to affect former friends, too. On a sad day in February 1656, Cromwell ordered his old ally Thomas Harrison to be imprisoned without trial. Along with his fellow Fifth Monarchist John Carew, Harrison had refused to swear he would not take up arms against what they saw as Cromwell's betrayal of the Commonwealth. Harrison and Carew were imprisoned on the Isle of Wight where they were soon joined by the irrepressible Harry Vane. Vane had published a pamphlet on government entitled A Healing Question, which Secretary of State John Thurloe saw as a veiled attack on Cromwell.[22] After Vane refused to refrain from further criticism, he was imprisoned. Under pressures from without and within, the great Puritan experiment in freedom was rapidly turning sour, as Cromwell himself acknowledged with his call for a national day of fasting to consider how the nation might be healed.

The pressure continued; hard on the heels of the Penruddock uprising, royalists hatched another plot to murder Cromwell. At the heart of the scheme were two former Levellers with royalist money raised from foreign sources. Edward Sexby and Miles Sindercombe shared the belief that if the monarchy was restored, the people would find it so objectionable that they would tear it down and re-establish rule by the Rump Parliament. They were both former soldiers in the New Model Army and had notable histories of opposition to the army grandees. Sindercombe had taken part in the Leveller mutinies in 1649 – doomed, small-scale rebellions against what they saw as the hegemony of the army grandees. Sexby had been an army agitator and had been vocal in the army debates in Putney, at which the Levellers tried, and failed, to make their case for universal male enfranchisement. He rose to the rank of colonel but was relieved of his command for allegedly withholding pay from his men. While languishing under an official cloud, he was dispatched on missions to Europe. Was Sexby deliberately disgraced so that he could forge links with royalist elements in Europe as a double agent? We don't know, but it seems likely. Despite his chequered career, he remained close to Cromwell until the latter became Lord Protector.

From then on, Sexby involved himself in various secret plans to oust Cromwell and restore the Rump. He developed links with exiled royalists close to Charles, whom he assured of his own royalist leanings. While Charles's courtiers did not necessarily believe Sexby's story, they felt they could use him. In turn, when Sexby met Miles Sindercombe in the Netherlands in 1654 or '55, he felt he had found someone he could use as an assassin. Sindercombe had been cashiered by General Monck, when sub-commander of the parliamentary army in Scotland, for allegedly taking part in a Leveller plot. This made him an unemployed radical with a good knowledge of weapons and a grudge to nurture.

Sexby realised that all previous attempts at insurrection had failed because they had featured no central action around which the rebellion could coalesce. To ignite rebellion, one single, exceptional act of violence was necessary. Only the murder of Oliver Cromwell would do it. Sexby commissioned Sindercombe to carry out the deed. The two men travelled to London. Once there, Sexby gave Sindercombe free rein to organise the assassination and gave him £1500. Since Charles was broke, this had to be obtained from the coffers of various royalist sympathisers.[23] There was also a degree of separation that way. Sexby left Sindercombe to it and headed for Paris.

Using the alias Mr Fish, Sindercombe hired a house in King Street, just to the north of St James's Palace. Realising he required more people to help with organisation and the assassination itself, he hired former soldier John Cecil and a dubious character called William Boyes. In an act of inspiration, he took on a member of Cromwell's life guard, John Toope, who had first-hand knowledge of the Protector's habits and movements. Sindercombe promised Toope £1500 – his entire funds – to betray Cromwell. In the event, Toope had to settle for £10 up front.

With Toope's advice, it was decided to shoot Cromwell as he went by coach to the state opening of Parliament. Sindercombe hired rooms in another house, the yard of which overlooked the entrance to Westminster Abbey. The idea was that a fusillade of shots would be fired over the wall at Cromwell as he left the abbey for Parliament. The plan had the virtue of simplicity.

Shortly after Sindercombe had hired the King Street house, word leaked out about his plans. One of Thurloe's agents had information from Brussels that an assassin was renting a house in that location. Thurloe took no action except to ask his agent for more information from his sources. This uncharacteristic lapse might have cost Cromwell his life.

On the morning of 17 September 1656, Sindercombe, Cecil and Boyes entered the yard, carrying an assortment of weapons. As the appointed marksman, Cecil stood on scaffolding which allowed him a vantage point from which he could see the street and the abbey door. What the conspirators had not appreciated was that crowds of people would be anxious to see the event. The streets quickly filled up and when Cromwell exited the abbey, Cecil could not get a clear shot. The plotters abandoned the plan.

Undeterred by the farcical attempt at the abbey, Sindercombe decided to try again. Reverting to a plan that had failed two years before, he determined to kill Cromwell en route to Hampton Court. This time, the preparations would be much more elaborate. Mr Fish hired a coach house in a narrow street in Hammersmith, down which Toope had assured Sindercombe the Protector would travel. He was able to supply other vital information – the exact place in the enclosed coach where Cromwell habitually sat.

Sindercombe believed the key to a successful assassination lay in the use of the most modern weaponry – and plenty of it. At an upstairs window he rigged up a frame to which he attached seven blunderbusses angled down to fire into any passing coach. The blunderbuss was a form of early shotgun, designed to deliver multiple shot. Seven fired simultaneously at short range would have a devastating effect.

Sindercombe and his gang set up their armoury in the morning and waited – and waited. Cromwell never came. Toope had revealed the plot to Thurloe, who was now keeping his eye unfailingly on events. Cromwell didn't make the journey.

After this, a lesser man might have been forgiven for thinking it was not his destiny to kill the Lord Protector – but not Miles Sindercombe. He made one more attempt. This time, there would be no problems with crowds, no inadequate intelligence on travel arrangements. The Protector was in the habit of riding in Hyde Park. All Sindercombe's gang had to do was keep close watch and when Cromwell was seen riding into the park, head in after him, shoot him at close range and gallop off. Again, Cecil was to be the marksman. The double-dealing Toope seems not to have been involved. Nothing could go wrong.

Sindercombe and his fellow conspirators duly spotted Cromwell entering the park. They attached themselves to the fringes of the crowds that always followed the Lord Protector on such occasions. To give themselves a clear escape route, they had previously broken the lock on one of the park gates. Cecil was mounted on a particularly fine horse capable of a speedy getaway. The only trouble was, the horse was so impressive that it attracted Cromwell's attention. A keen admirer of horseflesh, he called Cecil over to discuss the animal. Completely nonplussed at this turn of events, Cecil trotted over to Cromwell and, instead of producing his pistol and shooting him, made polite conversation until Cromwell continued with his ride. His nerves shattered, Cecil watched as the Lord Protector rode away.

True to the farcical nature of the enterprise, Sindercombe planned one last extravaganza: he would burn down Whitehall Palace and with it take Cromwell to a fiery grave. On the night of 8 January 1657, Sindercombe planted an incendiary device in the palace chapel with a slow-burning fuse designed to ignite its charge at midnight.

Thanks to information from Toope, government agents had Sindercombe and his men under surveillance. When they left the chapel after setting up their bomb, they were followed. Other agents then entered the chapel and neutralised the device. Cecil was arrested without a fight, Boyes escaped and Sindercombe stood his ground and tried to fight off his attackers with his sword. He was taken captive only after the end of his nose was cut off, a fitting conclusion to his comedy of errors. Given Sexby's links to the court of Charles II, there is little doubt that the plot was sanctioned by Charles himself, even though he publicly abhorred all suggestion of assassination as being ungentlemanly.

Thurloe, honest as always, admitted to Cromwell that he had received early intelligence about Sindercombe but had decided not to act on it. Furious, Cromwell threatened to sack Thurloe, who managed to deflate his ire by pointing out that rumours and false intelligence came in on a regular basis and if he followed up on every one he would have no time left for his main tasks as secretary of state.

When Thurloe told a packed meeting of Parliament about the full range of Sindercombe's plotting against Cromwell and the state, one

MP named John Ashe suggested Cromwell should become king in order to bring stability. Cromwell did not rise to the bait.

Miles Sindercombe, 'alias Fish', was tried in Westminster Hall in February 1657. He pleaded not guilty to high treason. His reasoning was by now familiar thanks to its use by both sides in the argument – that those in power were not the true authority, and so on. He was found guilty and sentenced to be hanged, drawn and quartered. But Fish had one last trick to play on the Protectorate. He might not have been the most efficient assassin ever known but he did know a way to cheat his captors out of their prized public execution. On 13 February, Miles Sindercombe committed suicide in his cell in the Tower by drinking poison.

Ten days later, a Bill deceptively called 'The Humble Petition and Advice' was brought before Parliament. This called for Cromwell to take the crown, for the restoration of Parliament's upper house and for the introduction of a national state Church. The aim was nothing less than to return England to its condition before the Civil Wars. While the Bill was widely supported within conservative Presbyterian circles, it was anathema to all supporters of a Commonwealth and of worship according to individual conscience.

Among those who drew up the Humble Petition was Lord Broghill, an Irish landowner who counted among his accomplishments the torture and murder of a Catholic bishop in Ireland during the Cromwellian offensive of 1650.* A more attractive supporter was Oliver St John, the Lord Chief Justice, who was a long-standing friend of Cromwell. Like Broghill, he now felt the country could only be brought to peace through the creation of a new establishment that looked and smelt much like the old one.

For the following weeks, the country was held in suspense. Was a constitutional settlement possible that was agreeable to most parties? While Parliament debated the petition, Cromwell received

---

* It is to the Puritans' shame that they saw no reason to punish any of their own for war crimes, whether in Ireland or elsewhere.

deputations from independent congregations and sections of the army urging him to reject it at all costs. On the other side, the government mouthpiece, *Mercurius Politicus*, ran a series of polemics urging the Lord Protector to accept the crown. Towards the end of March, the Commons voted in favour of a single national Church. If that were not controversial enough, the MPs went on to vote by a majority of 132 votes to 62 that Cromwell should be offered the crown. Always cautious, Cromwell replied with ambiguous and reluctant phrases.

In early May, several leading army officers, including Desborough, Lambert and Fleetwood, told Cromwell they could not support him if he became king. Two days later, Cromwell summoned Parliament to the Banqueting House to inform them of his decision. He must have enjoyed the theatricality of the location, knowing that Parliament would wonder quite what the symbolism represented. Under the great painted ceiling depicting the ascent of James I to heaven, the Lord Protector informed Parliament he would not take the crown.

A few weeks later, a pamphlet entitled *Killing No Murder* appeared on the London streets. Its author was given as William Allen and it was aimed squarely at Cromwell, suggesting it would be an honourable act to murder him. The broadside was notable for its sarcastic wit and use of historical references to the murder of tyrants. It was as if the wisdom of Milton had been subverted, deflected away from the House of Stuart and towards the Lord Protector. Mockingly dedicated to 'his Highness Oliver Cromwell', the pamphlet set out

to procure your Highness that justice nobody yet does you and to let the people see the longer they defer it the greater injury they do both themselves and you. To your Highness justly belongs the honour of dying for the people ... you will then be that true reformer which you would now be thought: religion shall be restored, liberty asserted and parliaments have those privileges they fought for ... all this we hope from your Highness's happy expiration.[24]

Among the candidates for authorship were the ubiquitous Edward Sexby and a Colonel Silius Titus. There were good reasons to attribute authorship to either man. Sexby's credentials we already know; Titus was a Presbyterian who had changed allegiance from the parliamentary to the royalist cause and harboured strong political ambitions. He had been educated at Christ College and the Inner Temple and was known to have a biting wit (which he was to deploy as an MP following the accession of Charles II).[25]

Killing No Murder posed three questions: who appointed Cromwell, was it right to kill a tyrant, and could the death of the tyrant (i.e. Cromwell) benefit the Commonwealth? The author left the first question open – sarcastically pointing out that as tyrants were appointed either by God or the people, it was impossible to say who had appointed Cromwell. The answer to the second and third questions was 'yes'.

The Protectorate immediately banned the publication. Three hundred copies were seized in London but it was too late and soon copies circulated on the Continent. Cromwell decided that the author was Edward Sexby. A line addressing the pamphlet 'To all those officers and soldiers of the army who remember their engagements and dare be honest' conjured up the younger agitator who had been so active in the army debates in the autumn of 1647.

Historians generally believe Sexby was the author, though there is a possibility that Titus had some input. Charles II seems to have believed Titus was the author. Titus later openly advertised himself as such. It is worth noting that notoriety as the author of a work promoting political assassination proved no hindrance to Titus's later career. After Charles ascended to the throne in 1660, he promoted Titus steadily from gentleman of the bedchamber to Keeper of Deal Castle and Colonel of the Cinque Ports. Charles could not recommend Titus more highly, saying of him, 'Nobody should make scruple of trusting' him and that he was 'very honest and entire to me'.[26] The friendship clearly gives us a picture of where Charles really stood on the vexed question of political assassination.

A month after the publication of *Killing No Murder*, Cromwell was reconfirmed as Lord Protector, to the fury of his enemies of all colours. He further outraged his adversaries by having the coronation throne dragged from Westminster Abbey and set up in Westminster Hall on the dais upon which the kings of England historically held court. Both royalists and radicals were incensed when he was installed on the throne dressed in regal robes. The only regal accoutrement missing was the crown (which, of course, had been torn apart along with all the other crown jewels, on Cromwell's orders). Despite the public pomp, the publication of *Killing No Murder* had rattled Cromwell. He took extra precautions over his travel plans and was rumoured to wear a breastplate under his tunic.

Although always surrounded by his life guards, the Lord Protector was not impervious to danger. Once, when he was driving a coach and four in a park for recreation, the horses bolted and Cromwell was thrown from the coach. As he hit the ground, a pistol shot was heard. It turned out that Cromwell always carried a pistol in his pocket for his own protection and it was this that had gone off, narrowly missing its owner.

Sexby was arrested while attempting to sail to France. He was interrogated, confessed and was imprisoned in the Tower, where he died a few weeks later, having gone insane. So ended the life of one of the most intriguing figures of the seventeenth century.

It seemed as if the era of plots had also come to a conclusion, but there was more to come. The year ended with dispiriting news for the Protectorate, that Charles was negotiating with the Spanish for an invasion fleet, even travelling to join the Spanish high command at Dunkirk. Meanwhile, Hyde informed royalist circles in England that a fleet could be ready by January. Thanks to intercepted letters, Thurloe was prepared and royalist activists were rounded up in a swoop on New Year's Eve.

The year 1658 did not begin well for the Protectorate. The war against Spain, which had begun in a trade dispute four years earlier, continued to take up huge resources and manpower. Cromwell's new, unelected upper house came under fire from republicans. There were rumours the army might move to take control. In February, Cromwell dissolved the Commons. Matters became increasingly chaotic. Members of Cromwell's own regiment refused to support the Protectorate, new plots involving Fifth Monarchy men emerged. Members of Cromwell's new Council of State refused to take the oath of allegiance. As the great work of the preceding fifteen years began to fall apart, Cromwell grew disillusioned.

With information coming from England that the time was right to carry out an invasion, Charles and Hyde implored the Spanish to prepare a fleet to sail as soon as possible. Rumours and intelligence flashed back and forth across the Channel, and both sides jockeyed for the initiative. The Protectorate ordered all Catholics and royalists to leave London and stay at least five miles from the city. Then in March, the Sealed Knot and the Action Party received devastating news: the Spanish would not send a fleet. Despite this, the round-up of activists continued, with more royalists and Fifth Monarchists arrested. A court was convened to try the royalists. In June two were beheaded and in July three were hanged, drawn and quartered.

By now, Cromwell's health, always brittle, had deteriorated due to the malarial fever that had plagued him for more than twenty years. One weekend in August when he was feeling better he went riding at Hampton Court. The Quaker George Fox described him as looking 'like a dead man'.[27]

7

AFTER OLIVER

September 1658–October 1659

Death finally caught up with Oliver Cromwell on a muggy summer afternoon in 1658. He died in a bedchamber in the crumbling glory of Whitehall Palace within hailing distance of the spot where the king had been beheaded almost a decade earlier. A bout of malaria that finally saw him relapse into a semi-conscious fever put paid to this most formidable of Englishmen. Cromwell had survived myriad battles, intrigues and assassination plots only to be laid low by an insect. He breathed his last on 3 September. It was on this date that, eight years before, he had won the Battle of Dunbar, his most stunning victory of the Civil Wars, while on the same day a year later he had crushed the royalists at Worcester and thus brought the wars to an end. Understandably he knew the date as 'a happy day'.

As Cromwell whispered his final incoherent words, England was buffeted by a fearsome gale that uprooted trees, blew down buildings and tossed ships on to the shore. The howls of wind and the roars of thunder over Whitehall were said to be the sounds of the Devil taking Cromwell's soul to hell. It was put about that to win at Dunbar and Worcester he had mortgaged his soul to Satan, who had returned on the anniversary of those victories to call in the debt.[1]

With the Lord Protector's death, God or Satan had claimed the souls of fifteen of the sixty-nine judges in the king's trial. The most prominent of the other dead judges was Henry Ireton, Cromwell's tireless son-in-law, who outlived Charles by just over two years, dying of fever while campaigning in Ireland. One more of the king's judges would soon be joining them – Thomas Pride, whose troops had notoriously purged Parliament of MPs opposed to putting their king on trial back in 1649. Pride died within three weeks of his hero, Cromwell.

The Cromwellian establishment laid on an awesome state funeral modelled on that of Charles I's father, James. The event radiated power and solemnity. It began with the lying in state at Somerset House, once the residence of Charles's queen, Henrietta Maria. Cromwell's corpse – a stinking mess after a botched attempt to embalm it – could not be displayed, so a life-sized figure carved in wood was used, the face moulded in wax. The effigy lay on a raised plinth dressed as a king in ermine, lace and velvet and spattered in gold ornament. According to the official account 'in the right-hand was a scepter; in the left, a globe ... Behind the head was placed a rich chair of tissued gold, whereon was placed an Imperial crown, which lay high, that the people might behold it.'[2]

On the day of the funeral the crown was placed on the effigy's head and the figure was borne out to a velvet-shrouded catafalque for the procession to Westminster Abbey. One of the pall bearers, Bulstrode Whitelocke, spied 'infinite' crowds jammed behind the lines of soldiers stretching along the route in their new red coats. Such was the draw of the event that people reportedly came from as far as the Orkney Islands to view the Protector's last journey.[3] The Knight Marshal of England headed the procession on horseback, bearing a black truncheon tipped at both ends with gold. Behind him were more mounted marshals, then, according to an account given to Parliament, forty lines of 'poor men in gowns', followed by hundreds of 'inferior servants', lines of drummers, dignitaries, officials of the court, commissioners, ecclesiastics, flagmen, stewards, officers of the army, and finally the rows of naval and military detachments seen at every state funeral to this day.[4]

Among the chief mourners were some of the most prominent of the military men who had sat in judgment of the king in 1649. They included the stern Puritan William Goffe, a major-general whom Cromwell had entrusted with the government of Berkshire, Hampshire and Sussex during his ill-judged experiment with military rule; Colonel 'Dick' Ingoldsby, Cromwell's easy-going cousin, the loyalest of the loyal according to Richard Cromwell; and Colonel John Barkstead, governor of the Tower of London, a feared and not a particularly savoury individual. Of these, Ingoldsby would play the most decisive role in the next two years, tossing away all vestiges of that reputation for loyalty.

Notably absent were the 'Commonwealthsmen', the uncompromising republicans who had been among Cromwell's closest collaborators in the Civil Wars, but who had parted company with him when he abolished the Commonwealth. The Fifth Monarchy leader General Thomas Harrison boycotted the funeral, as did the religious radical Sir Harry Vane and Edmund Ludlow. The only former allies from the ranks of leading republicans who did turn out were the sharp-tongued Sir Arthur Haselrig, who was one of the five MPs Charles had tried to arrest on the eve of the first Civil War, and the Cheshire lawyer John Bradshaw, president of the High Court of Justice that tried the king. Among royalists, Bradshaw was after Cromwell the most reviled of all the king's judges. His hectoring attitude to Charles during the trial remained a perpetual source of fury for them. Bradshaw exhibited 'all the pride, impudence, and superciliousness imaginable', wrote Edward Hyde, who might equally have been describing the lifetime characteristics of the king whom Bradshaw was trying. By 1658 Bradshaw was an ill man, but he still had a year to live; Haselrig, not far behind Bradshaw in the pantheon of royalist hate figures, would survive for a further year.[5]

Royalists were predictably venomous about the funeral. The poet Abraham Cowley bemoaned 'the folly and trouble of all public pageantry' and sneered at this particular example: 'Methought it somewhat represented the life of him for whom it was made: much noise, much tumult, much expense, much magnificence, much vainglory. Briefly a great show and yet after all this an ill sight.'[6]

It is a fair assumption that Cromwell's departure prompted wild celebration in Charles's court in exile. This notoriously riotous establishment had recently relocated to Brussels, in the Spanish Netherlands. The embittered Cavaliers who comprised much of the court must have exulted at the death of the man who had bested them on so many fields. The news was brought to Charles as he was playing tennis. An aide arrived shouting 'The devil is dead!' One imagines Charles's courtiers gathered before the delighted prince, toasting him many times over at the news that 'the devil' was no more, their single regret being that one of their own was not the agent of Cromwell's death.

Their hopes of a restoration lay in the expected inadequacies of Cromwell's nominated successor, his uninspiring son Richard. Few sons could have been more different from a father than the gentle, kindly Richard, who blanched at the thought of bloodshed and hadn't even commanded a platoon. The generals referred derisively to him as 'the young gentleman'. In anticipation that Richard would not last long in his appointed role, a confident call to arms was drafted in Brussels for Charles by his secretary of state, Sir Edward Nicholas. This denounced the new Protector and commanded all men 'of what[ever] condition, quality, religion, interest or persuasion . . . immediately to put themselves into arms and to resist, oppose and destroy the said usurper Richard Cromwell'. The declaration promised a free pardon to all former opponents who would pledge allegiance 'except the murderers of the King our father of ever blessed memory'.

The declaration was never issued. Whatever the doubts about Richard, England was hardly seething for change and certainly was far from ready for the return of the Stuarts. The historian N. H. Keeble writes: 'Many were coming to recognise that in significant respects the experience of Cromwellian rule was more liberal and humane than that of Charles I, particularly in the quite exceptionally generous policy of religious toleration, its allowance of an unusual degree of freedom of the press and its aspiration to reform the law.' Keeble concludes, 'All the indications were that the Protectorate would survive.'[7]

Charles's Chancellor Edward Hyde would not have disagreed. His analysis must have made grim reading for his royal master. Reviewing the situation from Brussels, Hyde wrote, 'We have not yet found the advantage by Cromwell's death as we reasonably hoped … Nay rather we are the worse for it and the less esteemed, people imagining by the great calm that has followed that the nation is united.' He added despairingly: 'In truth the King hath very few friends.' Revisiting that period some years later, he recalled that 'the king's condition never looked so hopeless, so desperate'.[8]

In these pessimistic circumstances Cavaliers were told to wait and hope. 'We know very well that this good change must be attended with other alterations before any eminent fruit will appear to the King,' wrote Hyde. 'His Majesty doth not expect that his friends should do any rash thing for him.'

There was one cloud darkening the Protectorate sky and uncovering a shaft of light for Charles – the army. Phrases like 'seething discontent' and 'badly demoralised' come to mind in attempting to describe the mood of the New Model Army in 1659. Oliver Cromwell had moulded it into the most formidable force in Europe, but he had left a legacy of unresolved grievances at every level that ate away at morale. Senior commanders were restless over their own loss of influence in government. Junior officers resented the repeated purges of their peers. And most dangerous of all, the ranks were mutinous over a huge build-up in back pay. This mix of grievances was fertile soil for the preachifying ideologues who dotted the army – Fifth Monarchy men, that new religious breed, the Quakers, and followers of a profusion of dissident sects such as the Ranters. The army was a nightmare to control.

As Protector, Richard was constitutionally commander-in-chief. Within days of his assumption of office, the two most senior generals, Charles Fleetwood and John Desborough – both of whom had married into the Cromwell family – were angling to wrest command of the army from Richard and vest it in Fleetwood. They aimed at complete army independence from the civil power, a state within a state. In the autumn, army petitions and mass meetings pushed the cause. However, the much-despised Richard fought the generals off. He surprised everyone by confronting restless troops and delivering thundering speeches. The words were probably written by John Thurloe, but they had the men cheering Richard Cromwell. Bolstered by this success, Richard took another brave – but ultimately disastrous – step. In need of money and hoping to reinforce his legitimacy as Protector through a parliamentary vote, he announced an election. This was to open the door for all his enemies, not least Charles Stuart.[9]

Three substantial groupings emerged from the election. The largest, at up to 170 seats, was the so-called Court Party, Cromwellians led by Oliver's workhorse secretary of state John Thurloe. Next was an amorphous group of around a hundred neutrals, mostly Presbyterians of various political hues, some ranged for and some against the Protectorate. Among them were what Edward Hyde called 'masked royalists', men who hid their monarchist views and were expected by such as Hyde to embarrass and impede the Cromwellians. Last, although anything but least, were fifty or so republicans hell-bent on pulling down the Cromwellian constitution and reinstalling the republic. Among them were seven unapologetic regicides including Edmund Ludlow and Thomas Scot, as well as Sir Arthur Haselrig and Sir Harry Vane.

Top military figures secured seats too. The cavalry leader John Okey – whose battlefield skill had rescued the parliamentary cause at the Battle of Naseby – was joined by the ambitious John Lambert and Lord Fairfax, the old war hero. Fairfax took to posting himself next to Haselrig in the House, which might have been understood as suggesting that the republicans had a mightily influential ally. Few would have suspected that before the year was out Fairfax would be plotting to bring back the monarchy; indeed perhaps the man himself would have disbelieved it.

The Parliament lasted eighty-six days. It was a roller-coaster ride of filibuster and obstruction as the republicans, led by Haselrig and Vane, attempted to tear off the Protector's wings and make the case for a return of the Commonwealth. Legislation confirming Richard's powers was repeatedly stalled, and progress was held up on tackling major problems, principal among them army pay. At the same time the Commons was becoming a forum for anti-military sentiment as Presbyterians and closet royalists unloosed their resentment at the years of military rule. One jibe against an old comrade-in-arms provoked John Okey to complain, 'I see it will be a crime to be an army man. Is the expense of our blood nothing?'[10]

Tensions between army and Parliament increased sharply in March after a parliamentary committee began to investigate specific allegations against army grandees. The most heinous of these was the shipping of some eighty suspected royalists into slavery in Jamaica without trial after the Penruddock uprising. Republicans and royalists joined in condemnation of the affair.

The crunch came in April. The General Council of Officers presented Richard with a petition demanding support for the 'Good Old Cause' and for Cavalier elements to be rooted out of the army, arrears of pay to be settled and steps taken to root out 'wickedness'. This was a scarcely veiled attack on Richard's conservative councillors. It was followed by more of the same at an emotional day of army fasting and prayer, with sermons delivered by radical republican ministers Hugh Peters and John Owen.

A day later, at a meeting of five hundred officers, John Desborough proposed an oath declaring the justice of the execution of Charles I. Instead, on 18 April Richard ordered the officers' council to dissolve and its members to disperse. From a Cromwell it was a feeble gesture – and the officers refused to obey.

Most of the leading republicans had kept a low profile while the army crisis developed. This puzzled Edward Hyde in Brussels. On 11 April he had written to John Mordaunt, the king's busiest agent, in London: 'I would be glad to know the reason why ... we have not heard the least mention of Bradshaw, Lambert, or Harrison, as if they were persons who have no parts to act.' Mordaunt replied that he couldn't explain it, 'but Ludlow, Lambert, and Harrison are deep in the army design, and no friends of ours, unless by accident'.[11]

In fact a bridgehead had just been established between the republicans and army grandees. Early in April, Edmund Ludlow, himself a lieutenant-general, visited Charles Fleetwood's headquarters, Wallingford House, and outlined the republicans' terms for an alliance. From his account these boiled down to a simple commitment on the part of the grandees to restore a republic and their support for Commonwealthsmen – republicans – in the army.[12]

At this point Parliament blindly raised the stakes by starting to debate disaffection in the army, a move guaranteed to infuriate the military. A test of wills began. Richard ordered Fleetwood to present himself before the bar of the House of Commons. Fleetwood refused, whereupon Richard ordered his bodyguard to arrest him. The bodyguard in turn refused. Finally the two sides called out their troops. Fleetwood ordered a muster of regiments at St James's and Richard ordered a rival one in Whitehall. Three of the king's judges among the military chiefs backed Richard – Edward Whalley, one of the heroes of Naseby, his son-in-law William Goffe and Richard Ingoldsby. When Goffe sent word for his four hundred men to come to Whitehall, however, they were already on their way to Fleetwood's muster in St James's. Of Richard Ingoldsby's six troops of horse, only one followed him to Whitehall. Whalley's men refused his order to his face. He begged them to shoot him, but they marched off to St James's. A biographer of Richard Cromwell wrote of 'this universal abandonment'.[13]

Richard was at the army's mercy, and one of the hidden dramas of British history was now played out by candlelight in Whitehall Palace, deep into the night. Richard's two in-laws, Desborough and Fleetwood, confronted him and apparently refused to depart. They insisted on a dissolution of Parliament, Fleetwood warning of a bloodbath if the sitting was allowed to continue. Desborough told Cromwell that if he ordered a dissolution the army would take care of him and his interests, but if he refused to do so the army would clear the MPs out and Richard would be left 'to shift for himself'.[14]

For hours the Lord Protector refused to dissolve his Parliament. Differing accounts suggest that at times he broke off discussions with Fleetwood and Desborough to consult with his council. One account has several of them urging him 'to remember that he was Cromwell's son, and to act as his father would have done'.[15] Another version has one of the council, Charles Howard, offering to 'rid' Richard of Fleetwood, Desborough, Lambert and Vane, 'the contrivers of all this'. It seems that the boldest of the advisors was Richard Ingoldsby, who offered to take personal responsibility for dealing with Lambert. The thirty-one-year-old 'young gentleman' wouldn't hear of it. Richard Cromwell explained 'that he neither had done, nor would do any person any harm; and that, rather than a drop of blood should be spilt on his account, he would lay down that greatness which was but a burthen to him'.[16]

At around four o'clock, as dawn was breaking, the Lord Protector finally caved in and agreed to a dissolution. Later that day the announcement was made and Roundhead troopers stood at the doors of the chamber to prevent MPs entering. Richard immediately ceased functioning as Protector and several weeks later officially resigned. The pathos of the scene was captured by Gilbert Burnet, Bishop of Salisbury, in his *History of My Own Times*: 'Without any struggle he withdrew, and became a private man. And as he had done hurt to nobody, so nobody did ever study to hurt him, by a rare instance of the instability of human greatness, and the security of innocence.'[17]

The grandees had not planned to overthrow Richard and probably would have preferred to retain him as a puppet. But no deal was possible between them and the affrighted Cromwellians in Richard's Parliament and, anyway, radical junior officers probably would not have allowed it. So, after some days, the army chiefs concluded an alliance with the republicans. They announced the recall of the Long Parliament, which was first elected seventeen years earlier, minus those MPs excluded in various purges. Some 120 members qualified, though fewer than 70 turned up in the House. The result was power for Haselrig, Ludlow and the other Commonwealthsmen, who commanded the largest group in the recalled Parliament. When a ballot was held to select a new Council of State, Haselrig came top, followed by Vane and Ludlow. In 1649, one of the MPs purged by Colonel Pride coined the phrase 'the rump' to describe what remained of the Long Parliament. Ten years later it was a term of abuse.*

There are violently different views of the Rump Parliament among historians. At one extreme, George Monck's biographer, François Guizot, called it 'a small faction of fanatical egotists, more important from their passionate activity than from their reputation or talents'. Guizot dismissed Sir Arthur Haselrig as 'a rapacious, headstrong, and conceited agitator' and called Scot 'almost as vain, and even more obstinate and Blind'. At the other extreme, John Milton's biographer David Masson portrays them as courageously naive:

> Remembering the great days of the Commonwealth between 1649 and 1653, and not inquiring how much of the greatness of those days had been owing to the fact that the politicians at the centre had then a Cromwell marching over the map for them ... they set themselves, with all their industry, courage, and ability, to prove to the world that those great days might be renewed without a Cromwell.[18]

---

* The MP Clement Walker called the remnants 'the veritable rump of parliament with corrupt maggots in it'. *Complete History of Independency* (1661).

The flaw in their vision was identified by Austin Woolrych in his *Britain in Revolution*: 'The Rumpers', he wrote, 'were dedicated to the republican principle that supreme power belonged of right to the chosen representatives of the sovereign people, yet most of the people did not want a republic at all.'[19]

The republicans began at a gallop. By June they had taken decisions to restructure the army, commission new militias, raise funds to ease the army arrears, pension off Richard Cromwell and his mother, vet the judges, sell the last remaining royal palaces and wind down the war with Spain. The self-consciously revolutionary Rump followed up with proposals for a host of more fundamental reforms. Press restrictions would be lifted, enabling the first issue of the *Weekly Post* to be published.* The rights of 'tender consciences', i.e. religious freedom, would be guaranteed – though not for Episcopalians or extreme sectarians, and needless to say not for Papists either. Cases of arbitrary imprisonment would be vetted and political prisoners of all kinds would be set free. Meanwhile, various groups got down to shaping a new constitution.

However, another preoccupation took up much of the parliamentary day from June to September – the purging of the army. This was a central feature of the republican insistence that the army must be subordinate to Parliament. Remarkably, an unhappy military hierarchy merely looked on as 1500 officers were displaced by Haselrig and company after being summoned to the House of Commons to be vetted. Most were casualties of their religion or their politics, though not all. In an England stuffy with unforgiving Puritans, morals were also scrutinised. Cornet Richard Hobson was put out because like Falstaff he was 'old and scandalous' and Cornet Thomas Mason for 'playing at table [on] the Lord's day'. Quartermaster Thomas Kitterd (or Riddard) shared the same fate,

---

* 'The *Weekly Post truly communicating the chief occurrences and proceedings within the commonwealth*' (3–31 May 1659), the first unofficial newspaper published under the Commonwealth.

not only for speaking words against the Council of State but because 'he was accused of keeping a woman and giving her £3 a month'.[20]

Edmund Ludlow conducted a similar purge in Ireland, where he had been appointed military commissioner or commander-in-chief. Although he was only there for three months, he reportedly dismissed and replaced eight hundred officers, largely with extreme Puritans.

In July the inevitable strains caused by the Rump's attempts to subordinate the army to parliamentary control saw relations breaking down. There was a confrontation between the dominant figure in the army hierarchy, John Lambert, and Sir Arthur Haselrig, the dominant voice in the Rump. Haselrig was increasingly convinced that the general aimed at becoming Lord Protector. But the confrontation between them had to be postponed thanks to another crisis, the long-expected royalist uprising. The two men had to sink their differences and face what threatened to be the most serious challenge to the republic in years. Haselrig, acknowledging Lambert to be Parliament's best general, took the risk of entrusting him with an army to put the royalists down.

The uprising had been planned in May. It was to be launched across the country in a series of insurrections scheduled to begin on 1 August. In recognition of the Stuarts' lack of appeal to Presbyterians, it was presented not as a royalist revolt but as a groundswell against republican misrule. There was no mention of Charles's name in the proclamations which the plotters prepared to issue on breaking cover. Their propaganda was all about unjust taxes and repression. It may have irked the exiled prince to be painted out of the picture, but it was not supposed to last. Charles was to land in southern England immediately a foothold was obtained. In mid-July he left for Calais accompanied by the Marquis of Ormond and two servants, ready to embark for Rye. His brother James – who had been promised several thousand French troops – was at Boulogne, from where he planned a landing in Hampshire.

In preparation, Charles furnished James with a letter instructing what he could offer individuals in return for support once he had landed. The letter is revelatory for what it says about Charles's attitude to his father's judges. In his desperation to regain the throne, he was now apparently ready to deal with the men he had vowed to hunt down. He authorised James to allow negotiations with 'any repentant judge' who offered 'an extraordinary service'. Such a man could not be pardoned but would escape prosecution and be allowed to go quietly into exile – 'to convey away his estate out of my domain'. It would seem that the cynical pragmatism that was to characterise Charles II's reign extended even to his treatment of the hated regicides.

In the event, Charles's readiness to treat with his father's judges remained a secret. Like so many earlier royalist plots, the insurrection ended in chaos, leaving the two royal brothers still on the wrong side of the Channel. The royalist plan had been betrayed by a spy close to Charles himself. Key plotters were arrested, and French support never materialised. As a result, the uprising was called off just two days before it was due to begin.

In some places the order to cancel failed to get through. Small bodies of armed horsemen gathered at appointed rendezvous only to be captured by republican militiamen or scattered. The exceptions were Lancashire and Cheshire, where substantial forces joined together under the command of Sir George Booth, a Presbyterian grandee who, having fought for Parliament in the first Civil War, was then excluded from Parliament by Pride's Purge. Booth's men quickly captured Chester, at which their numbers grew alarmingly, reaching upwards of six thousand.

Lambert was sent north to stop Booth, collecting militiamen and regular troops on the way. He caught the rebels at Winnington Bridge, near Northwich, where he defeated them with ease. There was a minimum of casualties thanks to Lambert, who ordered his cavalry not to pursue Booth's fleeing troops for fear of massacre. In what could be called the last battle of the blood-soaked Civil Wars, fewer than thirty men were killed. Sir George Booth was captured a week later, disguised as a woman, after he took rooms at an inn. A chambermaid, glimpsing his feet, realised that they had to be male.[21]

Officers serving with Lambert were exultant at their easy victory; too much so. Shortly after their triumph a group of them, swollen-headed in victory, drew up a memorandum calling for constitutional changes that Lambert and other army leaders had been pressing on the Rump for months. Since Parliament had just vetoed these same proposals, it was an ill-judged and provocative move. But Sir Arthur Haselrig's reaction was more provocative still. Ignoring the pleas for restraint from his long-time ally Sir Harry Vane, and apparently oblivious to the Rump's ultimate dependence on army support, Sir Arthur had the Rump cashier Lambert and other generals. Lambert responded by leading troops into Whitehall to close Parliament down. For the second time in six months, MPs were locked out of the chamber in an army coup.[22]

The army then set up what was seen as a puppet government, a junta it called the Committee of Safety. This body, twenty-three strong, was to exercise all the functions of the executive and was dominated by the army grandees Lambert, Fleetwood and Desborough. But it included Rumpers willing to go along with the generals, notably Harry Vane, Bulstrode Whitelocke and Archibald Johnston, Lord Wariston. Its priority was the production of a new constitution without delay, but the committee would collapse before New Year and London would be plunged into chaos. Before summer the republic would be dead.

8

THE INVADER

October 1659—February 1660

A week after the coup John Bradshaw died, like Oliver Cromwell reportedly a victim of malaria. The last public act of the man who had presided over the trial of King Charles was to drag himself from his death bed to Whitehall to denounce the army coup and reaffirm his republican beliefs. He let it be known that if called upon to try the king again he would be the first man in England to do it.

Bradshaw's republican comrades in the Rump were divided over how to react to the coup. Sir Arthur Haselrig and Thomas Scot headed the irreconcilables among them, insisting on army sub-servience to the civil authority and vowing punishment for the grandees. On the other side, Sir Harry Vane and the Rumpers who had agreed to join the Committee of Safety saw unity between the army and Parliament as the prerequisite for the republic's survival. 'Shocked' by the coup, Edmund Ludlow returned from Ireland and tried vainly to reconcile the contending sides. It proved a futile task. The always fractious personal relationship between the principal players, John Lambert and Haselrig, had become too poisonous. Lambert told Ludlow that 'Sir Arthur was so enraged against him, that he would be satisfied with nothing but his blood.'[1] Haselrig seems to have been equally enraged by the stance of his old friend Harry Vane.

No one of the stature of Oliver Cromwell was available to knock heads together. But a figure of considerable if meaner talents was waiting in the wings. This was the short, overweight George Monck, commander-in-chief of the English army in Scotland and the ultimate hero – or villain – of this history. Monck was the most enigmatic of Cromwell's generals. His background was royalist. He came from an impoverished family of West Country gentry and had earned his military spurs in the king's service in the 1630s. He was briefly employed as a royalist commander in the first Civil War until his capture in 1644. Thereafter, he spent more than a year as a prisoner in the Tower, resisting blandishments to accept a command from Parliament. Eventually he said yes and went on to distinguish himself in the second Civil War, after which he was appointed commander-in-chief in Scotland. An ardent admirer of Oliver Cromwell, to whom he was unflinchingly loyal, he was an equally fierce oppressor of suspected royalist conspirators and dutifully reported several approaches made to him by the exiled Charles II. Yet there were doubts about this monosyllabic, solitary man. He was married to a loud-mouthed royalist, and the suspicion remained that at heart he was still as loyal to the Stuarts as his indiscreet wife. Shortly before his death, Cromwell made a laboured joke on the matter after Monck had informed him of a royalist attempt to recruit him, writing in response: 'There be [those] that tell me that there is a certain cunning fellow in Scotland called George Monck, who is said to lay in wait there to introduce Charles Stuart; I pray you, use your diligence to apprehend him, and send him up to me.'[2]

Cromwell's joke was later to turn sour. For years Monck had been high on the list of Cromwellians whom the royalists viewed as potential turncoats. His royalist background and personal acquaintance with the Stuarts encouraged hopes that he could be persuaded to the cause, and the exiled Charles Stuart courted him by letter. In 1658 Charles wrote to Monck:

One who believes he knows your nature and inclinations very well assures me that notwithstanding all ill accidents and misfortune you retain still your old affection for me and resolve to express it upon the first seasonable opportunity which is as much as I look for from you. We must all patiently look for the opportunity which may be offered sooner than we expect. When it is let it find you ready, and in the meantime have a care to keep yourself out of their hands who know the hurt you can do them in a good conjuncture.[3]

Monck did not reply, and he was discouraging when approached to change sides during the Booth uprising. In the weeks before the uprising Charles put out feelers to several Cromwellians, again including Monck. In a rather plaintive letter he wrote:

I cannot think that you wish me ill, nor have you reason to do so; and the good I expect from you will bring so great a benefit to your country and to yourself that I cannot think you will decline my interest ... If you once resolve to take my interest to heart I will leave the way and manner of it entirely to your judgment and will comply with the advice you shall give me ... It is in your power to make me as kind to you as you can desire, and to have me always your affectionate friend.[4]

Monck again did not reply, and he proved a disappointment when two of Charles's emissaries appeared at his headquarters in Dalkeith. The first was Colonel Jonathan Atkins, an old comrade in Ireland. According to John Price, one of Monck's two chaplains and also his biographer, Atkins told Monck of plans by 'gentlemen of the north' to back Sir George Booth and asked him to join them. Monck turned him down. If these gentlemen did appear, he said, he 'would send a force to suppress them ... by the duty of his place he could do no less.'[5]

However, two days later there arrived a very different emissary.

Monck's younger brother Nicholas was a country parson in Cornwall. His story was that he had journeyed four hundred miles ostensibly to bring back his daughter, who was staying with her uncle and was due to marry. That was a cover. The curate, a fervent royalist, had been picked to carry a mouth-watering offer to his brother. If George Monck helped Charles gain the throne he would be rewarded with land and honours plus £100,000 a year for life, 'to be disposed of at his own discretion'.

Nicholas bore an introductory letter from Charles, but the money offer was conveyed by word of mouth. The curate had promised to give the message to Monck alone, but his brother was busy with dispatches when he arrived, and Nicholas was unable to contain himself. He poured it all out to John Price, his fellow clergyman. Price later recalled continually going to and fro to the door to check that there were no eavesdroppers in the vicinity.

Monck was not overly welcoming to Nicholas. They met later that night and after the older man was given the letter and told of the offer, his attitude changed. The younger Monck explained how Sir John Greenville, a cousin deeply involved in the royalist underground, had set up his mission. He also revealed plans for Presbyterians and Cavaliers to widen the uprising, with insurrections across the country, plans involving no less a figure than Lord Fairfax. The loquacious Nicholas emerged from the meeting to tell Price that his brother liked what he had heard, especially the involvement of Fairfax. 'From this time on,' wrote Price, 'I do believe that his resolve was fixed for the King's restoration.'

Monck's decision would not become apparent for many months. Secrecy was, of course, essential. George Monck's officers, many of them Puritan radicals, were also mostly republicans, and Monck, or 'the General' as his entourage called him, was fearful lest any of them should overhear his conversations. Price witnessed his fear and embarrassment at the loudly proclaimed royalism of his wife Nan. She had once been married to a body servant of the Stuarts and was fiercely partisan for them. After dinner, when her husband's officers had retired, leaving the General drinking with Price, she would sometimes appear and rant against the enemies of the king. 'I have often shut the dining room door and charged the servants to stand without,' Price recalled.[6]

Next day, a Sunday, Monck convened a council of war comprising himself, his brother, his adjutant Major Smith, and his two chaplains, Price and Thomas Gumble. The conclave continued into the night and the momentous decision was eventually reached to come out against the 'fanatics' of the Rump and join Booth. Price was to draft the justification, a declaration for distribution among the troops expressing the people's 'dissatisfaction' with the Rump and the need for a new Parliament. That was to be backed up by a letter to the army grandees in London and by immediate military moves. Smith was ordered to seize Edinburgh Castle and the citadel at Leith.

Monck told Price 'that he was resolved to commission the whole Scotch nation against Parliament and the army and all before he would be taken tamely by them'.[7] The General had not lost his caution: as Smith made ready to depart for Leith, Monck disappeared, only to rush back to recall Smith and the declaration. He wanted everything to be put on hold till receipt of the post in the morning, which would bring news from the battlefronts. Price protested. There should be no delay, he insisted. At which the General 'laid his hands on my shoulders, frowned and paused and then in some anger spake thus: What Mr Price, wilt thou thus bring my neck to the block . . . and ruin our whole design by engaging too rashly.'

The post brought news of Lambert's victory at Winnington Bridge and of the poor turnout among other insurrectionists. Monck immediately faced about. The dispatch to Parliament and the proclamation appear to have been destroyed. Edinburgh Castle and Leith were left undisturbed and Monck put the fear of God into his brother as to what would happen if ever he talked. According to Nicholas, he was warned by Monck that 'if ever this business was discovered [revealed] by him or Sir John Grenville he would do his best to ruin both of them.'[8]

A few nights afterwards, Monck's officers held a thanksgiving dinner to celebrate the victory of their comrades in England. Monck, the guest of honour, led the toasts. For a long time no one, either among his own men or in the government, would be given cause to doubt his loyalty to Parliament.

For Charles, there were more setbacks after the disappointments of August. He dispatched the dependable Marquis of Ormond to Paris to try to raise support from Cardinal Mazarin and decided to travel south himself to Spain to remind the Spanish of their promised help. In France, the Cardinal slapped down Ormond before he could complete his flowery introduction, saying, 'I know that there is a King of England exiled from his kingdom. I know all his misfortunes so it is useless to tell me any more. I can do nothing for him.'

As for Spain, Charles arranged to rendezvous with Ormond at Fuenterrabia on the Franco-Spanish border. Negotiations were under way there between France and Spain to end the Thirty Years' War and it was hoped that Charles would make his presence felt. Instead, at this crucial moment, he went on holiday, vanishing en route to Spain in early September along with two companions. He was out of touch with Hyde and everyone else for nearly three months. Surfacing in November, he wrote to Hyde explaining that they had been unable to go by sea because of the weather and so had travelled by coach and horse. He had obviously had a splendid time, describing 'the pleasant accidents of the journey and not one ill one to any of our company, hardly as much as the fall of a horse . . . By all reports I did expect ill cheer and worse lying, and hitherto we have found both the beds and especially the meat very good.'[9]

Sir Edward Nicholas, a dry stick, was not amused. 'Reputation', he told Ormond, 'is the interest of princes . . . and he has lost much of it by his unseasonable delay.' The Spanish were hospitable when Charles arrived, but all that he left with was a sum of money to help him back to Brussels.[10]

George Monck had kept his head down for the two months following the Booth fiasco. Then on 18 October the news reached him of the new coup mounted by the army grandees. Monck responded with a virtual declaration of war on the military junta. In a letter to Speaker Lenthall he wrote, 'I am resolved, by the grace and assistance of God, as a true Englishman to stand to and assert the liberty and authority of Parliament.'[11] He also wrote to his opposite number in Ireland, Edmund Ludlow, asking for his support, a letter Ludlow did not know about for months.

Monck acted quickly. The great garrisons of Edinburgh and nearby Leith were secured by his men, parties were dispatched to take Berwick and Newcastle and a purge of officers began. Colonels, majors and captains said to be of dubious fidelity to Parliament were summoned to meetings, only to find themselves arrested en route or cashiered on arrival. Monck's men were ordered to stop short at the border but there was no doubt that Monck was seriously preparing to invade.

His fellow generals, not expecting such belligerency, were both placatory and defiant. In his reply to a terse letter from Monck, Lambert wrote, 'Nothing seems more desirable than to have a good understanding and union among ourselves.' Charles Fleetwood, the nervous and gentlemanly commander-in-chief in England, wrote: 'My Lord, I love and honour you but give me leave to say, no man of sober principles throughout this Nation will otherwise interpret this action of yours then [sic] a way to bring Charles Stewart [sic] amongst us again.'[12]

Centuries later, historians cannot agree on whether or not the restoration of the Stuarts was Monck's intention from the moment he opposed the junta. At the end of October, the Committee of Safety dispatched Lambert to stop Monck, just as he had stopped Sir George Booth. On 4 November, Lambert headed north with an army of Ironsides. The confidence of a victor must have coursed through him, especially when it was clear that he far outnumbered his opponent. All told, he had mustered twelve thousand troops after picking up militiamen on the way. Monck had only about five thousand men, and was especially lacking in cavalry. He was lacking in trust too. Despite the purges, there were too many Anabaptists for Monck's liking among his officers and men, and too many with loyalties to the army rather than to him. Monck told his brother-in-law that there were still some 140 'oppositionists' among his officers. He needed a minimum of six weeks to replace them and reshape the army. Then he would be ready.[13]

To buy that time, Monck grabbed at an offer of talks from the army grandees. He proposed that each side appoint a three-man delegation to meet in London to hammer out an agreement. 'I shall not despair of a happy issue from their endeavours,' he wrote to Fleetwood, adding that he was 'confident your Lordship does not intend by the offer of this mediation to ensnare us'.[14]

It was Lambert who would be ensnared by the illusory prospect of peace that Monck fostered. He had reached York when he met the three peace envoys sent by Monck to London. They apparently convinced Lambert of Monck's sincerity. In a haze of optimism he ordered the army to hunker down in Newcastle and wait. Bulstrode Whitelocke, then presiding over the Committee of Safety, warned Lambert not to trust Monck. He sent a dispatch encouraging him 'to advance with all his forces ... to attack him before he could be better provided'.[15] According to John Price, 'if Lambert had not lingered so long at Newcastle, but, with his horse only, advanced ... he could then have met with little or no resistance.' Instead Lambert waited weeks, and meanwhile his war chest emptied.[16]

Monck's tactic of keeping peace talks going till he was ready for war and his rival was weakened worked perfectly. Lambert's army became icebound and paying them difficult, then impossible. Lambert's colleagues on the Committee of Safety were so hard put to raise money from a hostile City of London that they had to raid naval funds. The fleet was ordered to ride offshore because there was no money to pay off the crews on landing. Lambert's unpaid army began to melt away. As for Monck, he concentrated on purging more of those worrying 'oppositionists' among his own men and mounting a highly effective propaganda campaign of leaflets and declarations, presenting himself as a liberator intent on redeeming the 'laws and liberties of Parliament'.[17]

While Lambert's army shivered on the banks of the Tyne, in London Sir Arthur Haselrig and Thomas Scot were stirring again. After the coup, they formed a secret cabal of members of the old Council of State to plot for Parliament's return. Their first move was on 14 November. Taking the view that the Council of State was still in being, making its members the only legitimate government, they drew up a secret commission appointing Monck commander-in-chief of the armies of England and Scotland, and awarding him extensive powers. The ferociously worded commission authorised him to 'kill, and destroy, or by any ways put to death all such who are in hostility against the Parliament ... ' The document, headed 'Council of State' and signed 'Thos. Scot, President', was smuggled to Monck in Scotland. He was in no position to make use of it immediately, but he would do so before the year was out.

Monck was ready to move at the end of December, however, but his intervention was no longer needed. A combination of factors was destroying the junta. Thanks to the years of war in Europe trade had slumped, and the City of London wouldn't or couldn't lend to the military government. Collection of taxes to pay the army was resisted and London looked increasingly ungovernable. Mobs of apprentices materialised from nowhere and confronted troopers. Newsletters reported 'citizens arming themselves ... great disorder ... the highest discontents I ever knew'. It was a tinderbox atmosphere that threatened a bloodbath. 'Divisions grow worse and worse,' a correspondent wrote to Monck's secretary William Clarke. 'Citizens ... expect to be in blood every hour ... fears and jealousies multiply. Nothing will serve the rude multitude but to have a free Parliament.'[18]

Blood did flow after a one-eyed colonel named John Hewson was dispatched to control demonstrating apprentices. Sixty-year-old Hewson was among several 'humble' men whose careers had been made by the Civil Wars, in which they had proved outstanding soldiers and fought their way up to command a regiment. A shoe-maker by trade, Hewson described himself as beginning life as a 'child of wrath' from a 'wicked and profane family' before a 'Godly' preacher converted him.

Hewson was another regicide. His signature was the eighteenth on Charles I's death warrant, and he must have guessed that he would be one of the first targets if the Stuarts ever regained the throne. Now, as London seethed, he made a Stuart return a little more likely by ordering his troops to fire on stone-throwing apprentices who made the demonstrations very personal by using old shoes as ammu-nition to throw at Hewson's soldiers. Two apprentices were killed and twenty more were injured. London never forgave Hewson. Six weeks later, a gibbet was erected in Cheapside with a picture depicting Hewson hanging from it.[19] The city's antagonism towards the army would prove crucial in the months to come, and for the fate of the regicides.

The news grew worse: revolt in the fleet, a coup in Ireland and military humiliation in the south. This last item was down to Arthur Haselrig, who with other Rump leaders contrived to seize the citadel of Portsmouth from the army and then persuade successive forces sent against them to switch sides. Haselrig announced that if the army persisted in blocking sittings of Parliament at Westminster, Portsmouth would host the legislature. In the meantime, he marched on London with three thousand men.

With the crisis deepening, Charles Fleetwood proved a broken reed. The restiveness of those troops who were still loyal demanded personal appearances and rousing speeches from the commander-in-chief, but 'he could hardly be prevailed with to go to them.' When Fleetwood did make an appearance, he would suddenly interrupt himself, go down on his knees and invite the troops to prayers. He became known for lamenting 'that God had spit in his face'.[20]

The critical moment arrived on 22 December. Events in Portsmouth and London left a group of prominent Presbyterians worried for their necks, and a deputation went to Bulstrode Whitelocke, Keeper of the Great Seal. They suggested that Fleetwood be used to finalise a deal with Charles before Monck did. Whitelocke readily agreed. According to his diary he had 'a long discourse' with the commander-in-chief, during which he hammered home the message that 'all their lives and fortunes would be at the mercy of the King and his party' unless terms were agreed in advance. If it was left to Monck they all faced 'destruction'. Whitelocke suggested contact be made immediately with Charles in Breda.

The usually hesitant Fleetwood concurred and asked Whitelocke to be the emissary. Whitelocke volunteered to go to Breda that night. After details were discussed, Whitelocke made to depart, but as he was on his way out he met Harry Vane, John Desborough and a third officer coming in and he was asked to wait. After about a quarter of an hour Fleetwood emerged from the meeting with his visitors and 'in much passion' told Whitelocke, 'I cannot do it.'

Whitelocke said, 'Why?'

Fleetwood answered, 'These gentlemen have reminded me and it is true that I am engaged not to do any such thing without My Lord Lambert's consent.'

Whitelocke rejoined that Lambert was too far away to be consulted on something that had to be 'instantly acted'.

Fleetwood said, 'I cannot do it without him.'

Whitelocke: 'You will ruin yourself and your friends.'

Fleetwood: 'I cannot help it.'[21]

Next morning, Fleetwood surrendered the keys of the Houses of Parliament to the Speaker. He gave notice that the guards on the doors had been withdrawn, and that members 'might attend the discharge of their duty': That put the Rump back in power.

Just over a week later, on 2 January 1660, Monck invaded. There was no opposition. His first night in England was spent peacefully at Wooler, thirty miles into Northumberland. There a messenger from the Speaker of the House caught up with him with a letter containing news that the Parliament he had sworn to restore was now indeed restored. It conveyed 'hearty thanks' to him for what he had done. The messenger also brought an order to Lambert to withdraw and send his men back to their positions before the coup.

Had George Monck possessed no hidden agenda, no thought of making himself master of the country for whatever purpose, this was the moment for him to halt. He did no such thing; there was no order to withdraw in the message and so on his army came. As yet, he had no authority for an invasion, but he justified his advance on the grounds that Lambert still posed a threat. Monck wrote to the Speaker that he had 'intelligence which was certain that Lambert was marching back to London to oppose your sitting in freedom and honour' and was raising fresh troops.[22]

In jumpy, rioting London there was a fear of civil war, but it was not to be. Across the country, garrisons were declaring for Parliament while Lambert's demoralised army had disintegrated. In the first few days of January a messenger from London found Lambert at Northallerton, his twelve-thousand-strong army shrunk to himself, two officers and fifty troopers.[23] This would not, however, be John Lambert's lowest moment. George Monck had worse to hand out to the would-be Cromwell a few months later.

On 4 January, Monck reached Morpeth, half a day's march from Newcastle. There to greet him was the first of hundreds of dignitaries who would turn out to cheer and petition him at every crossroads on his way south. Invariably he was greeted as a liberator, the man who had stood up to the army and might restore harmony. At Morpeth it was the Sheriff of Northumberland who led the local welcome, but a more important emissary was from the City of London. The Lord Mayor had sent William Man, the ceremonial sword bearer, with a message praying for Monck to deliver a 'full' and 'free' Parliament. That was code either for the restoration of MPs excluded by Pride's Purge or for a new election to fill the empty seats in Parliament – either of which could open the door to the Stuarts. As yet there was little sign of an upsurge in royalist support but every sign of public dissatisfaction with the republican government. As ever, Monck himself would not be drawn on his own aspirations for the country. To all the petitioners awaiting him on the trek to London with the same message he would reply by restating his commitment to the Commonwealth – and, by implication, to the Rump.

Still no one, Roundhead or Cavalier, knew his real purpose. 'Monck, no flesh understands,' wrote John Mordaunt that January. 'What he really is none knows.' Pepys made the same judgment. 'All the world is at a loss to know what Monck will do,' he noted.[24] James Butler, Earl of Ormond, advised fellow royalists not to count on Monck as their man. 'What his further intentions are, or for whom, I will not so much as guess.' Monck was a man who had learned during his life that he could best survive by blowing with the wind. His famed inscrutability stemmed from his fear that he might misread the weather.

The invasion was legalised a few days later. A fulsome letter from the Speaker thanked Monck again for his 'never to be forgotten faithful service' and authorised him 'as speedily as you can to come to London'. Somewhat astonishingly, given the Rump's distrust of the military, the letter gave Monck *carte blanche* as to the size of his invading army. It invited him to bring 'what forces you think fit to march with or after you'.[25]

'Old George' ignored the injunction to hurry and took his time. He spent four days in Newcastle and five in York, purging suspect militia officers and continuing to weed out 'fanatics' from his own ranks. In York, he held a long meeting with a gout-ridden Lord Fairfax, before enjoying the hospitality of the latter's mansion at Nun Appleton eleven miles away. The great Civil War leader was now a barely disguised royalist and is said to have pressed on Monck the Stuart case. According to the French biographer Guizot, 'Fairfax even urged him to remain at York, and to declare at once for the king.' Did the guest respond? Did he, one old soldier to another after a boozy late-night feast, unburden his soul on the matter of the one question everyone would soon be asking? Given the habitual secrecy of the man it seems unlikely. No outsider was in his counsel yet.

George Monck's next obstacle to overcome was the Rump. When he crossed into England over the deeply frozen Tweed, Haselrig, Scot and the Rump had been back in power a week. The mercurial Sir Harry Vane was no longer among their number; having been cast into the outer darkness for colluding with the junta, he was about to be banished. His disgrace left Arthur Haselrig, whose standing had been enhanced by the Portsmouth affair, more than ever the republicans' leading light. The day after his arrival Haselrig easily topped the poll of members for a new Council of State. He and Thomas Scot were to dominate the Rump in what would prove its final months.

The other big beast in the republican ranks, Edmund Ludlow, was now a lone wolf under attack. Six months earlier he had been appointed military commissioner – commander-in-chief – in Ireland with a larger army behind him than Monck or Fleetwood. Then came the grandees' coup in October, which sent him hurrying back from Dublin to London. All that he subsequently achieved through his attempted bridge-building between army and Parliament was the distrust of both sides. To cap it all, in mid-December came the coup in Dublin. The castle was seized by pro-Monck officers, and their allies took over strategic centres throughout the province. An uneasy alliance now controlled the island – on one side a council of officers chaired by the regicide Sir Hardress Waller, whose life depended on keeping out the Stuarts; on the other two local power-brokers, Sir Charles Coote and Lord Broghill, both of them in contact with the royalists and intent on bringing the Stuarts back.

In a vain attempt to restore his authority, Ludlow returned to Dublin on 31 December, only to find the city and every other town except Duncannon in hostile hands. Ludlow spent fruitless days on a man-o'-war outside Duncannon trying to muster support. Then came news that his Irish enemies had launched treason proceedings against him in Parliament. He was accused of deserting his post in Ireland and of plotting with the army junta. That sent him at full speed once more to Westminster to defend himself.

In Westminster, a struggle had begun over the so-called secluded Members of Parliament, those who had been dragged out of the House in the course of Pride's Purge in 1648 and thereafter excluded. They had favoured an accommodation with the king then and probably favoured a similar arrangement with his son now in 1660. Crucially they could outvote the Rump if allowed back in. At their head was the bizarre figure of William Prynne, the lead attack dog in the parliamentary campaign that led to the execution of Archbishop Laud. Prynne had become a Puritan martyr in the 1630s when he lost his ears as punishment for alleged sedition, having written a pamphlet which called women actors 'notorious whores'. Coincidentally or deliberately, it had appeared at a time when Queen Henrietta Maria had shocked convention by acting in a theatrical extravaganza staged before the king. Prynne's remark was seen as being aimed at her. Hauled before the Star Chamber, he was fined a colossal £5000, jailed and had both his ears clipped. Despite these punishments there was no let-up in his pamphleteering and Prynne was hauled up before the Star Chamber a second time. The remnants of his ears were cut off, his nose was slit, the letters 'S' and 'L' (for 'seditious libel') were branded on his cheek and he was fined another £5000. Thereafter Prynne wore his hair long, covered with a close-fitting cap. He was not a comfortable sight. John Aubrey described him as having 'the countenance of a witch'.[26]

Though Prynne was hailed as a parliamentary hero, he had opposed putting the king on trial and was one of the members of the Long Parliament purged in 1648. By 1659 he was openly a king's man and unarguably the royalists' most effective propagandist. He launched a blitz of news sheets and pamphlets denouncing the Rump and asserting the rights of the excluded members. A letter to the future Charles II's secretary of state, Sir Edward Nicholas, enthused about Prynne, 'His quill doth the best present right to our edge and though his ears are lost he hears now very well and speaks more loyalty to a general reception than any other.'[27]

In April 1659 Prynne had attempted to barge his way into the House the first time the Rump took power. He tried again in December when the Rump returned. Both times he failed, but both attempts furnished wonderful propaganda material.

Monck pulled out of York on 16 January and made for Nottingham. Before his departure, the news reached him that he had been made a member of the Council of State and would be required to take the oath abjuring the Stuarts. His only reply was that he was sending two regiments back to Scotland and bringing four thousand foot and eighteen hundred horse to London – which, as François Guizot puts it, was 'a sufficient force to overawe, without raising suspicion'.[28] His priorities at this point were first to keep the Rump in line and second, as his chaplain later revealed, to secure military domination in London.

In Nottingham two of Monck's key informants were waiting, his brother-in-law Thomas Clarges and one of his chaplains, Thomas Gumble, who had been sent to seek out potential allies in London. They drew a picture of an isolated, deeply unpopular Parliament that had to rely on troops to restrain the mobs. Monck was told that two colonels with regiments in the capital, Herbert Morley and John Fagge, were secretly prepared to offer him their support. That night Monck had Gumble compose a letter to the Speaker asking to be allowed to garrison the capital with his own men, claiming that all but Morley's and Fagge's regiments were unreliable. He withheld the letter for the present and decided to spring the idea on the Rump at the last possible moment.

The next day a coach bearing two more men from London caught up with Monck somewhere between Nottingham and Leicester. Thomas Scot and Luke Robinson had been sent by the Council of State, ostensibly to welcome him. Their real mission was to make sure the General took the oath abjuring monarchy well before he reached London. Little is known about Robinson, who just scraped through in the last place on the Council of State. Scot, however, remained second only to Haselrig in influence within the Rump. A regicide and proud of it, he had been an unbending opponent of Cromwell since 1653, and after the Lord Protector's death became a leading figure in the Parliaments of 1658 and 1659. In this latest incarnation of the Rump, Scot was secretary of state. His presence on the mission was testament to its importance.

Monck treated the two with the deference a Stuart king might demand. 'The highest honours were prepared for their reception,' wrote Guizot. 'Monck spared no demonstration of humility, becoming the most obsequious servant of the Parliament.' The emissaries insisted on accompanying Monck to London. At every stop he took a back seat, allowing Scot and Robinson to treat with the petitioners who were invariably waiting for Monck at every stopping place.[29]

It was not a comfortable journey. Mutual distrust reigned behind the civilities. According to Dr Skinner, another of Monck's chaplains, the two parliamentary emissaries managed to take rooms adjoining his at every stopover and 'always found or made some hole in the door or wall to look in or listen (which they practiced so palpably that the general found it out and took notice of it to those about him reflecting on their baseness and evil) that they might more nearly inspect his actions and observe what persons came to him'. Monck called the two 'my evil angels'.[30]

The column from Scotland arrived at St Albans, twenty-five miles from the capital, at the end of January, and was ordered to bivouac. Among the great and the good awaiting them here was Hugh Peters, Oliver Cromwell's favourite preacher and a hate figure for monarchists. Peters delivered a long sermon of welcome in which he likened Monck to a Moses leading his people out of the wilderness.

For those still suspicious of him, Monck produced more reassurance. He ordered one of his own officers to be thrashed for claiming that he planned to bring in the king. And he slapped down petitioners from his native Devon who called for the secluded members to be brought back.

At St Albans Monck dispatched a messenger to Parliament carrying the letter, composed three weeks earlier, in which he asked that, the London-based troops being allegedly 'untrustworthy', some regiments be removed from London to make way for his own men. Many months later Monck revealed that his strategy had been to split up individual regiments, quartering some units here, others there, so as to minimise the chances of coordinated action against his plans.

Unsurprisingly, the letter caused a heated debate in Parliament. The Rump had spent months hand-picking individual army officers, many of them radicals. Under Monck's proposal they would be replaced by units whom Monck had spent months trying to purge of exactly such elements. Nevertheless Parliament accepted the proposal.

The handover was tense and almost took a bloody turn when outgoing troops briefly staged a mutiny and refused to leave without payment of arrears. The difficulty was overcome by a promise of payment at the first stop, and Monck's four regiments marched briskly in. Observers were struck by the silence of the watching Londoners. The unpopularity of the army in the capital was palpable. So was the unpopularity of the Rump Parliament: on 7 February Pepys noted, 'Boys do now cry "kiss my Parliament" instead of "kiss my arse", so great and general a contempt is the Rump come to among all men.'[31]

Monck was allotted rooms at the Palace of Westminster, the 'Prince's apartment'. Edmund Ludlow persuaded an old friend of Monck, Vice Admiral John Lawson, to go with him to see the new arrival. When they arrived he treated them to 'many ... protestations of zeal to the common cause with many professions of friendship to ourselves', recalled Ludlow. Admiral Lawson was reassured. 'He said to me', Ludlow wrote, 'that since the Levite and the Priest had passed by and would not help us, he hoped we had found a Samaritan that would do it.'[32]

'It was not yet time to undeceive, and yet it was becoming difficult to blind them,' writes Guizot of Monck's position as he faced his supposed political masters in Parliament. 'Monck, now exposed upon the stage, and urged from all quarters by impatient observers, could no longer betake himself to his favourite resource of silence. Taciturnity no longer served the purpose of disguise, and falsehood became necessary.'

Nan, Monck's royalist wife, was part of the deceit. Having travelled down from Scotland by sea weeks earlier, she now played the part of the dedicated republican hostess. She 'took especial care to treat the wives of the members that came to visit her,' writes Ludlow, 'running herself to fetch the sweetmeats, and filling out wine for them; not forgetting to talk mightily of self-denial, and how much it was upon her husband's heart that the government might be settled in the way of a commonwealth.' Presumably the words stuck in her throat.

Four days after his arrival, Monck was put on the spot. Pressure on the Rump climaxed in a declaration from the Common Council of London that no more tax would be levied until the nation was represented by a freely chosen Parliament. Faced with bankruptcy, the Council of State issued a punitive rejoinder. It authorised Monck to arrest eleven London burgesses and destroy defensive posts and chains erected at the city gates to keep the army out. Portcullises were to be wedged open and the great gates of the city themselves unhinged.

Monck perceived a threat to his own position. Refusal to carry out the orders would lay him open to dismissal from his command, and possibly worse. According to a leak attributed to Thomas Scot's son, his father had made arrangements to throw Monck in the Tower should he defy the orders.

The General's aides were all for defiance. But early on 9 February Monck headed a column of troops into the City and by nightfall had arrested nine of the eleven burgesses, and removed all the posts and chains. Next day, on further orders from the Rump he burnt the gates. Haselrig was ecstatic. Monck had proved himself the servant of Parliament. 'All is our own,' he exclaimed. 'He will be honest.'[33]

The joy was short-lived. A day later, Monck went to the Guildhall to show the Lord Mayor a copy of a letter he had written to the Rump. It was devastating. The letter attacked the use of force against London, complained that John Lambert and Sir Harry Vane were still in the city and that supporters of the junta still retained commands, and reprimanded the House for allowing men accused of high treason to sit among them. This was a dig at Edmund Ludlow. But what had Sir Arthur Haselrig storming out of the House in rage was a call on the Rump to issue writs for an election almost immediately. The letter requested it be done by 18 February – under a week.

The atmosphere in London was transformed when the import of the letter circulated. Samuel Pepys, then clerk to the Naval Board, captured the excitement in his diary entry for 11 February. He was present in Westminster Hall to see the reaction of MPs. 'I went up to the lobby, where I saw the Speaker reading of the letter; and after it was read, Sir A. Haselrig came out very angry, and Billing [a prominent Quaker who a few days earlier had been beaten up by some of Monck's soldiers], standing at the door, took him by the arm, and cried, "Thou man, will thy beast carry thee no longer? thou must fall!"'

Pepys then made for Guildhall, where Monck had gone to explain his letter to the Lord Mayor and the aldermen. The General apologised to them for what had happened on the preceding two days and declared that the work which he had been ordered to carry out was 'the most ungrateful he had ever performed in his life'. The Rump, he told them, would not sit beyond 6 May. It was a transformative moment. Monck had entered the city's headquarters a villain and left a hero. Pepys was just in time to see him departing and was deafened by the crowd when it glimpsed the presumed liberator. 'Such a shout I never heard in all my life,' the diarist recorded, 'Crying out, "God bless your Excellence."'

After a protracted visit to an alehouse – one of many that day – Pepys walked home through a London that seemed on fire:

In Cheapside there was a great many bonfires, and Bow bells and all the bells in all the churches as we went home were a-ringing. Hence we went homewards, it being about ten o'clock. But the common joy that was everywhere to be seen! The number of bonfires, there being fourteen between St. Dunstan's and Temple Bar, and at Strand Bridge, I could at one view tell thirty-one fires. In King Street, seven or eight; and all along burning, and roasting, and drinking for rumps. There being rumps tied upon sticks and carried up and down. The butchers at the May Pole in the Strand rang a peal with their knives when they were going to sacrifice their rump. On Ludgate Hill there was one turning of the spit that had a rump tied upon it, and another basting of it. Indeed it was past imagination, both the greatness and the suddenness of it. At one end of the street you would think there was a whole lane of fire, and so hot that we were fain to keep still on the further side merely for heat.

A hiatus of ten days followed as Parliament's leaders struggled to bring the General back on side. They sent Thomas Scot and Luke Robinson to his lodgings with a pacifying message of thanks for his work in the city. The duo whom he had treated with such obsequiousness on the road from Nottingham found difficulty even getting an audience. The Rump then performed a humiliating U-turn to appease the General by dropping the oath abjuring monarchy. An amendment replaced the oath with a mere 'engagement' to be 'faithful to the Commonwealth . . . without a King'. The worried parliamentarians also scurried to satisfy the General by getting Harry Vane and John Lambert out of London. Vane, though accounted too sick to travel, was ordered to be 'carried' over one hundred miles to his house in Lincolnshire. Lambert was given four days to surrender to the Council of State or suffer loss of his estates.[34]

Monck now moved to break the bar on the secluded Presbyterians taking their old seats in the Commons. On 21 February, he met their leaders secretly and agreed terms for their readmission the very next day. The Presbyterians were to settle the government of the army and provide money for its maintenance, issue writs for a new Parliament to meet on 20 April, and dissolve the Long Parliament as speedily as possible. It was also understood that they would not alter the form of the government.

What happened in the following hours is unclear. According to one account, Monck wavered all night over whether or not to back the secluded members and betray the Rump, finally being persuaded to do so by his wife and aides. According to another, the Council of State got wind that secluded members planned to force entry into the House but were reassured by Monck that although he didn't believe it, he would double the guard on the House.[35]

Next morning the guards were indeed doubled. However, their orders were not to stop the secluded members entering but to ensure that they did. Under Monck's protection, seventy-three MPs purged in 1648 pushed and laughed their way to the seats they had been prevented from occupying since before the king's death. They were led by William Prynne.

The forces favouring an accommodation with the king's son were now a majority in Parliament and the General was evidently behind them. The seven regicides in the house that day must have shivered. Time was running out for them.

9

THE ROUND-UP BEGINS

February–April 1660

Events were moving even faster in Ireland than in England that February. In the space of a fortnight the argument over the secluded members led to the seizure of Dublin Castle and an Irish declaration for a free Parliament – and the first arrests of regicides took place.

The arrests were ordered by Sir Charles Coote, the ambitious president of Connaught and George Monck's chief ally in Ireland. He was acting on the prompting of Sir Arthur Forbes, one of Charles's Irish agents. As the issue of the secluded members came to the boil, Forbes urged Coote to declare for a free Parliament and arrest 'those persons who had a hand in the murder of the King'.[1]

Coote eagerly complied. He was one of many rats leaving the Commonwealth's sinking ship. In the 1650s he had been 'a scourge of the King's supporters ... hanging royalist commanders, killing bishops and profiting vastly from confiscated royalist estates'.[2] But for a year he had been co-operating with Irish royalists and was desperate to curry favour. Edmund Ludlow, during his four months' rule in Dublin, had become so wary of Coote that at the time of the Booth emergency he ordered the Irish magnate not to leave Dublin. Ludlow was right to be suspicious – Coote had a force assembled ready to proclaim the king had Booth's insurrection not been so firmly crushed. Four months later Coote was to play a key role in the coup that ousted Edmund Ludlow's commissioners. A month after that he laid the treason charges against Ludlow, alleging that he had deserted his post and plotted with the army.

Now Coote hoped to play kingmaker by encouraging Charles to make his bid for the crown through a landing in Connaught. There, an Irish army led by Coote would be waiting. The negotiations with Sir Arthur Forbes which led to his hunt for regicides had begun with Coote making the case for an Irish landing. 'His own restoration agenda, after dispatching Ludlow,' suggests Geoffrey Robertson, 'was to have the King come first to Ireland, receive a rapturous welcome and progress on to London with Coote at all times at his triumphant side.'[3]

Acting on the royalist agent's prompting, Coote tracked down five men who had been involved in some way in the king's trial and were now in Ireland: prosecuting counsel John Cook, judge John Jones and the army officers Hercules Huncks, Robert Phayre and Matthew Tomlinson, who had been on duty guarding the king. The five were quietly seized by Coote's men. There appears to have been no legal sanction for the arrests but all were held in Athlone or Dublin preparatory to being sent to England.

The star catch was fifty-two-year-old John Cook, the brilliant legalist who had compiled the indictment of the king and served as lead prosecutor at the trial. Charles's refusal to recognise the court meant that Cook's role had been confined to reading out the indictment to the seated monarch. Nevertheless, he was probably top of the royalist hate list now that John Bradshaw was dead. Charles had once included him with Cromwell and Bradshaw as men who were 'incapable of forgiveness'. Ironically, Cook had just written – though anonymously – a pamphlet defending his friend Edmund Ludlow from charges of treason and attacking Coote, whose 'design must be first to bring in the excluded members from 1648 and then – ding dong bells – will come in king, lords and commons'.[4]

Another military figure from the king's trial soon ended up in Coote's dungeons too. This was Sir Hardress Waller, whose signature was eleventh on the death warrant. The senior figure in the Council of Officers in Ireland, Waller had watched developments in England with mounting alarm. He tried to persuade the officers' council to declare against readmitting the secluded members. The officers turned him down. In some desperation Waller formed a plan to seize his opponents but was betrayed. Waller and his supporters were forced to barricade themselves in Dublin Castle.

Next day, while the defenders of the castle prepared for an attack, the Council of Officers called for the immediate admission of the secluded members. It was a huge psychological blow against the Rump and in favour of the Stuarts. The day after that, a convention organised by Coote's rival Lord Broghill endorsed the officers' declaration and the Dublin Castle garrison gave Hardress Waller up. He was held at Athlone, together with John Cook and the four others seized by Coote. They would remain in confinement in Ireland for months before being briefly released, then arrested again.

In England, George Monck's decision to reverse Pride's Purge and readmit the secluded members ushered in a brief new era in which members of the Rump were bit players and Parliament was controlled by Presbyterian grandees. These were the men who had fought against Charles I alongside the Rump but who, believing that a deal could be done, had negotiated the Treaty of Newport.

The terms of the treaty had involved parliamentary control of the military and the right of Parliament to nominate the great offices of state, the king's councillors and the judges, and to raise taxes, if need be without permission of the king. The Presbyterian grandees, men like the Earls of Manchester and Newcastle, believed they could bring back the king's son on the same terms. After taking their seats on 22 February the Presbyterians wasted no time. They fulfilled a commitment to Monck by appointing him supreme commander of the armies of England, Scotland and Ireland, with the title Lord General. They then turned the legislative clock back nearly a dozen

years, annulling over a period of twenty-six days much of the most
radical legislation passed since 1649 – including the orders legitimis-
ing the purge of the House and their own exclusion. Presbyterianism
was established as the state religion. The Westminster Assembly's
Confession of Faith was imposed as standard doctrine and the
Solemn League and Covenant of 1643 tying England to Scotland's
form of Presbyterianism was reinstituted. And, crucially, the declaration of fidelity that required new members to pledge loyalty to a
government 'without King or House of Lords' was abolished.

All this had to be achieved quickly because of the deal with
Monck, which obliged the Presbyterians to keep the Long
Parliament going to allow enough time to prepare for the election of
a 'free' Parliament. They set themselves 16 March as the date for dissolution of the Parliament they had striven so long to enter.

After the secluded members' first dramatic appearance in the
House, Haselrig, followed by Scot, had stormed out and hours later
led a delegation to confront George Monck. According to Edmund
Ludlow, the fat little man was as civil as ever and treated them to
more protestations of loyalty to the Commonwealth. He explained
feebly that he had let the secluded members in to get them off his
back – 'free himself from their importunity' was Ludlow's phrase –
and insisted he would ensure they did no damage. Charles would be
kept out. As Ludlow reports it, Monck took off his gloves at this junc-
ture, grasped Haselrig by the hand and said, 'I do here protest to you,
in the presence of all these gentlemen, that I will oppose to the
utmost the setting up of Charles Stuart, a single person, or a house of
peers.'

Yet the direction in which the country was travelling was unmistakable. The growth of royalism was signposted daily. 'Everybody
now drinks the King's health without any fear, whereas before it was
very private that a man dare do it,' Pepys observed.[5]

The differing fates of the two men who had rebelled against
Parliament and fought each other at Winnington Bridge just six
months back offered a more personal sign of the times. On 22

February Sir George Booth, the Presbyterian leader of the crypto-royalist revolt in August, was released on a bail of £5000. Nine days later John Lambert appeared before the Council of State and was told to pay four times as much, £20,000, as a security for his freedom. Lambert was reputed to be a wealthy man but he was unable to find £20,000 and was sent to the Tower.

In the first week of March there was speculation about the return of Richard Cromwell. Edward Montague, Samuel Pepys' patron and number two at the Admiralty, let drop to Pepys that 'there was great endeavours to bring in the Protector again'. The exiled court picked up the same gossip. There was talk too of offering Monck the crown. According to one account, republican leaders had pressed the proposal on him but he had refused. Some of the regicides among them were seemingly promoting the idea that anyone was preferable to Charles Stuart.

There were desperate republican attempts to reverse the tide. Propagandists poured out pamphlets, tracts and broadsides warning against the Stuarts. Puritan preachers like Barebone, Peters and Owen prayed for the godly to unite in the Good Old Cause and Edmund Ludlow's republican comrades plotted an uprising.

Predictably, the most powerful warning came from the Secretary for Foreign Tongues. John Milton switched for a moment from composing his masterpiece *Paradise Lost* and at the end of February thundered out six thousand horrified words on the prospects of a restored monarchy. *The Ready and Easy Way to Establish a Free Commonwealth* threatened, 'if we return to kingship, and soon repent, as undoubtedly we shall, when we begin to find the old encroachments coming on by little and little ... we may be forced perhaps to fight over again all that we have fought, and spend over again all that we have spent.' The poet was no democrat in the modern sense of the word. But he implored the citizenry not to backslide into autocracy and with uncanny accuracy forecast the decadence England would invite if it said yes to Charles: 'a culture of servile deference to a King who must be adored like a demi-god with a dissolute and haughty court about him, of vast expense and luxury, masques and revels ... among the perpetual bowings and cringings of an abject people'. The poet sent a letter to George Monck enclosing a copy and a summary of the tract. It is not known whether the General replied, or if he even read it.

The booksellers in St Paul's Churchyard were equally well fed by the royalist propagandists. It was still too risky to call openly for a restoration, but the streets were flooded with lampoons of the Rump and broadsides calling for a free Parliament, which everyone knew meant a Stuart restoration. Prynne alone published more than twenty pamphlets in 1660, mostly against the Rump. According to Thomas Rugge's *Diurnal* (daily diary), 'Rump ballads' were being given 'for nothing to poore Girles for to sell'.[6]

Significantly, royalist literature downplayed vengeance. When a group of royalist gentry in Worcestershire daringly published a tract in favour of monarchy, they declared that they had no thought of revenge and wished only for peace and unity. Royalists in other counties began issuing honeyed declarations. Later, when the restoration had been secretly agreed, a declaration signed by ten earls, four viscounts, five lords and a host of baronets, knights and squires denied any thoughts of vengeance. That would change completely, and soon.

On Saturday 17 March, three weeks after George Monck had taken Sir Arthur Haselrig by the hand and reiterated his fidelity to the Commonwealth, the General met the royalist agent Sir John Grenville late at night in his chambers in St James's Palace. Having employed Monck's brother Nicholas as a go-between during the Booth uprising, this time Sir John gained access to Monck himself through Sir William Morrice, a kinsman and aide of the General whom a contemporary described as his 'elbow-Counsellor'. Morrice persuaded the General to receive Grenville secretly and escorted him into Monck's chamber.[7]

Grenville brought Monck the same offer as that conveyed the previous August. In return for effecting a restoration, Monck was again promised £100,000 a year to distribute as he liked between himself and the army, along with the choice of any high office he liked – Grenville suggested Lord High Constable. As with the earlier offer, the details were passed by word of mouth. All that was written down was a short message: 'I cannot think you wish me ill, for you have no reason so to do; and the good I expect from you will bring so great a benefit to your country and to yourself, that I cannot think you will decline my interest.' Charles had written a commission to Grenville, which perhaps he was also supposed to show to the General, and which perhaps he did: 'I am confident that George Monck can have no malice in his heart against me, nor has done anything against me which I cannot easily pardon', it read; 'and it is in his power to do me so great service, that I cannot easily reward; but I will do all I can.'

Monck's response was unequivocal. According to notes of the conversation which Grenville transcribed later, 'he pledged his life' to the king. Monck then called in Morrice, who had been told to wait outside. From then on Monck would use his kinsman as an 'indirect and deniable channel to the royal court'. Deep into the night the three men discussed the way to effect a restoration. Monck appears to have counselled against Charles indulging in open displays of vengefulness such as had characterised earlier proclamations issued in his name. He suggested that Charles forestall people's fears by promising a free and general pardon to all who swore allegiance to him. He advised the king to counter other fears by confirming land settlements made since the wars and proclaiming freedom of conscience. Monck told Grenville to write it all down but also to commit it to memory. The meeting then broke up.

The following Monday they met again, and Monck checked that Grenville had memorised every detail before taking the paper from him and burning it. He insisted that no one else save Charles himself should know about the meeting. Grenville was then packed off to Brussels with Monck's proposals. He took with him Monck's assurance that 'his consistent object had been the King's restoration', an account accepted by his admirers ever since.[8]

Grenville was now launched on weeks of secret negotiation, shuttling between Monck and Charles as plans for the restoration matured. The only outward sign that something was moving was Charles's abrupt departure from Brussels and relocation in Breda in the Dutch Republic. This move was made on the advice of Monck, who counselled him against remaining in the Spanish Netherlands while England was still at war with Spain.

Given the temper of the army, Monck's insistence on security was understandable. Monck had launched a new purge in the officer ranks soon after arriving in London, getting rid of radicals like Francis Hacker. He had also replaced distrusted regiments in London with his own men. But the army, and indeed the navy, still bulged with republican sectarians, and crucially remained deeply imbued with hatred for the Stuarts. As a correspondent put it in a letter to Prince Charles dated 20 March, 'the army is not yet in a state to hear your name publicly.'[9] Monck himself would later refer to being 'involved in many and great difficulties' because of the republicanism of the army.

Monck's most persistent army opponent was now John Okey, another of the king's judges. Active in marshalling army opposition when the Presbyterians dropped the requirement on members to sign an engagement against single-person rule, Okey also led opposition to a new Militia Bill which invested command of the militia in local dignitaries and revived old fears that the army was to be disbanded. On 8 March he appeared at the head of a delegation of officers presenting a remonstrance to Monck. This was accompanied by talk of officers mounting another 'interruption' like Lambert's six months earlier. It caused 'a general damp over men's minds and faces', remarked Pepys.[10] 'They were high [angry] on both sides', a royalist noted. 'It is feared we shall have some combustions.'[11]

The furore soon abated. Monck, aware as ever of what he could get away with, felt strong enough to slap Okey and the officers down. In Clarendon's words, 'He told them that he brought them not out of

Scotland for his nor the Parliament's counsel, that for his part he should obey the Parliament and they should do the same.'[12] He followed up with a general command to officers to return to their regiments and banned them from holding political meetings. Thus he closed down what had been treasured as a right since the first Civil War. Pepys sighed in relief. 'I was told, that the General had put a stop to it, so all was well again.'[13]

Shortly afterwards, Monck took the final step to control of the military. He circulated a declaration for officers to sign in which they promised obedience to whatever Parliament decreed. Okey was among the minority who refused to sign. But officers from forty regiments did sign it. Remarkably, the deeply political New Model Army had been taken almost out of politics.

Publicly, Monck continued to reiterate his commitment to a Commonwealth. Such was his apparent sincerity that royalists became convinced that he was at heart a republican. 'Monck is, God knows,' a correspondent complained to Hyde. 'He comes once a day into the Council of State. Time will discover whether he be a wise man or a fool. He lately wished his right hand might rot off if he were reconcileable to the King.'[14]

Among republicans fearing the personal consequences of a vengeful monarchy, the talk was of mounting a coup. Edmund Ludlow's memoirs reveal that from late February he and other increasingly panicked republicans were discussing military intervention. His memoirs admit that the plotters came together not just 'for the public interest' but also because of the 'dangerous condition of their affairs and ... their own preservation'. Ludlow proposed calling together members of the Rump's old Council of State and raising rebellion in their name. He revealed that he already had the promised backing of two regiments in the Home Counties and a commitment from Herbert Morley, commandant of the Tower. He also had hopes of John Lawson and the fleet. By mid-March the plot had reached the stage of attempting to raise money. 'A considerable party of those who had been engaged against the King' agreed to contribute money for troops, Ludlow recalled. However, the plot stopped there. It was scuppered because, it seems, Sir Arthur Haselrig had sold the pass.

Slingsby Bethel, a member of the Council of State, was sent to Haselrig's chambers with plans for the uprising. When he arrived he found Haselrig with his head in his hands moaning, 'We are undone.' If George Monck is to be believed – and in this instance he may not have lied – Haselrig had concluded a Faustian pact with the General. The story was detailed in a sensational letter Monck wrote to the Speaker many months later when Haselrig was facing execution. He claimed that Haselrig's friends had asked him to write it to save his life. It described an agreement by which Haselrig was to get out of Monck's way in return for his life. According to the letter, some time after the secluded members were readmitted to the House, Sir Arthur had concluded that a Stuart restoration was inevitable and had come to beg for Monck's protection. He told Monck that a restoration would mean 'ruin to his person, family, and fortune'. Monck, it seems, was only too happy to help if that would put Haselrig out of the game. 'At this conjuncture in time,' he wrote, 'no man was so capable to obstruct my designs as Sr Arthur Hasilrig.' He explained that Haselrig had under his immediate command 'the government of Berwick, Carlisle, Newcastle, and Tynmouth, with a regiment of foot and one of the best regiments of horse in the Army'. Moreover, Haselrig had the biggest hand in selecting officers during a massive purge in the army the previous year and so had a huge 'influence upon all the rest of the regiments in England'.[15]

George Monck's price for saving the republican leader was Sir Arthur's retirement from the fray. 'I told him that if he would engage to me to go home to his own house and live quietly there, I would undertake to secure his life and estate; whereupon he did so engage.'

Haselrig's despair seems to have been the signal for others to give up hope. Ludlow writes:

Mr. Scot also informed me, that he had lost all hopes of getting such a number of our council of state together, as should be necessary to put in execution the design which I had proposed; and that, having notice that the new council of state had resolved to seize his person, he designed to retire into the country, as well to secure himself, as to endeavour to be elected into the ensuing convention ... These things put me in further doubt of my own safety, and moved me to provide for myself as well as I could. To that end I seldom lay at my own house after Mr. Scot's departure from London.

Scot managed one more republican trumpet blast before he departed. The day before the Long Parliament finally dissolved itself, Presbyterian MP John Crew moved that the House bear witness against the 'horrid murder of the king'. One member who plainly feared that fingers might be pointing at him protested that he had neither hand nor heart in the king's death. A furious row over monarchy developed and, disastrously for him, Thomas Scot was unable to keep his sharp tongue out of it. In a speech justifying the trial he declared: 'Though I know not where to hide my head at this time, yet I dare not refuse to own that not only my hand, but my heart also, was in that action.' He concluded by declaring that he should desire no greater honour in this world than that the following inscription might be engraved on his tomb: 'Here lieth one who had a hand and a heart in the execution of Charles Stuart, late King of England.' He was announcing his own death warrant and obviously realised it.

The day ended memorably for royalists. In the evening a man with a ladder, paint and brushes approached the quadrangle of the old Royal Exchange where a row of statues of all the monarchs of England except Charles I stood. After Charles's execution his statue had been pulled down and an inscription put in its place, reading *Exit Tyrannus Regum Ultimus, Restitutae Angliae Libertatis Anno Prime Die. XXX Januarii MDCXXXXIIX* [*sic*] (So ends the rule of the last tyrant. Liberty was restored to England on the thirtieth day of January 1648).* Soldiers and others watched the painter climb his ladder and cheered lustily as he painted over the inscription, descended his ladder and shouted 'Long live King Charles the Second.'[16]

On cue, royalist supporters came out into the open. 'Hesitation suddenly ceased everywhere and the torrent was at its full,' writes Masson. 'They were drinking Charles' health openly in taverns; they were singing songs about him everywhere; they were tearing down the Arms of the Commonwealth in public buildings and putting up the king's instead.' In the Commons, Edward Stephens took the risk of making a speech enthusiastically in favour of monarchy and was applauded for his pains.

Anglican clerics, so long restrained, came out into the open too. On 5 April, Matthew Griffith was briefly jailed for publishing a zealously royalist sermon, *The Fear of God and the King*, taken from Proverbs 24.21: 'fear thou the Lord and the King'. Blind John Milton replied with *Brief Notes upon a late sermon*: 'so wide [is] the disjunction of God from a King,' he wrote, 'we could not serve two contrary masters God and the King.' Griffith's pamphlet was technically treasonable; a few weeks later the world would be turned upside down and Milton would be dubbed the traitor.

A handful of republicans fought the election, including Ludlow and Scot. Both felt themselves to be in jeopardy but risked a last show of defiance. Ludlow contested the Hinden seat in his native Somerset which he had previously represented, and noted that he was now a bogey man. Local Cavaliers 'had printed the names of the late king's judges, of which number I had the honour to be one' and they issued warnings to the electors that they 'should certainly be

---

* In the seventeenth century England and Scotland still adhered to the old style or Julian calendar, according to which the new year began not on 1 January but on 25 March. The New Style or Gregorian calendar was not adopted until 1752. Hence, from our modern perspective, Charles I was executed on 30 January 1649. As is usual when writing of the period, we have used modern dating throughout.

destroyed by the king if they elected me'. Nevertheless he won a clear majority over a royalist, Sir Thomas Thynne. It was a Pyrrhic victory. Thynne later had some of Ludlow's votes declared invalid and was awarded the seat.

Scot's old seat was in Buckinghamshire, where his opponent was a royalist baronet. According to Henning's *History of the House of Commons*, 'No efforts were lacking to ensure his [Scot's] defeat including the production of an alleged bastard during the election campaign.' Nevertheless, Scot tied in votes with his monarchist opponent. After the election, however, the House, now with a royalist majority, ruled that his votes were invalid and ordered the local mayor into custody for a false return.[17]

Increasingly, Ludlow felt personally threatened:

I continued my course of passing sometimes through Westminster Hall that they might see that I had not withdrawn upon any design yet not so frequently or publicly as formerly, lodging sometimes at one friend's house, sometimes at another. And when I lodged at my own home I took special care that the outer gates should be kept closed and that he who attended at them should not permit any to enter of whom he had the least suspicion before he had first given me notice that if I saw cause I might withdraw myself which by reason of back doors I had opportunity to do.[18]

On the evening of 11 April at about eight o'clock, John Lambert, his hands bound with cloth, slid down a rope that was tied to his window and escaped from the Tower of London. Six men were waiting by the wall. They hustled him on to a barge that vanished into the night. He wasn't missed till morning, because a maid put on his nightcap, lay in his curtained bed and managed a convincing 'Good night' when the warder came to lock up. It was said that the rope he used was of silk woven by a lady.

Lambert was not seen for some days, finally surfacing in

Warwickshire. The auspices must have seemed propitious with reports suggesting that soldiers were flocking to him. 'The defection appeared general,' wrote François Guizot, 'an attempt was made, for the purpose of securing the soldiers, to oblige them to sign the address from their officers; but they deserted in crowds: the army of London alone remained entire.'[19]

Monck sent Richard Ingoldsby in pursuit of Lambert. One of a small band of Cromwellian turncoats who had switched allegiance after Richard Cromwell's fall, Ingoldsby was now a king's man, falling over himself to disavow his past. He was particularly anxious to impress because he was also a regicide.

The Lord General does not appear to have been especially confident. After Ingoldsby's force had departed, he summoned Charles's envoy Sir John Grenville and told him, 'If Ingoldsby is beaten, and the army revolts to Lambert, I shall declare for the king, publish my commission, and raise all the royalists to arms in England, Scotland, and Ireland: be in readiness to receive orders.' He then wrote also to thank the king, and to engage himself formally in his service.[20]

Lambert's men were scouring England for support. A major sent to find Edmund Ludlow discovered him in a safe house in Somerset, where he had gone to ground on hearing news of Lambert's escape. The major seems to have given a breathlessly upbeat description of troops flocking to join Lambert in the Midlands: already he had a thousand horse, and the greater part of the army was going to come over to him. After imparting this information to Ludlow, the major explained that they looked to him to raise the west and had arranged a rendezvous in Oxfordshire. Ludlow duly dispatched messengers to trusted commanding officers in Dorset, Somerset and Wiltshire, asking them to be ready to march. But he held back from a public declaration till Lambert's prospects were clearer. Distrust for Lambert was widespread and Ludlow shared it. He had risked his life opposing the proposal to give the throne to Oliver Cromwell and was one of those who feared that Lambert had similar Cromwellian ambitions. Before joining him he wanted to know what Lambert's agenda was. The major answered 'that it was not now a time to declare what we would be for, but what we would be against, which was that torrent of tyranny and popery that was ready to break in upon us'. Ludlow replied that 'the best way to prevent those mischiefs, would be to agree upon something that might be contrary to them'. Ludlow was still waiting for a reply a week later when Ingoldsby caught up with Lambert near Daventry.[21]

It was now that Monck's insistence on quartering suspected regiments in different parts of England and dividing them into sections paid off. Dispersal made concerted action that much more difficult. Haselrig's horse was spread over five towns, Francis Hacker's regiment over three Midland counties. When the call came from Lambert, one of Colonel Hacker's units saddled up ready to go, while others marched through Nottingham swords drawn, but the end result appears to have been that just a dozen or so men actually set off. Reports of isolated handfuls of soldiers and officers being arrested on the roads to the Midlands suggest that it was the same everywhere.

One of Haselrig's troops did get through, only for its captain – no less than Sir Arthur's son – to switch sides. According to a field report from one of George Monck's officers, a few hours before the denouement at Daventry one of Ingoldsby's officers captured Captain Haselrig, but released him on his promise to send his whole troop over to join Ingoldsby, 'which he faithfully performed'.[22]

In the end, when Ingoldsby caught up with Lambert the escaped general had no more than seven squadrons of cavalry and a very small body of infantry, totalling less than a thousand. They were posted behind a little brook which became the line separating the two forces. There was a standoff for some four hours as both sides harangued and shouted, loath to fight former comrades, endeavouring instead to prise men away from the ranks opposite.

Ingoldsby, dressed as a common trooper, reportedly infiltrated Lambert's line and persuaded twenty-five horsemen to cross over. Eventually Ingoldsby gave the order to charge; his infantry fired, wounding two of Lambert's men. In turn Lambert advanced, commanding his cavalry to reserve their fire till they closed in on the enemy; but when they arrived within pistol shot, they stopped and lowered their guns. The final battle of the Civil Wars was over.

Ingoldsby reportedly rode up to Lambert, shouting, 'You are my prisoner.' Lambert asked to negotiate but his plea was refused. Lambert's officers, led by Daniel Axtell and John Okey, are said to have pressed Ingoldsby to let their leader escape. But Ingoldsby was immovable. He was going to keep his prize and prove his new loyalty. According to one report, 'Lambert put his horse to a gallop to save himself; but Ingoldsby, darting off in pursuit, closed upon him, with his pistol in his hand, calling on him to surrender, or he would shoot him. Lambert's fortunes had too often failed him; he had no longer a hope left to sustain him; he lost his courage, stopped, vainly requested his liberty, then submitted.'[23] It has to be said that the accounts of Lambert's pathetic end probably originated from Ingoldsby or one of his lieutenants and are inconsistent with the accounts of courage that Lambert exhibited time after time in his career. But of course it suited Monck for the aura around the army's great hero to be destroyed.

Lambert was brought back to the Tower less than a week after he had quitted it. On his way, Ingoldsby obliged his prisoner to stand under the gallows at Tyburn. The following week there was a great military review of London and surrounding militias in Hyde Park – twelve thousand men from various regiments, in white, green, blue, yellow and orange, but not it seems in the scarlet of Cromwell's New Model Army.

All was over for this revolutionary army and its allies. Samuel Pepys was one of many who celebrated, seeing Lambert's defeat as a decisive blow against the 'fanatics'. On 24 April, he wrote: 'Their whole design is broken and things now very open and plain and every man begins to be merry and full of hopes.'

IO

EXODUS

April–May 1660

John Lambert's abject defeat, followed by his humiliating treatment at Tyburn, marked the end of the republican era. Three days after his capture the new Convention Parliament met and proclaimed Britain a monarchy.* The Lords were re-established too. Some thirty peers simply occupied their old chamber and acted as if the upper house had never been abolished. The final piece in the jigsaw, the proclamation of Charles Stuart as monarch, would not be in place for a further week, but everyone knew that the restoration was unstoppable. A frightening summer was ahead for the men associated with the execution of Charles I.

A sign of things to come arrived on 27 April when a party of militiamen descended on the Staffordshire home of the Fifth Monarchist leader General Thomas Harrison and took him away. He was the first of Charles I's judges to be arrested in England. No one had more to do with the king's death than Harrison. He had pressed for the trial,

---

* Constitutionally, only the sovereign can summon Parliament in England. On the occasions when Parliament has convened without royal summons, it is called a Convention Parliament.

he had been in charge of security at the trial, he had attended every session, he had even taken charge of the dead king's funeral. Not surprisingly his name topped the lists of the king's 'murderers' that royalists now took to scattering around.

Harrison was arrested by Colonel John Bowyer, one of the secluded MPs. Well provided with horses and arms, he could have made a show of resistance or escaped. He did neither. He would have counted it an 'action of desertion of the cause in which he engaged, to leave his house', explained Mark Noble, the first biographer of the king's judges.[1] George Monck sent an order to convey Harrison to the Tower. His horses were impounded and sent to London for the use of the king. The king would lay claim to the property and estate of every so-called regicide, most of it going to his brother James, Duke of York.

Edmund Ludlow, who was well aware that he might be the royalists' next target, attempted to secure what he could of his estate before the authorities acted. He tried to make over to his brother-in-law £1500 of livestock on his property in Ireland and to have tenants' rents collected. But his old enemy Sir Charles Coote, without any authority from Parliament, seized it all, taking control of the estate and forcing Ludlow's tenants to pay rents to him. Colonel Theophilus Jones, Coote's chief collaborator in wresting control of Ireland from the Rump, took away the pick of the livestock, presumably for himself.

In London, the business of restoring the monarchy occupied a fraction of the time it had taken to displace it. This mighty political turnabout was achieved in just over a week. The process began on 1 May with an elaborate charade. Charles's trusted middleman Sir John Grenville presented himself at the door of the council chamber in Whitehall flourishing a letter. It bore the royal Stuart seal and was addressed to General George Monck. The General affected not to know Grenville and theatrically commanded the guards to hold him while the document was examined. Grenville announced that it was a declaration from the king and that there were similar missives for the Commons, the Lords, the City of London, the army and the fleet.

The document, the Declaration of Breda, contained Charles's promise of clemency to most of his enemies, and those of his father, if they swore fealty. It was an astute document that breathed forgiveness. The crucial passage announced a 'free and general pardon' to all who within forty days offered their loyalty and obedience to the king, 'excepting only such persons as shall hereafter be excepted by Parliament – these only to be excepted'. The declaration then repeated the assurance:

> Let all our subjects . . . rely upon the word of a King, solemnly given by this present Declaration, that no crime whatsoever, committed against Us or our Royal Father before the publication of this, shall ever rise in judgment, or be brought in question, against any of them, to the least endangerment of them, either in their lives, liberties, or estates.

Charles undertook to settle army pay arrears and to confirm land settlements made since 1648. Remarkably for a son of Charles I, he also pledged to guarantee 'liberty for tender consciences', or freedom of worship.

The forty-day countdown for former enemies to pledge allegiance began on the day the declaration was published, 1 May. The wording would persuade some of his father's judges that if they pledged in time (by 10 June) they would qualify for clemency. It wasn't so. They were misled, or they misled themselves. A flurry of activity followed the reading of the Breda document in the Lords and the Commons. Peers and commoners hastened breathlessly in and out of joint meetings in the Painted Chamber and back to their own chambers as the two houses raced to be first to declare England a monarchy again. In mid-afternoon the Lords won. Their statement read: 'The Lords do own and declare that, according to the ancient and fundamental Laws of this Kingdom, the Government is, and ought to be, by King,

Lords, and Commons.' The Commons had to follow suit: 'this House doth agree with the Lords ... that, according to the ancient and fundamental Laws of this Kingdom, the Government is, and ought to be, by King, Lords, and Commons.'

The statement had the bonfires burning, the drink overflowing and the maypoles going up for the first time in a dozen years of grey Puritan rule. The giant maypole set up at the traditional point in the Strand was said to have been erected by John Clarges, a blacksmith from the Savoy, who was not only an ardent royalist but also George Monck's father-in-law. 'Transcendant was the Joy all over England which issued from this good News,' wrote the monarchist historian William Howell nearly two decades later.[2]

Three days after the declaration of a monarchy, the royal arms were restored to the Courts of Justice, and the statue of Charles was returned to Guildhall. Throughout the following month the effigy of Cromwell, which only eighteen months before had been crowned with a royal diadem, draped with a purple mantle, and borne with all imaginable pomp to Westminster Abbey, was exposed at one of the windows at Whitehall with a rope fixed round its neck.

The next eight days saw a battle between the Presbyterians and the new, wildly royalist intake in the Commons over the limits to be put on royal power. The Presbyterian grandees in the Lords, the Earls of Manchester and Newcastle and Sir Thomas Wharton, were determined to impose conditions on the incoming king and pushed for those accepted by Charles I in the Treaty of Newport in 1648. Those had denied the king control of the army and reserved for Parliament the appointment of council members, judges and other officials. The Presbyterians wanted no less. They were set on preventing any more favourites like a Strafford or the Duke of Buckingham taking the helm.

A year earlier, young Charles would have accepted almost any terms. Around Easter 1659 his courtiers were so desperate that they had canvassed the idea of him securing the throne by marrying a daughter of John Lambert, who would then play kingmaker.

Apparently Charles had gone along with the proposal. But Lambert wanted no part of it. Now, in April 1660, emboldened by George Monck's commitment to him, Charles felt so strong that he pressed for an unconditional restoration. He let it be known that his 'honour' demanded no less.

All eyes were on Monck. 'The General hath been highly complimented by both Houses,' wrote the courtier Henry Coventry to the Marquis of Ormond, 'and without doubt the giving the King easy or hard conditions dependeth totally upon him; for if he appear for the King, the affections of the people are so high for him, that no other authority can oppose him.'[3] The Presbyterians tried to set up a committee in the Commons to consider putting the Newport terms to the king. This proposal was seconded, but got nowhere. According to one contemporary account, 'It was foreseen that such a motion might be set on foot' and Monck was 'instructed how to answer it, whensoever it should be proposed.'[4] Instructed is probably the wrong word, but Monck played the saboteur anyway – first by suggesting that Charles could be trusted to be accommodating when he assumed the throne and then by frightening Parliament. He told the Commons that he could not answer for the peace 'either of the nation or the army' if there was any delay in bringing over the king. Although universal peace reigned all over the nation at the moment, 'many incendiaries stood ready to raise the flame'. The portly general referred dramatically to information he dared not release and talked of 'the blood or mischief' that delay might produce. The speech ended with a warning that the consequences would be upon Members' own heads; this 'was echoed with such a shout over the house, that the motion was no more insisted on'.

So Charles got his way. On 8 May the still absent prince was officially proclaimed 'the most Potent, Mighty and Undoubted King of England, Scotland and Ireland', with no conditions attached.

By common consent among historians, this was a disastrous decision. William Cobbett wrote: 'To the king's coming in without conditions may be well imputed all the errors of his reign.'[5] In the opinion of Edmund Burke,

> The man given to us by Monck, was a man without any sense of his duty as a prince; without any regard to the dignity of his crown; without any love to his people: dissolute, false, venal, and destitute of any positive good quality whatsoever, except a pleasant temper, and the manners of a gentleman. Yet the Restoration of our monarchy even in the person of such a prince, was every thing to us, for without monarchy in England, most certainly we never can enjoy either peace or liberty.[6]

How little truth there was to Monck's warning about urgency was evident from Charles's own reaction. He could hardly have moved at a more leisurely pace. A man who all his life loved symbolic gestures, Charles opted to delay his arrival in England, finally making a triumphal entrance in London three weeks later on his thirtieth birthday.

Over those weeks Parliament lavished spending money and compliments on the Stuarts, and worked on how to deal with the alleged killers of the king. The Commons voted £50,000 in immediate cash for Charles, £20,000 for his brother James and £10,000 for brother Henry, topped up by £10,000 from the City of London and a £3000 personal gift – a bribe – from William Lenthall, the Speaker in the Long Parliament. Samuel Pepys was in the party sent to The Hague to accompany the Stuarts back to England. His diary for 16 May 1660 notes the poverty of the royal entourage – 'their clothes not being worth forty shillings the best of them' – and their relief at suddenly being in funds. 'How overjoyed the King was when Sir J. Grenville brought him some money; so joyful, that he called the Princess Royal and Duke of York to look upon it as it lay in the portmanteau before it was taken out.'

While Charles dawdled in The Hague, the manhunt he had always promised himself got under way in London. The hunt would

dominate the first year of the new king's reign and was still to res-
onate during that of his brother. The legislation authorising it was a
'Bill of General Pardon, Indemnity and Oblivion' introduced into
the Commons by the solicitorgeneral, Heneage Finch, on 9 May.
This was to be the focus of the regicide battle, specifying all those
deemed guilty enough to die, those guilty enough to lose everything
but their lives and those to be let off with minor punishments.

During the first debates on the Bill, the king's 'inclination to
mercy' was stressed repeatedly, not least by Charles himself. But
those who suspected that they would be targets recalled the ferocious
threats of revenge attached to his name in earlier years. They were
faced with stark choices – fleeing for their lives, keeping their heads
down and praying for the best, or standing their ground as martyrs for
the cause.

Those who fled were arguably the wisest. Charles exhibited
moments of ruthlessness that boded ill for anyone judged an opponent. While preparing the ground for his landing in England, he
dispatched a letter to Monck telling him to stop appeasing
opponents. He wrote, 'There are many persons still contriving ...
against me and you and who must be rather suppressed by your
authority and power than won and reconciled by your indul-
gences. ... it may be a little severity towards some would sooner
reduce the rest than anything else you can do.'[7] Later he told
Parliament: 'The same discretion and consequence which disposed
me to the clemency I have expressed ... will oblige me to all rigour
and severity towards those who shall not now acquiesce but continue to manifest their sedition and dislike of the government, either
in words or deeds.'[8]

Among the first of the King's judges to flee were William Goffe
and his father-in-law Edward Whalley. Had they lingered they would
undoubtedly have been leading targets for arrest. A report to
Charles's Chancellor, Edward Hyde, pinpointed them as particular
enemies – Whalley 'as a great stickler against the King and Goffe [as]
another'.[9] On 4 May the two managed to slip unnoticed out of the

country just as the last pieces confirming the Stuart restoration were falling into place. The former major-generals kissed their families goodbye and took horse for Gravesend, where passage awaited them on the *Prudent Mary*. She was bound for Boston.

The two refugees would no doubt have heard that Monck had just secured another endorsement from their former comrades in the army. On 2 May the Declaration of Breda was read to a mass meeting of army officers who applauded it. The meeting repeated the army's recent commitment to abide by the will of Parliament and recorded the officers' satisfaction with Charles's promises. There was a similar commitment from naval officers at a meeting aboard the *Naseby*, and of course this was marked by celebratory cannonade from the entire fleet.

That evening the House of Lords ordered the restitution of all statues of the dead king and of the blue and gold royal coat of arms of the Stuarts. A statue of George Monck was also proposed.

Goffe and Whalley had booked their passages under the names of Edward Richardson and William Stephenson, but their real identities became known to some of their fellow passengers quite quickly. Fortunately these other passengers were sympathisers. New England was a bastion of Puritanism and admirers of Cromwell, and most of the passengers on the *Prudent Mary* would have been no different. The fugitives made friends on board with two prominent colonists who were en route for home, Captain Daniel Gookin of the Massachusetts Bay Colony and William Jones of New Haven Colony. They would prove godsends in the troubled years ahead.[10]

A third judge, John Dixwell, would later join Goffe and Whalley in America. Most of the other fugitives either attempted to hide in England or made for Europe.

Cornelius Holland and John Barkstead, both of them also judges, fled for the Dutch coast. The Netherlands was an obvious place in which to lose themselves. The great trading city of Amsterdam was the base of numerous English merchants, most of them Puritan and sympathetic to the Good Old Cause. There were numerous other potential havens in the country too. The great university city of Leiden was one of a dozen or more places with substantial English and Scots populations. These émigré enclaves had first grown up during the Spanish war, when garrisons from both countries were stationed throughout the Low Countries. A by-product of this military presence was the provision by treaty of churches for British subjects in Dutch towns. These were non-episcopal and nonconformist and enjoyed the same privileges as the Dutch Reformed Church. In Leiden, the pastor received at least part of his salary from the municipality, while the town magistrates provided a meeting house for use by the English-speaking congregation.

Barkstead appears to have reached a Dutch port without trouble. Cornelius Holland, on the other hand, was nearly caught. He later told how he had planned to stop in his native town of Colchester on his way to the coast and on arriving took rooms at an inn. He explained that he had come to collect money owed him by a friend, a local merchant. One assumes he needed every penny he could get to fund his life in exile. Holland left his horse at the inn while seeking out the merchant. Mysteriously, he then vanished from sight until the early hours of the following morning. Someone at the inn appears to have become suspicious of the absent guest, and Colchester's major of militia was brought out of bed by news that a suspected person might have booked in at the inn. There was excited talk of it being John Lambert, though of course Lambert was being held in the Tower. At around 4 a.m., Holland's rooms were raided in his absence. Holland heard of the raid and did not return for his horse. His friend smuggled him out of town. Eventually he escaped across the Channel and joined other exiles at Lausanne in Switzerland.

John Milton chose to hide, realising correctly that although he had no direct role in the king's death, Cavaliers would be after his blood. He left his home in Petty France on 7 May, borrowed the tidy sum of £400 for emergencies and went to ground in a house near Smithfield. Friends are said to have dissuaded constables from making a thorough search for him by putting out a story that he was dead. They even held a pretended funeral. The poet avoided arrest for nearly four months.

Edmund Ludlow stuck around precariously, spending much of his time on the run. He had 'timely warning' of the order to arrest all who had signed the death warrant, and the night before it was issued he quit his house in London to stay with the first of a long line of relatives and friends who would shelter him till he finally left the country. A day later a warrant for his arrest was circulated throughout the land. He breathed in relief that he hadn't followed his usual route. If his way had taken him near the Guildhall, he would have seen the statue of Charles being re-erected and, outside the Courts of Justice, the installation of the royal arms.

The manhunt began to focus on its quarry on 12 May, nearly two weeks before the king stepped back on English soil. That day, extracts from the official report on his father's trial, dated December 1650, were read aloud in the Commons. The ten-year-old report congratulated 'the persons entrusted in this great service, of the trial of the late King' for having 'discharged their trust in them reposed with great courage and fidelity'. Four or five of the men in the new Convention Parliament had been among the king's judges. They sat uncomfortably as the praise accorded them was quoted ten years later. The record states that several of these former judges rose to their feet to 'express how far they were concerned in the said proceedings'.[11] What they said is not recorded, but as David Masson puts it: 'Happy were those who could say that, though named among the commissioners for the trial, they had never sat in the court, or had discontinued their sittings before the fatal close.'[12]

Passions began to run so high that, according to Edmund Ludlow, men dared not show moderation lest it be called disaffection to the king. Yet in private, he says, various members of both houses declared in favour of a general indemnity covering everyone without exception. Ludlow's memoirs quote the gout-ridden Lord Fairfax as asserting that if any man must be excepted, 'he knew no man that deserved it more than himself, who being general of the army at that time, and having power sufficient to prevent the proceedings against the king, had not thought fit to make use of it'.

On the opening day of debate on the Bill, Sir John Lenthall, son of the former Speaker, roused fury when he tried to spread blame beyond the judges. 'He that first drew his sword against the King committed as high offence as he that cut off the King's head,' Sir John declared. Strictly that was true, but his words prompted an outraged rebuke from his father's successor as Speaker, Sir Harbottle Grimston. There was 'much poison' in young Lenthall's words, Grimston claimed. They were spoken out of a design to 'set the house on fire'. Lenthall was forced to withdraw the words and was briefly imprisoned.

The first principle dealt with was numbers – how many were to die, how many to be imprisoned for life. Monck, careful not to stir up opposition needlessly, had discussed the matter with Charles's envoys, urging the king to forgo vengeance and pardon everyone. Not so merciful as claimed, the prince was not to be persuaded. Monck then accepted that there should be up to five 'exceptions' from pardon – meaning executions – among the judges. In an increasingly bloodthirsty atmosphere, five deaths was considered inadequate and almost immediately it was agreed to raise the total of judges excluded from pardon to seven. This unlucky handful, together with whoever among the wider community Parliament chose to make examples of, would constitute an initial death list. There was also to be a much longer list of men subject to heavy punishment short of death. However, none of this would be set in stone before the Bill was enacted. Until that happened there would be a desperate struggle to have enemies included on the two lists and friends removed. Behind the almost non-stop celebrations of the returning royals and their supporters, dozens of life and death struggles would be waged.

A bulging House of Commons committee of fifty-two members handled the Bill after the preliminaries. William Prynne and the solicitor-general, Heneage Finch, headed the hard-liners pushing for harsh, widespread punishment, while Arthur Annesley, a late convert to royalism, was the leading moderate.

All the known paperwork from 1648–9 was transferred to Prynne and John Bowyer, the man who had arrested General Harrison. Prynne ferreted endlessly through it to produce evidence on who exactly had done what in the prelude to the trial and beyond. Whole libraries seem to have been sent to him to burrow through. Later he was appointed Keeper of Records at the Tower of London, a post he called 'most suitable to my genius'. In a letter to the Speaker, Sir Harbottle Grimston, he wrote: 'whilst you are sucking in the fresh country air, I have been almost choked with the dust of neglected records (interred in their own rubbish for sundry years) in the White Tower; their rust eating out the tops of my gloves with their touch, and their dust rendering me, twice a day, as black as a chimney sweeper.'[13]

Meanwhile, the king's legal officers were dispatched to load the dice against the regicides by weakening the rules of evidence that were to apply when they were brought to trial. A series of secret meetings with senior judicial figures took place in the Inns of Court. They were attended by the king's attorney, Sir Geoffrey Palmer, and his solicitor, Sir Heneage Finch, together with the Duke of York's attorney, Sir Edward Turner, the Chief Baron of the Exchequer, Sir Orlando Bridgeman, and three senior judges. These lawyers agreed to charge the alleged regicides under the ancient law of treason, which made 'imagining' the death of the king or his heir punishable by death. 'Imagining' could cover a range of acts from direct involvement in a royal death to advocating it. They then agreed to drop the requirement under common law for two witnesses to prove an action. In the forthcoming trials one witness was to be deemed sufficient.

Three of the accused regicides swiftly wriggled off the hook. Richard Ingoldsby was the first of them, quick to capitalise on his capture of John Lambert. Before Charles was even proclaimed Ingoldsby's friend, the Earl of Northampton was lobbying the king on his behalf. In a letter to Charles dated 29 April, the earl portrayed Ingoldsby as a deeply honourable man misled by others but now a real convert to the crown. The letter asserted that no one else in the army could have crushed Lambert with so small a force. He wanted no reward, only 'His Majesty's pardon and forgiveness of his former errors'.

The repentant Ingoldsby was summoned before Parliament on 14 May. In tears he presented himself as horrified at what he had been part of. He claimed that, although he had been named as one of Charles I's judges, he attended none of the sessions, 'always abhorring the action in his heart'. The day after the pronouncement of what he called 'the horrid sentence', he had come across Cromwell and other judges in the Painted Chamber where they assembled to sign the warrant. His story was that Cromwell saw him and ran to him, forcing him over to the table and saying that although he had escaped the trial he would be made to sign the warrant along with the rest. Ingoldsby claimed to have refused, saying that he was forcibly held while 'Cromwell, with a loud laugh, taking his hand in his, and putting the pen between his fingers, with his own hand wrote Richard Ingoldsby.'[14] His performance was called a 'whining recantation'. It served its purpose, however. Ingoldsby would be made a baronet. It is worth noting that his signature on the warrant is bold and florid.

Another judge to be freed early in the hunt was Colonel Matthew Tomlinson, the man whose courtesy and attentiveness in guarding the king to and from the court each day had so impressed Charles that he presented the officer with a gold toothpick. Luckily for Tomlinson, Charles had let others know of his considerate behaviour.

The third of the judges to get off relatively lightly was Colonel John Hutchinson, the former governor of Nottingham Castle who had just been returned as a member of the Convention Parliament. Hutchinson, the well-connected son of a baronet, had been as zealous as anyone in killing the king, attending every day of the trial as well as signing the death warrant.[15] He escaped retribution eleven years later after, like Ingoldsby, providing support for George Monck in the critical months of January and February. But there were – and still are – unanswered questions about the man and his escape from the scaffold. After his death four years later, his wife Lucy wrote an adulatory memoir about him, casting him as an unflinching embodiment of honour. He was hardly regarded as such by former comrades at the time, for he sent to the Speaker an abject letter that grovelled in apology for his part in the king's death. 'I acknowledge myself involved in so horrid a crime as merits no indulgence,' it said. The letter went on to claim a 'real, and constant repentance' arising from 'a thorough conviction' of his 'former misled judgment and conscience', not from a regard for his own safety. He also seems to have produced a wealth of supportive testimony from kinfolk and aristocratic friends that he had aided the royalist cause at a much earlier date. He had, he asserted, 'endeavoured to bring the King back'.

The day after interviewing Hutchinson, the committee examined the list of sixty-seven judges, dead and alive, who had attended the last session of the trial and heard the sentence of death pronounced. Those most hated by the royalists were dead of course – Oliver Cromwell, Henry Ireton, John Bradshaw and Thomas Pride. The committee took the first step towards punishing them posthumously. It voted to except them from pardon and 'attaint' them as traitors. Attainder was medieval England's great disincentive to treason. It was seen by many as a punishment equally dire as execution. As well as condemning the individual to a traitor's death, it condemned his bloodline to ruin by declaring all titles, property and estate held at the time of the treason forfeit to the crown. The near-contemporary historian Roger Coke described the punishment facing the judges as 'terrible ... for tho' they did not all suffer in their Persons, scarce any of them but forfeited their Estates'. Pauper-making went with widow-making.

An Act of Parliament conferred the regicides' estates on the king's brother James, Duke of York. One of the recurring matters occupying parliamentary time in the months ahead was the nodding through of land and property transfers to the future James II.

A start was made with Oliver Cromwell's property. The Council of State ordered the seizure of the late Protector's team of horses and the 'grand coach' which he had commissioned before his death. This was followed later by moves to take back from the Cromwells the great estate in Monmouthshire that Parliament had voted to Oliver for his military achievements. Cromwell's widow Elizabeth was the first to suffer. She was rumoured to have planned to finance life in exile with a cache of valuables – gold, jewels and paintings – that were allegedly royal property. The hoard was supposedly hidden in a Thameside warehouse owned by a friend of the widow. In a report dated 12 May, the *Parliamentary Intelligencer* announced that the council was 'following up information that there were several of His Majesty's goods at a fruiterers' warehouse near the Three Cranes in Thames Street London which were there kept as the goods of Mrs Eliz Cromwell, wife of Oliver Cromwell deceased, sometimes called Protector'. The report added: 'it being not very improbable that the said Mrs Cromwell might convey away some such goods, the council ordered persons to view the same.' There was a follow-up report in *Mercurius Publicus* on 16 May: 'Amongst goods that were pretended to be Mrs Cromwell's at the fruiterers' warehouse are discovered some pictures and other things belonging to His Majesty.' What the pictures and 'other things' were was never revealed.

A few weeks later, a much larger repossession exercise began after a list was produced of properties formerly owned by Henrietta Maria, the Queen Mother. They ranged from the palace of Somerset House, which the Commonwealth had used as a barracks, to a string of stately manor houses sequestered by the state and sold to government supporters. The buyers had included John Lambert, now in the Tower, Edward Whalley, now on his way to America, and Edward Dendy, probably in Rotterdam. All the properties and everything else they owned were liable to be seized from their families. It was the same for every attainted fugitive.

A line of men-o'-war bearing Charles and his brothers James and Henry hove to at Dover on 23 May. The royal party was carried on what had been the flagship *Naseby*, but was now *The Charles*. During their passage across the Channel the king had ordered not only her name but those of four similar vessels to be changed: *The Richard* became *The James*, *The Dunbar* became *The Henri*, *The Lambert* became *The Henrietta*, and *The Speaker* became *The Mary*.

George Monck was first to greet his sovereign. He began to bow, making as if to prostrate himself, only to be swept into an embrace by the king, who kissed him. After that there unfolded scenes of fawning comparable to those envisaged by John Milton. Dignitaries jostled to kiss the hems of Charles's garments and to deliver the most humble and joyous declarations. A leisurely progress to London followed, interrupted by a three-day stopover at Canterbury where a new royalist council was appointed and Monck was invested with the Order of the Bath, the first of many gifts to him from the grateful king.

While the king paused, the destruction of republican symbols went on. In New Palace Yard, Westminster, in Cheapside and at the Old Exchange, copies of the Solemn League and Covenant were ceremoniously burned by the common hangman. 'The executioner ... did his part perfectly well', reported the *Kingdom's Intelligencer*,

> for having kindled the fire he tore that Solemn League into very many pieces, first burned the Preface and then cast each parcel solemnly into the fire, lifting up his hands and eyes, not leaving the least shred but burned it root and branch. What a damnable wicked Covenant was this ... that fatal oath born in Scotland and fed in both kingdoms with the blood and livelihood of more thousand Christians than this oath had words.[16]

The king and his two brothers rode through cheering multitudes and were hailed outside London by a reported fifty thousand troops drawn up on Blackheath. This was the prelude to a magisterial parade into London that enthralled the crowds and sickened republicans. As David Masson wrote:

At the skirts of London itself there were the kneeling Lord Mayor, Aldermen, and Common Council, and thence through the City, the trained-bands and City Companies ... a troop of three hundred in cloth of silver ... next a marching mass in purple velvet ... next, a troop in buff, with silver sleeves and green scarfs ... smaller troops, in blue and silver, grey and silver, and pure grey, all with trumpeters before them ... the Sheriff's-men, in red cloaks and with pikes in their hands ... six hundred picked men of the City-companies, in black velvet suits with chains of gold ... then kettledrums, trumpets, and streamers ... the Knights of the Bath and their esquires ... then more kettledrums and trumpets, preceding his Majesty's life-guard of horse ... then, in a blaze of various colours, the City-marshal, the City-waits, and all other City-officers ... the two Sheriffs, the Aldermen, the Heralds ... the Lord Mayor carrying the sword ... then Lord General Monck and the Duke of Buckingham; then, O then, His Majesty himself, between the Dukes of York and Gloucester.

No doubt the excited rush and bustle made it easier for furtive men going the other way. It is believed that Thomas Scot and John Okey managed to leave the country somewhere during the period around Charles's return. Scot's was a heart-stopping escape. He claimed not to have feared arrest but murder: 'Some unreasonable men designed no less than a bloody assassination upon me,' he said.[17] An assassin would have found it easy to track him down. A well-known figure, he lived ostentatiously with his family in a wing of Lambeth Palace across the river from Whitehall. In May or June a passage to the Continent was arranged for him, probably from Portsmouth. His vessel set off, but her route was through waters notorious for the presence of pirates and sure enough Scot's vessel was boarded. According to Scot's own account, the pirates 'plundered' him and set him ashore somewhere on the Hampshire coast. The hunt for regicides must have been in full swing by now, but somehow Scot avoided capture. He got aboard another vessel, this one shipping Spanish prisoners of war back to the Spanish Netherlands. It is more than possible that Scot's friendship with the Spanish envoy in London helped him secure a berth on the ship.

Ludlow continued to hang on. He even watched the king's entry into the city, the soldier idealist in him quailing at the sight. He wrote:

> I must not pass over the folly and insolence manifested at that time by those who had been so often defeated in the field, and had contributed nothing either of bravery or policy to this change, in ordering the soldiery to ride with swords drawn through the city of London to Whitehall, the Duke of York and Monck leading the way; and intimating, as was supposed, a resolution, to maintain that by force which had been obtained by fraud.

He then reflected bitterly on the changed role of the army he had been proud to lead. 'It was a strange sight to me, to see the horse that had formerly belonged to our army, now put upon an employment so different from that which they had at first undertaken ... they had not been raised out of the meanest of the people, and without distinction, as other armies had been; they ... had engaged themselves from a spirit of liberty.'

Edward Hyde, Charles's Chancellor, was equally struck by the welcome, though from a different perspective. 'At Whitehall the two Houses of Parliament cast themselves at his feet with all vows of affection to the world's end. Well might the King exclaim, as he saw the fervency of welcome, It had been his own fault he had been absent so long; for he saw nobody that did not protest he had ever wished for his return.'[18]

The pageantry went on for days. Across the country there was a 'delirium of joy . . . peals of bell-ringing, bonfires and shouting mobs, public feasts, wine running from the spouts for the general benefit' and burnings of Oliver Cromwell in effigy, usually accompanied with effigies of the Devil.[19]

The exodus of judges would go on too.

II

DEATH LIST

May—September 1660

While the country celebrated, a hue and cry was unloosed for the men who had judged the king. A decision was taken to attach the terrible label 'regicide' to those who had been present in the High Court as Charles I's death sentence was pronounced and from their number to select the death list of seven. Thirty-seven of these men were still alive, and the order went out to sheriffs and other law officers across the country to seize them and seize their property.

The seven were deemed to be unpardonable and were wholly 'excepted' from the Bill of Indemnity. They could expect the full savagery of a traitor's death – hanging, castration and disembowelment before the victim was beheaded and the trunk quartered so parts could be displayed across the land.

The remaining judges were to be on a list of men who could expect severe future punishment short of death; the phrase used was 'pains, penalties, and forfeitures'. What that punishment was to consist of would be decided by Parliament at a later stage. For a lucky few this would turn out to mean a fine and perhaps a bar from future public office; for most it would mean incarceration for life and the seizure of their estate and property by the king.

A rhetorical blast from the Speaker, Sir Harbottle Grimston, let Parliament know how the regicides were to be viewed. In judging them, Sir Harbottle told the Commons, they 'were looking over a long, black, prodigious, dismal roll and catalogue of malefactors ... monsters, guilty of blood, precious blood, precious royal blood, never to be remembered without tears'. There was, he thundered, an absolute necessity to except such men from pardon 'that they may be made Sacrifices to appease God's Wrath, and satisfy Divine Vengeance'.[1]

The first of the judges to be selected for execution was the flamboyant Fifth Monarchist Thomas Harrison. On 4 June Parliament announced that he was to be 'excepted out of the Act of general pardon for life and estate'. The choice of General Harrison was no surprise. Apart from his several roles at the trial of the king, his status at the head of the Fifth Monarchists made him look the most dangerous of surviving republican leaders and a man for royalists to be rid of.

A day after Harrison was named, six more judges, major figures from the republican past, were listed with him as wholly beyond pardon. They were the military men John Jones and John Barkstead, the lawyer John Lisle and the parliamentary politicians Thomas Scot, Cornelius Holland and William Say. Edmund Ludlow narrowly escaped inclusion after George Monck received a letter alleging a plot by Ludlow to mount an insurrection. Ludlow managed to put down that nonsensical claim and Barkstead, the once feared military governor of the Tower, was voted in by a narrow margin as the seventh man on the death list.[2]

The list was supposed to stop at seven, the number of men that Parliament had agreed should bear the guilt of King Charles's death by being totally excepted from pardon. However, that restriction was immediately disregarded. On 8 June, three days after announcing the identities of the seven, the Commons put five more on the list: the prosecutor, John Cook, one of the clerks of court, Andrew Broughton, the sergeant-at-arms, Edward Dendy, and the two so far unidentified executioners.

The same day, Parliament decided to add men other than judges to the list of partial exceptions – individuals who, though not stained by the guilt of the king's death, had shown such 'mischievous activity' in the recent troubles they deserved to suffer. The Commons voted that there should be 'twenty and no more' on this list.

At the beginning of June only three of the twelve men on the death list were in government hands – Harrison, John Cook and John Jones. The last two had been seized by Sir Charles Coote in Ireland back in February. Coote had held Cook until a few weeks earlier when George Monck ordered his return to England. John Jones had been released about the same time only to be picked up after a few weeks, this time in England. Jones evidently expected the worst, for he spent the time after his release putting his affairs in order. He was found by constables 'taking the air' in a London park.

Of the other nine on the list, the two executioners were still unidentified, while the remaining seven men had slipped away to Europe. A stop on the ports had been ordered in mid-May and thorough searches were undertaken. However William Say, John Lisle, Cornelius Holland and Andrew Broughton escaped through the net and were either in, or on the way to, Switzerland, while Thomas Scot was in Brussels, Edward Dendy was probably in the Netherlands and John Barkstead in Germany.

Others of the king's judges who, fearing the worst, scattered abroad included John Hewson, the apprentices' hate figure in London who ended up in Germany; Sir Hardress Waller, who had also been held in Ireland by Sir Charles Coote but was now in France; and Edward Whalley and William Goffe, who must have been more than halfway across the Atlantic. All told, nineteen of forty-four men whose arrest had been ordered were abroad, seemingly out of Charles's reach. The rest remained in England to brave it out.

Around them the country boiled with righteous animosity against all those described as regicides. As recently as April, royalists had issued public declarations disdaining 'any thoughts of rancour or revenge' once the king was restored. The pledge was forgotten immediately Charles was back in England. His return saw a deluge of bloodthirsty royalist broadsheets inciting action against the 'phanatics' who had 'murdered' the king. A *Hue and Cry after the High Court of Injustice* set out the names of the 'traitors' and the estates they owned. *Lucifer's Lifeguard* listed 'the anti-Christian imps who have been murderers and destroyers of the best religion, the best government and the best King that ever Great Britain enjoyed'. *The Royal Martyrs* listed 'Lords and Gentlemen that were slain in ... defence of their King' and *Royal and other Innocent Blood* called to heaven 'for dire vengeance'.

At this stage the number of captured regicides could be counted on one hand. After Harrison, Cook and Jones the next to be seized was sixty-four-year-old Gregory Clement, whose signature on the death warrant was number fifty-four. He was caught at the end of May hiding in London, in what was described as a mean house near Gray's Inn. Clement had never been a discreet individual and this characteristic was his downfall. In 1653 he had been discharged from the House of Commons for 'offensive and scandalous' behaviour after being discovered in bed with a maidservant. Now he made the mistake of not acting the poor man in a poor man's neighbourhood. He ordered in provisions only the well-to-do could normally afford, and a suspicious neighbour reported him. The militia was called out and Clement was brought from the house to be questioned by officers in front of a gaping crowd. One of the interrogators knew him but was evidently a friend, for he failed to divulge Clement's identity. Clement survived the questioning and the militia were eventually prevailed upon to let him go. But Clement had a very distinctive voice and the story is that before he could get away, a blind man in the crowd recognised it and challenged him. At this, Clement evidently broke down and admitted his identity. He was sent to the Tower.[3]

Colonel Daniel Axtell was betrayed by a friend who had agreed to hide him. Axtell had been on the run since John Lambert's fiasco at

Daventry six weeks earlier, having stuck loyally with Lambert till the moment the latter allowed himself to be arrested by the eager Richard Ingoldsby. Only then did Axtell make his own escape. Even without the Lambert connection, Axtell would have been a prime royalist target. It was he who had allegedly roused the halberdiers under his command to shout 'Justice, justice' as the king passed by during his trial; it was claimed, too, that he had ordered his men to shoot the masked woman in the gallery – identified by many as Lady Fairfax – who had barracked the judges. The friend who betrayed Axtell agreed to hide him, but thought better of it: as soon as the search for regicides was launched he contacted the nearest constable and turned his guest in.

Officers caught Sir Henry Mildmay as he tried to escape through Rye on the Sussex coast. Keeper of the King's Jewels under James I and Charles I, Mildmay had retained his post to become a disposer of royal treasure under the Commonwealth having taken Parliament's side in the Civil War. Enemies accused him of growing rich by dipping into the treasures he was supposed to be guarding. In fact he sold them all on Parliament's orders, but in the way of such office holders probably secured a goodly cut. Although not a signatory to the death warrant, he attended several sessions of the trial, which was enough to damn him in royalist eyes. On the report of his arrest, the Council of State, sniffing royal gold, ordered his captors to take particular care to guard whatever 'monies and goods' he and his servants had about them.

Two wanted men from the New Model Army completed the government catch in May. The brilliant general John Desborough, the hard man of the Wallingford House group, was caught on the Essex coast, and the bluff, unbribable cavalry officer Francis Hacker, another who commanded the guards at the king's trial, was arrested in London.

June saw the search launched for the two masked executioners. William Prynne chaired a parliamentary probe into their identities, while Charles's secretaries of state made their own enquiries. The first suspect investigated in England was the most obvious, the Common Hangman of London himself, Richard Brandon, who had died six months after the king. At that time one rumour had it that he was paid £30 for the execution; another put his fee at £300 to do the grisly work. At Brandon's burial later in 1649 crowds had packed the churchyard yelling abuse – among other things threatening to quarter the corpse in retaliation for the killing of the king.[4]

Prynne's committee uncovered witnesses who claimed that Brandon had admitted to being the headsman. One recalled him saying, 'God forgive me I did it, and I had forty half-crowns for my pains.' Prynne found a waterman on the Thames who claimed to have been forced by soldiers to ferry the hangman away from Whitehall immediately after the execution. Apparently his passenger was terrified of the crowd spotting him – and so was the waterman:

> He shook every joint of him. I knew not what to do. I rowed away a little further, and fell to a new examination of him when I had got him a little further. Tell me true, said I, are you the hangman that hath cut off the king's head? I cannot carry yon, said I. No, saith he, I was fetched with a troop of horse, and ... truly I did not do it: I was kept a close prisoner all the while, but they had my instruments.

Another witness told an intriguing story about Brandon's next major engagement, the beheading of the Earl of Holland, Lord Capel and the Duke of Hamilton in Palace Yard, Westminster. The witness heard Lord Capel ask the hangman: 'Did you cut off my master's head?'

> 'Yes', saith he. 'Where is the instrument that did it?' He then brought the axe. 'This is the same axe. Are you sure?' saith my lord. 'Yes, my lord', saith the hangman, 'I am very sure it is the same.' My lord Capel took the axe, and kissed it, and gave him

five pieces of gold. I heard him say, 'Sirrah, were thou not afraid?' Sayeth the hangman, 'they made me cut it off, and I had thirty pounds for my pains.'

The evidence against Brandon was considered inconclusive and two well-known republicans – George Joyce and Hugh Peters – were canvassed as alternative suspects. Both were named by Cromwell's favourite astrologer, William Lilly, when he was brought in to Westminster on 2 June to be questioned by William Prynne and two others. Lilly himself was in danger of being excepted from pardon. A rival astrologer, John Gadbury, charged that he had promoted Charles's execution through his almanacs and other writings, specifically *Observations on the Life and Death of King Charles*, in which Lilly justified Parliament's stance against the king.

Predictably, he was given a rough ride by younger members of the overwhelmingly royalist House of Commons when he arrived to meet Prynne, and he must have been a frightened man. 'At my first appearance, many of the young members affronted me highly, and demanded several scurrilous questions,' he wrote. Prynne quizzed him for an hour before the astrologer was allowed to say his piece. It was sensational. He told Prynne that a week or so after the execution he had hosted a supper at which Robert Spavin, Oliver Cromwell's secretary, was a guest. The talk that evening was taken up with speculation and gossip about the identity of the man who swung the axe, with the most unlikely names being floated alongside serious candidates. When the eating was done Spavin drew Lilly aside and said, 'These are all mistaken; they have not named the man that did the fact; it was Lieutenant-Colonel Joyce. I was in the room when he fitted himself for the work – stood behind him when he did it – when done, went in again unto him. There's no man knows this but my master [Cromwell], Commissary Ireton, and myself.'[5]

George Joyce was hated by royalists. He was the bumptious young junior officer who could be said to have sealed Charles's fate in 1647, two years before the king was put on trial, when he lay in 'protective custody' at Holmby House in Northamptonshire. Joyce was a lowly cornet of horse, the most junior rank of officer in the army. Sent with five hundred troopers to take charge of weaponry in Oxford, the royalist capital in the Civil Wars, Joyce instead collected the king, diverting his column to Holmby House in order to seize the monarch. On his arrival he allegedly barged into the king's bedroom and curtly informed him that he was being moved to army headquarters at Newmarket. The king protested and asked to see the officer's commission. Joyce pointed to the troopers behind him. 'There is my commission. I hope that will satisfy your majesty.'

Joyce proceeded to deliver the king to Newmarket and thus to Cromwell. He claimed later that he was acting under Cromwell's orders, but Cromwell disputed it. Whatever the truth, the king was now in Cromwell's hands and, unknown to anyone, the first step to the scaffold had been taken. As for Joyce, he was later promoted to the rank of colonel, but was ever afterwards known as 'Cornet Joyce' in recognition – or in horror – that one of the most junior officers in the army should have had the nerve to kidnap a king.

On 7 June, after hearing Lilly's account, William Prynne had a warrant issued for Joyce's arrest. The colonel is thought to have been still in England, but he avoided the bloodhounds and joined the list of military men, lawyers and politicians who evacuated to the Netherlands.

During Lilly's testimony another well-known name was dropped. This was Hugh Peters, the excitable Puritan preacher who was close to Cromwell. Peters had visited the king frequently during his imprisonment and was thanked by Charles for his kindness, but his brilliant and sometimes venomous sermons made him yet another royalist hate figure. Peters became a suspect in the search for the axemen because Lilly reported that mention of him had been made during that supper. This was enough for William Prynne to issue a warrant. The idea that the ungainly old Puritan had been one of the hefty figures on the scaffold was ludicrous. But he had been such a celebrant of republicanism – and of Cromwell's victories – that he was a natural target for the royalists. He went into hiding in London and managed to stay undiscovered for weeks, but his enemies would pursue him to the scaffold. A rhyme was taken up by newspapers: 'The best man next to Jupiter/Was put to death by Hugh Peter.'[6]

In Ireland, the inquiry was handled by the recorder of Dublin, who was able to yield another suspect whom Prynne also had arrested. He was a bearded army veteran, William Hulet (or Hewlet). A sergeant testified that in 1649 he and Hulet had been in a unit drafted into Whitehall for the trial. He reported that, a day or two before the execution, a colonel gathered a group of nearly forty men together and asked whether any would behead the king for £100. He also promised preferment in the army. None of the men put their hand up. On the day of the execution, however, the sergeant was posted by the window to the Banqueting House; from here he saw the heavily disguised executioner kneel and overheard him ask for the king's forgiveness, which of course was refused. The sergeant claimed to have recognised the voice as that of William Hulet. A short time after the execution, Hulet's promotion came through. He was made up to captain-lieutenant. Several other soldiers were found who had served with Hulet and were willing to claim that he had admitted being on the scaffold. Hulet was held pending trial.

Throughout June, the Commons laboured over the punishment lists, while those who knew they were possible targets trembled. If they were to be added to the list of those wholly excepted they would be as good as dead; if added to the secondary list of the partially excepted, they faced attainder, probably incarceration and the destitution of their families. If they were very lucky, they might escape with a fine and a permanent ban on holding office.

After agreeing the twelve-strong death list, the Commons took less than two weeks to choose the 'twenty and no more' men who, though not regicides, were to join the bulk of the judges a step away from the gallows in the partially excepted category. Predictably the twenty included the most troublesome figures of the old republican establishment, Sir Harry Vane and Sir Arthur Haselrig. Also among them were the former Speaker, William Lenthall, and the former generals John Desborough, Charles Fleetwood and John Lambert, as well as Daniel Axtell.

Gossip augured badly for them – and for that other former general Edmund Ludlow, who recorded:

> My Lady Vane told my wife, that Mrs. Monck had said, she would go upon her knees to the King, and beg, that Sir Henry Vane, Maj Gen. Lambert, and Lt-Gen. Ludlow, might die without mercy and one of my friends, who frequented the court, assured me, he heard Monk saying to the King, that there was not a man in the three nations more violent against him, or more dangerous to his interests than I was.[7]

On 18 June two more men – William Hulet and Hugh Peters – were added to the death list. Peters was indicted on the strength of a statement from William Young, a doctor from Pwllcrochan in Pembrokeshire. According to the *House of Commons Journal*, Dr Young claimed that he had attended Peters in Plymouth when he returned from Ireland dangerously ill and that Peters had told him that 'he and Oliver Cromwell, when the said Cromwell went from the Parliament unto the Army in 1648, did in a field … none being present besides, contrive and design the death of his late Majesty, with the change of the Government.'

The bloodlust was mounting and this can be attributed at least in part to the king's personal arrival on the scene. As Charles's Chancellor Edward Hyde coyly put it, 'the actual presence of the King and his court and the exuberant ebullitions of loyalty which burst so vehemently from assembled myriads had not tended to diminish their detestation of regicides or to impart a merciful calmness to their deliberations.'[8]

How bloodthirsty was Charles himself? Since his much-applauded declaration from Breda, his consistent posture had been that of the merciful prince, the reconciler. Gone was the furious figure of earlier years, thundering for revenge. However, he stood back as the numbers on the death list mounted, and was to help ensure that some were added to the list. Republicans like Edmund Ludlow inevitably put the worst construction on Charles's actions. Recalling the numbers of his friends lined up for punishment or death in June and July 1660, Ludlow wrote:

> Tho' the message from Breda had declared the King would be satisfied, if some few persons who had an immediate hand in the death of his father, might be excepted from the indemnity; yet finding himself now possess'd of the throne, 'twas visible to all men that he used the utmost of his endeavours to influence the House of Commons to greater severities than were at first pretended.

The king's motives, Ludlow decided, were 'partly revenge and partly rapine', in other words, the royal seizure of the estates of those who were excepted.

Bribery and enmity, and, of course, influence and family, played their parts in the selection of who was excepted and who escaped. The diaries of that arch political fixer of the Commonwealth period, the lawyer Bulstrode Whitelocke, show all those elements at work. Whitelocke had made some very dangerous enemies from his time as Commissioner of the Great Seal and president of the Committee of Safety. They included George Monck, William Prynne and Heneage Finch. No more frightening a trio could be imagined, given the influence each wielded. Prynne, the barrack-room lawyer, hated to be found in error on any fact and during the Long Parliament Whitelocke, the genuinely learned lawyer, caught him out several times. The little man had borne him a deep animosity ever since and, according to Whitelocke, searched the Parliament journals to find something against him. Whitelocke's wife, who apparently had helped Prynne when he was in poor straits, tried to intercede for her husband. She waited for hours to see Prynne, only to be treated to an outburst of invective from him. He told her that her husband should be excepted and he would see to it that he was excepted. She was then dismissed 'more like a kitchen wench than a gentlewoman'.

It is not clear why Finch was an enemy, but George Monck's antagonism stemmed from Whitelocke's warning to the Common Council the previous winter that he, Monck, was planning the restoration. This, the General complained, might have ruined the whole enterprise. He and Whitelocke had been friends but when Whitelocke went to see him to plead for his backing he was snubbed.

In his now desperate battle for survival, Whitelocke found himself paying out a fortune in bribes. The Earl of Berkshire, whose daughter had been imprisoned by order of the Committee of Safety, which was sometimes chaired by Whitelocke, demanded £500; if the money was not forthcoming, he would persuade the Lords to have Whitelocke excepted. Thomas Napper, Whitelocke's former clerk and now a royalist colonel, arranged for Whitelocke to have an interview with the king and expected £500 for the favour (he got £250). Near the top of the tree 'Ned' Hyde, the Chancellor and a purported friend, was bought off with 'a present' of £250, plus 'fees' totalling £37 18s 8d. And right at the top, the king was graciously pleased to accept treasures from the royal library which Whitelocke said he had saved for His Majesty. They included the fifth-century *Codex Alexandrinus*, which Whitelocke claimed he could have sold for £4000 overseas.[9]

On 14 June, William Prynne, true to his threat, tabled a motion in the Commons proposing Whitelocke's inclusion on the 'twenty and no more' list. It may be hard to believe that sentiment played a part in deciding the fate of this wily man, but during the debate much was made of the plight that Whitelocke's family would face if he was excepted or partially excepted – he had sixteen children to support.

The vote went Whitelocke's way by 174 votes to 137.[10] His escape cost him 'a great deal of money in gratifications and buying out of enemies from their designs of destroying him', Whitelocke wrote.

Midway through the compilation of the death list, on 16 June, the king issued a proclamation authorising the arrest of John Milton and the minister John Goodwin. The poet was still in hiding and couldn't yet be found. But his books could. Charles ordered a public burning of Milton's *Eikonoklastes* and *Pro Populo Anglicano Defensio* (in defence of the people of England). The king proclaimed that both books 'contained sundry treasonable passages against us and our Government, and most impious endeavors to justify the horrid and unmatchable murder of our late dear father, of glorious memory'. The burnings, which were carried out with great solemnity by the common hangman, began on 27 August and enough copies were found to enable him to repeat the performance every day throughout the next two weeks.

Milton remained at large for nearly two months. He was finally taken into custody at about the time of the book burnings and remained in jail until 15 December. Then he was released without any charge. Monarchy's most vibrant critic was neither excepted nor subject to any sanction. That 'amazed' people, wrote Milton's biographer David Masson. Their incredulity was understandable. As another biographer put it, Milton's offence was worse than that of the regicides, for 'they had only put the King to death, he attacked the very office and memorialized posterity against the very idea of Kingship'.[11]

It seems that the poet was saved by the lobbying of his very powerful political friends, Sir William Morrice and Sir Thomas Clarges, and by the support of royalist poets Andrew Marvell and Sir William Davenant, the Poet Laureate. Milton is said to have intervened to save Davenant's life in 1650 when he was in the Tower facing a possible treason trial, and Davenant was determined to return the favour. Another of Milton's biographers wrote: 'A life was owing to Milton, and 'twas paid nobly.'[12]

Throughout the list-making William Prynne was at his busiest, serving on more committees and speaking more often than anyone else, a man driven by 'a pathological desire for revenge on regicides and Cromwellians', according to one historian.[13] During the first discussions he came triumphantly into the Commons brandishing data on eleven judges who had not been involved in the sentencing of Charles but who, he said, had been active enough during the trial to qualify as regicides. The Commons immediately put them on the partially excepted list. Then Prynne turned to those who had not participated as judges. On one day alone, 18 June, he moved to except from pardon all the MPs who had drawn up the key Cromwellian statute, *The Instrument of Government*, and then successively moved to exclude Charles Fleetwood; Richard Cromwell; Major Selway, an ardeut republican; Bulstrode Whitelocke; William Godwin and John Thurloe.[14] He failed this time, but Selway and Fleetwood were to be included on the list of twenty in the end.

In July, Prynne backed proposals to fine and disable whole classes of republicans and Commonwealthsmen from public or private office – all those who had sat in High Courts of Justice since 1648, all of Cromwell's major-generals, anyone who had petitioned against the king, and whole sections of MPs and officials from the Protectorate. One proposal would have had them all refunding their salaries. It was likened to a 'hand-grenado thrown into a barrel of gunpowder'.[15] Charles's wiser advisors managed to defeat the more extreme proposals, but according to Edward Hyde they were hard put to do it.

Three of the four most prominent Scottish Covenanters were among the men swept into prison in July and regarded as regicides. First came the leader of the Campbell clan, once the most powerful man in Scotland, the pious, squint-eyed, brilliant and much feared Marquis of Argyll. Eight years earlier at Scone he had crowned Charles king of Scotland in return for the young prince's uncomfortable adoption of the Covenant. At the time, Charles promised 'on the word of a King' to make Argyll a duke when he assumed the

English throne. Subsequently, their ways had parted, Charles fleeing Britain after the Battle of Worcester and Argyll reaching agreement with Cromwell. Nine years later, Argyll could no longer expect that dukedom, but nor did he expect the reception he was given when he arrived in Whitehall at the beginning of July. He asked for permission to see the king in order to kiss his hand.[16] On hearing this, Charles petulantly stamped his foot and sent the Garter King of Arms to arrest the marquis for treason.

Later that month, two more of the leading Covenanters, Sir John Swinton of that ilk and James Guthrie, the minister of Stirling, were seized. An attempt was made to arrest the other great Covenanter, Archibald Johnston, Lord Wariston, but he escaped to Germany and while there he was safe. A fifth Scot, one William Giffen (or Govan), was also seized, upon a false allegation that he was one of the king's executioners.

Edmund Ludlow spent these fearful summer days mainly in hiding, although he made fleeting appearances in London, and kept occasional contact with the sergeant-at-arms to show that he hadn't fled. He retained the dreamer's hope that the storm would abate and that he yet might be able to protect his family from the sequestration of his estates. 'I found it difficult to resolve what to do,' he confessed, as he weighed up his chances of survival if he were to give himself up to the sergeant-at-arms and present a petition to Parliament arguing his case. Others among the king's judges, including normally courageous men, had submitted grovelling, sometimes tearful apologies to the House for their opposition to monarchy. Needless to say, Edmund Ludlow intended to apologise for nothing. The nearest he came to expressing regret in his petition was to claim that he had always acted with 'as much tenderness to those of the contrary party as my fidelity to the parliament would permit'. The petition was shown by Ludlow's wife Elizabeth to his old friend Arthur Annesley, who was close to the king. He told her that her husband 'should do better to say nothing'.

Of all the fugitive judges, Thomas Scot was probably the most wanted. If his prominence in republican government had not until now made him the top target, his suicidal outburst just weeks earlier justifying the king's execution ensured it. He did, however, seem to be safe in Brussels when he eventually reached the city after his brush with pirates. Scot's luck was not to hold. A gloating pamphlet put out later in 1660 by a royalist MP reports his capture after just six days in Brussels.[17] According to this account, Scot was seen visiting the house of Don Alonso Cardenca, the former Spanish ambassador in London. The authorities were approached by royalists and authorised Scot's arrest. He was duly seized, but a stand-off developed when Don Alonso intervened on Scot's behalf. It is not clear what happened next, but the story goes that the British resident in Brussels, Sir Henry de Vic, eventually persuaded Scot to return to England and give himself up. The timing suggests that, like others, Scot may have been misled by the wording in the king's deadline proclamation – which called on the wanted men to surrender within fourteen days 'under pain of being excepted from any pardon or indemnity for their respective lives and estates' – into believing that compliance with the deadline would bring mercy. It seems that Sir Henry de Vic encouraged him to think so.

The clear implication of those sixteen words was that those surrendering on time would be treated with clemency, but the position was not spelled out. Years later, the likely author of the document, Edward Hyde, later Earl of Clarendon, admitted in his autobiography to an 'ambiguity of expression'. He lamented that because of it, 'acts of retributive justice to which otherwise few could have objected were sullied with the imputation of a breach of faith'.

It is hard to escape the conclusion that the ambiguity was deliberate, worded carefully to deceive the fugitives into the Stuart net. Whether deliberate ploy or carelessly drafted phrase, the lure worked. At the expiry of the deadline the House was told that twenty of the regicides till then at large had surrendered themselves. They included Henry Marten, Lord Monson, John Carew and – according to the sergeant-at-arms – Edmund Ludlow and John Dixwell. Neither of the last two had physically handed themselves in, but both had given assurances that they would do so. Most of the other eighteen who had surrendered were held in Lambeth House. According to Lucy Hutchinson in her memoir of her husband, they had an eminent visitor there. George Monck, who had just been ennobled as Duke of Albemarle, 'came gloatingly' to look them over.[18]

Eleven of the fugitives preferred not to trust their lives with the king and stayed away. They were added to the primary death list, bringing the total to twenty-three. Edmund Ludlow would soon be added to the list. But for the moment he was reported to have surrendered and so was neither a wanted nor a condemned man.

Others who were persuaded to surrender included Sir Hardress Waller and Adrian Scroop, the latter of whom would turn out to be the most ill served of the judges. The former republican governor of Bristol, Scroop was rumoured to have helped snatch the king from Holmby House and had been an ardent attender at the king's trial, two reasons why royalists might hate him. Nevertheless, after he handed himself in on time, the Commons examined his plea and voted to deal lightly with him. Scroop was fined the value of a year's rent on his estate, banned in perpetuity from holding office and released. However, when the Lords began reviewing the Bill of Indemnity a few weeks later, they insisted on arresting and wholly excepting him. He had talked too freely to Richard Browne, once a Cromwellian major-general, now Lord Mayor elect of London and a supposed friend. Browne reported that in a private conversation Scroop appeared to justify the king's execution; he had suggested to Scroop that the death of Charles I was a sad affair, but Scroop had refused to pronounce it murder, observing, 'Some are of one opinion, and some of another.' The Commons fought briefly for his removal from the death list but eventually gave him up.

Thomas Scot's fate was not quite sealed after he was persuaded to return to England. As intelligencer for Cromwell and more recently for the Rump, he had a wealth of information with which to bargain for his life. On 12 July the House of Commons excepted him from pardon, but 'some promise of life' seems to have been made to him if he would unmask the men who betrayed royalist plans to him. Scot appears to have baulked at that, but did disgorge some titbits. He answered questions from Sir William Morrice and Sir Anthony Ashley Cooper and submitted a note on his activities, telling them of the men who kept him abreast of Charles's negotiations with the Presbyterians, of the Dr Jansen in France who offered to 'have the King brought into my power', of one or two other agents around Europe including the Anglo-Irish adventurer Joseph Bampfield, who spied for everyone, and of the amazing cipher breaker, Dr Waller of Oxford, who deciphered all the mail, apparently for the fun of it. The doctor 'never concerned himself on the matter but only in the art and ingenuity'. Scot called him 'a jewel for a prince's use'.[19]

Like Ludlow, Scot was not a man to apologise. He would not retract his parting words in Parliament, confessing only to 'rash and over-lavish language' and 'an intemperate tongue', which could be blamed, he said, 'on a misguided conscience which I heartily repent'. It was not enough to save the former spymaster. He was already on the death list, absolutely excluded from pardon, and he remained on it. One wonders what went through the mind of Sir Anthony Ashley Cooper, the future Earl of Shaftesbury, as he left Scot in the Tower after the interrogation. Only months before he and Scot had been comrades, and more recently Ashley Cooper had reassured another worried republican that no lives would be lost when the king returned. He'd 'be damned body and soul if ever I see a hair of any man's head touched ... upon this quarrel'.

June had been a month of roistering and ceremonial as well as of the compilation of death lists. At night the king and his two brothers were relentlessly feasted. Monck led the way, laying on for them a 'great supper at his residence in the Cockpit'. There followed a nightly round of banquets in the mansions of triumphant royalists like George Villiers, Duke of Buckingham, and more nervous aristocrats like Philip Herbert, Earl of Pembroke, who needed to convince the king that his support for Parliament in the Civil Wars was much-regretted madness. This first round of celebration climaxed at the Guildhall with an elaborate pageant, 'London's Glory Represented by Time, Truth, and Fame', followed by a City feast. John Evelyn saw 'his Majesty go with as much pomp and splendour as any Earthly prince could do'.[20]

By day, Charles was intent on re-establishing the mystique of royalty. He reintroduced the Ceremony of the Royal Touch, in which a brush of the hand from the monarch was supposed to cure the diseased, principally of scrofula (the disease known as 'the King's Evil'). On 19 June *Mercurius Publicus* reported that crowds 'of poor afflicted creatures ... many brought in chairs and baskets' flocked to the Banqueting House, where the king in a chair of state

> stroked all that were brought to him and then put about each of their necks a white ribbon with an angel of gold on it. In this manner His Majesty stroked above 600 and such was his princely patience and tenderness to the poor afflicted creatures that though it took up a long time the King being never weary of well doing was pleased to make inquiry as to whether there were any who had not been touched ...

The following month it was announced that in future, the king would perform this service only on Fridays, and to crowds of no more than two hundred, and they had to apply to the Royal Surgeon for tickets.

Some people placed boundless faith in the king's messianic powers of healing. John Aubrey's *Miscellanies* featured an Avis Evans who had a 'fungus nose and said it was revealed to him that the King's hand would cure him. And at the first coming of King

Charles II into St James Park he kissed the King's hand and rubbed his nose with it which disturbed the King but cured him'. The following April, Charles claimed to have touched between fifteen and sixteen thousand people, but no longer. He announced that on his physicians' advice he was 'to forbear for the present to touch anyone'.

Charles was besieged with petitioners. The state archive is stacked with petitions dated May 1660 from aspiring state servants – among them would-be chamberlains, clerks of the Mint, clerks of the Exchequer, tellers, messengers of the chamber or council, masters of requests, clerks of the Pells, comptrollers, coiners and engravers. John Evelyn's diary records how he arrived at Whitehall with letters from Henrietta Maria to deliver to the palace, but was unable to get through the human scrum. 'It was indeed intolerable as well as inexpressible, the greediness of all sorts of men, women and children to see His Majesty and kiss his hands in so much as he had scarce leisure to eat for some days, coming as they did from all parts of the nation.'

In July and August, the demands for retribution reached a peak – and not only retribution for the king. Across the country royalists demanded redress or revenge for their own individual losses, human and material, at the hands of Parliament. None were more persistent and passionate than Arundel Penruddock, whose sense of injustice at the execution of a beloved husband would leave its mark not just on Charles's reign but on that of his successor too.

Arundel Penruddock had petitioned unsuccessfully for her husband's life five years earlier. Now she was back, along with the widows of some of her husband's men, petitioning for retribution over their deaths. The similar wording of the petitions suggests that this was a coordinated campaign. Full of anger and bitterness, the petitions were targeted at the officer who, the widows said, had promised their men quarter and the members of the Cromwellian judiciary who tried and condemned them. These included the Lord Chief Justice Lord Rolle and the regicide John Lisle. The widows wanted them excepted from pardon and pressed for their arraignment for murder and high treason. They took their campaign to the House of Lords, a still more vengeful place than the Commons, and they were to find eager allies there.

On 9 July the Commons finalised the Bill of Indemnity and passed it on to the Lords. The death list had leapt again and again as the Bill passed through the Commons. The list of five proposed by George Monck in May, which had become seven, and then twelve in June, now stood, with the addition of those who had vanished abroad, at twenty-five. But that was not blood enough for the young Cavaliers in the Lords, and perhaps not for the young king either.

The hand of Charles was felt from the moment that the Lords began debating the Bill. He dispatched a letter to the peers which damned Daniel Axtell, the halberdier colonel who had been on duty in Whitehall with his men on the day that Charles was beheaded. The letter was from an old servant of Charles I, expressing surprise that Axtell was to escape with life. The writer said that he could testify to having heard Axtell incite his soldiers in Westminster Hall to cry out for the king's execution.

A second piece of evidence against Axtell was then submitted by the Council of State, in effect by the king. This was an allegation that Axtell had been talking treasonably in prison. He had forecast that 'Monck's reign would be short', and that the king and council 'would involve the kingdom again in blood'. Axtell's journey to the block had begun; after this nudge from the throne, the Lords voted to wholly except him from pardon.

During the rest of July and most of August, the political temperature reached boiling point as the Lords listed more individuals they wanted to be excepted. On 23 July they discovered the whereabouts of the smoking gun, the warrant for the king's execution. This bore the bold signatures of John Bradshaw, Lord Grey and Oliver Cromwell at the top and of fifty-six more beneath them. It was unearthed after peers asked for the paperwork on the trial and learned that the warrant had been left in the keeping of another of the officers present at the execution, Colonel Francis Hacker. He had already been arrested, and so his wife was asked to go home and retrieve the forgotten piece of parchment. Alas for both of them, she complied and dutifully returned with the warrant. On the back of the document, held today in the Parliamentary Archives, there is written in a seventeenth-century hand, 'The bloody Warr[an]t for murthering the King'. On the other side, in addition to the judges' signatures it carries that of Hacker, authorising the execution. On noting his name, the Lords voted to exclude him too from all hope of pardon – ensuring that he would in turn be attainted and executed with his wretched wife left destitute.[21]

Graphic fragments of evidence kept surfacing to stir the punitive venom of the Lords. The sight of the fatal death warrant was one. The allegation that soldiers had spat at the king was another. And there was the report of how the carpenter who constructed the scaffold, a man named Trench, had dipped his handkerchief into Charles's blood after the deed was done. On the day the Lords had their first glimpse of the death warrant, they produced a list of all the judges present when sentence was pronounced and a second list of all who signed the warrant, and immediately voted to have all the men on both lists wholly excepted.

It was all taking too long for the king. He wanted the Bill of Indemnity out of the way so his council could get on with the potentially explosive task of disbanding the army. For all George Monck's regimental purges, there was a real danger of a backlash from republican officers if retribution were to be visited on too many people, which was what the peers' bloodlust threatened to achieve. On 27 July Charles came down to the House to urge it to complete its deliberations quickly. In a speech that challenged the Lords to defy him, he said, 'I do earnestly desire and conjure you, to depart from all particular animosities and revenge ... and that you will pass this Act, without other exceptions than of those who were immediately guilty of that Murder of My Father.'

On the day that the king was delivering his injunction to the Lords, the *Prudent Mary* was disembarking Edward Whalley and William Goffe in Boston. New England was as yet unaware of the reversal of fortunes in England. No one in America, including the two newcomers, yet knew of the hue and cry unleashed all over England in pursuit of the king's judges. The two men were war heroes and stars of a revolution of which Massachusetts heartily approved, and the colony's Puritan establishment opened its arms to them.[22] No one of their status had ever visited the colony before, and they were wined and dined by the great and good almost from the moment they landed. The governor of Massachusetts, John Endecott, set the pace, receiving and feasting them in their first week in Boston. Other prominent colonists, including the president of Harvard, followed suit. So did the governor of New Haven, William Leete, who put them up in his home. Captain John Crowne, an angry royalist, later reported that the regicides 'were treated like men dropped down from heaven'.[23]

It was a honeymoon which should have been short-lived, for news of the restoration came hard on the regicides' heels. Less than two weeks after the arrival of Whalley and Goffe, their host Daniel Gookin showed them a paper brought by the latest ship to dock. It reported the House of Lords' order to arrest sixty-six members of the High Court of Justice and seize their estates. Goffe wrote in his diary, 'Went to Boston lecture, heard Norton, Scotch ship brought threatened recognition.' The two were subsequently challenged in the street, apparently by someone from the same ship, while another royalist, Thomas Breedon, demanded their arrest. Yet such was the climate of opinion in the colony that nothing was done. Governor Endecott told Breedon that he would not 'meddle with them' without an executive order.

Breedon later returned to England and unloaded his outrage on the Council of Foreign Plantations, the embryonic Colonial Office presided over by the Duke of York. Captain Breedon told the council that when he demanded action against Whalley and Goffe, the marshal-general in Massachusetts had grinned in his face and taunted him: 'Speak against Whalley and Goffe if you dare, if you dare.' Even after another Scottish ship berthed in Boston, bringing Breedon copies of the final Act of Pardon and Oblivion and the king's proclamation, he was vilified for showing them around. The copies were dismissed as 'being more malignant pamphlets that he had picked up'. Whalley and Goffe remained utterly unmolested. The remarkable honeymoon of the two supposedly hunted men would last beyond Christmas.

Back in England, the Lords voted to except three more men who had nothing to do with Charles I's death: Sir Harry Vane, Sir Arthur Haselrig and the once-feared general John Lambert. The additions were made in the presence of James, the king's brother. He and the youngest Stuart brother, the Duke of Gloucester, regularly attended these sessions, no doubt reporting back to the king and ensuring that his real wishes were transmitted to the floor.

Aristocratic bloodlust was anything but sated by the lengthening death list which the peers were building, apparently with royal approval. The Lords took up the Penruddock campaign and found more victims there: 'In the House of Lords, much striving there is of several parties to increase the number excepted,' Edmund Ludlow recorded. 'Mrs Penruddock and Dr Hewitt's widow and several others solicit for particular satisfaction for the death of their relations ... And much ado they make.' Still greater ado was created when an altogether more celebrated widow, the Countess of Derby, joined in. She was bent on vengeance for the execution of her husband, the Earl of Derby, who was beheaded with other Cavaliers after a court-martial at Chester in 1652.

When she surrendered a stronghold on the Isle of Man upon receiving the news of her husband's death, Lady Derby had earned the distinction of being the last royalist commander in the British Isles to submit to Cromwell's Commonwealth. Man was effectively a fiefdom of the earldom and, come the restoration, Lady Derby took revenge on the local Roundhead leader on the island who had besieged her, exercising her power as de facto queen of Man by executing him. Then she targeted the four members of her husband's court-martial, which included Colonel Harry Bradshaw, a brother of John Bradshaw. A petition from the countess prompted the House of Lords to summon Bradshaw and accuse him of breach of privilege. Grasping at the furthest reaches of their prerogative, the Lords held that for commoners to condemn a peer to death was unlawful. Luckily for Harry Bradshaw, he managed to convince their Lordships that he had tried to save the earl from the block.

The Lords turned to other aristocratic 'martyrs' executed on Parliament's orders in 1649 – the Duke of Hamilton, the Earl of Holland and Lord Capel. Justices, prosecutors and others involved in their trials, and in Derby's trial too, were arrested and hauled before the House to face the most vindictive proposal so far – that a kinsman of each dead peer pick one of their judges or prosecutors to be executed. Clarendon called it an 'odious' and 'disgusting' course of action.

The battle of the death lists came to a head in mid-August, when the Commons addressed the Lords' final version of the Indemnity Act. The solicitor-general, Sir Heneage Finch, was dispatched to seek a compromise. It was hard going. Their Lordships now wanted a total of forty-three of the judges to be completely excluded from pardon, also Vane, Haselrig, Lambert, Hacker and Axtell. The Lords insisted furthermore on exacting vengeance for the four executed aristocrats by executing a man for each of them. At first the peers wouldn't budge on anything. Indeed, on the last matter it was claimed that the peers were showing their moderation by taking 'no more than one a-piece'.[24]

'Blood requires blood,' asserted Heneage's namesake Lord Finch, the Lords' spokesman, referring to the forty-three regicides. 'The shedding of royal blood had brought infamy upon the nation' and their Lordships 'did not think it fit nor safe for this kingdom, that they should live.' They could not live in England and would be a danger to the Kingdom if allowed to live abroad. The negotiators conferred and reported back again and again throughout a highly charged week.

A compromise heavily favouring the Lords was eventually forged. The Lords dropped their demand for eye-for-an-eye vengeance and in return the Commons retreated on much more. They acquiesced to the total exception of thirty judges and agreed to the exception of Lambert, Vane, Axtell and Hacker too. However, what appeared to be a life-saving deal was made for Vane and Lambert. In return for putting them on the death list, the Commons secured the Lords' agreement to a joint petition to the king to remit execution in the event of the two men being attainted and facing death. The king agreed. The *House of Lords Journal* for 8 September records the Lord Chancellor reporting that 'His Majesty grants the desires in the said petition.' Charles was not to keep his word.

Sir Arthur Haselrig avoided the death list thanks to a letter from George Monck, explaining his pledge made six months earlier to save Haselrig's life. This time the great dissembler kept his word and Sir Arthur survived. After a rancorous debate, the Commons voted by 141 to 116 not to except him. It made little difference. Haselrig died a prisoner in the Tower before the year was out.

Edmund Ludlow's time was up. His memoirs do not mention the date on which he decided to escape, but it must have been late August. Ludlow asked his wife Elizabeth to seek the advice of friends. This led to a rancorous exchange with one of them, no less than the Speaker, Sir Harbottle Grimston, who urged Elizabeth to make Ludlow give himself up. Ludlow's memoirs describe the argument after she pointed out that there was no guarantee of Ludlow's life if he physically surrendered to the authorities. Ludlow wrote:

> The Speaker seemed much offended with this discourse, and going down the stairs with her, told her he would wash his hands of my blood, by assuring her, that if I would surrender myself, my life would be as safe as his own; but if I refused to

hearken to his advice, and should happen to be seized, I was like to be the first man they would execute, and she to be left the poorest widow in England.

Others advised flight. 'Another of my friends who was well acquainted with the designs of the court, and had all along advised me not to trust their favour, now repeated his persuasions to withdraw out of England, assuring that if I stayed I was lost; and that the same fate attended Sir Henry Vane and others.'

When Ludlow finally departed, his preparations were typically thorough. He had grown a beard as a disguise; a guide and horses were laid on at a rendezvous south of the river; a merchant in the port of Lewes was to lay on a ship to take him to Dieppe. There was a choice of safe houses in Dieppe and arrangements with banks provided access to plentiful funds in Europe. But, as we know, it nearly went wrong. In Lewes, which he reached in the early hours of the morning, searchers boarded the vessel hired to take him. Thanks to the weather, Ludlow wasn't aboard. A violent thunderstorm had prompted him to seek better cover in another boat and this vessel drifted on to a sandbank with the lieutenant-general in it. None of the search party bothered with the beached boat and Ludlow could relax. Two days later his vessel set sail, braving the still stormy Channel successfully to land him in Dieppe.[25] He learned that the same craft had taken Richard Cromwell into exile some weeks earlier. He stayed there for several days until letters arrived from England. One included a printed proclamation offering a £300 reward for his arrest. Ludlow decided to make for somewhere far distant from England – Geneva. Switzerland would become his base and within two years was the Mecca for republican opponents of the Stuarts.

On 29 August Charles signed the Bill and it became law. The legislation divided the 'regicides' into living and dead. First were the dead: Bradshaw, Cromwell, Ireton, Pride and twenty others who had died since 1649, all of whose 'lands, tenements, goods, chattels, rights, trusts, and other hereditaments' were to be subject to such

'pains, penalties, and forfeitures' as should be specified by another
Act of Parliament.

Then came the living. The Act set out a readjusted death list of
thirty-two men. Twenty-three were among the king's judges: John
Barkstead, Daniel Blagrave, John Carew, William Cawley, Thomas
Challoner, Gregory Clement, Cornelius Holland, Miles Corbet,
John Dixwell, William Goffe, Thomas Harrison, John Hewson, John
Jones, John Lisle, Sir Michael Livesey, Nicholas Love, Edmund
Ludlow, John Okey, William Say, Thomas Scot, Adrian Scroop,
Valentine Walton and Edward Whalley. The remaining nine com-
prised officials, officers and those said to be culpable in other ways:
Daniel Axtell, Francis Hacker, John Cook, Andrew Broughton,
Edward Dendy, William Hulet, Hugh Peters, and those two persons
'who, being disguised by frocks and visors, did appear upon the scaf-
fold erected before Whitehall'. All thirty-two were to be absolutely
excepted from pardon 'for life and estate'.

A further nineteen living regicides – those who surrendered by the
deadline believing they would be treated mercifully – were excepted
with a saving clause. The Act stated that if any of them be 'legally
attainted for the horrid treason and murder', they would be executed
only after a special Act of Parliament.

It was now September 1660 and the first trials were to be in
October. But first another of the fugitives was captured – the hapless
preacher Hugh Peters.

At the beginning of September, Peters was reported to be in
Southwark and two royal heavies, 'messengers of His Majesty's chamber', were dispatched to apprehend him.[26] Peters was being sheltered
in the house of a Quaker family called Mun. A lurid account in
Mercurius Publicus describes how the officers arrived and searched
the house, and how Peters escaped detection by hiding in the bed of
his host's daughter. She had given birth two days before, and the
royal messengers were described as too delicate to enter her room,
thus allowing Peters to go undetected. Rashly, he decided to stay on
in the house, and when the searchers returned several days later

they forced their way in to discover him in a room upstairs. A struggle followed and, according to *Mercurius Publicus*, it took the combined efforts of the two officers, the local constable and a number of neighbours to restrain Peters. He hotly denied that he was Peters and pleaded with his captors not to allude to him publicly by the name. 'For, said he, if it be known that I am Hugh Peter, the people in the street will stone me.' He eventually only agreed to go along with the officers after being allowed to down two quarts of ale, the paper sneered.[27]

Hugh Peters did not receive a fair showing in the press, and he would be treated no better in his trial the following month – nor would those tried with him.

12

'THE GUILT OF BLOOD'

8–12 October 1660

The trial of the regicides was a sensation even before it opened. London talked of nothing else: a mass trial of those who only months before had ruled the land and were now accused of treason for killing the king. Thanks to meticulous preparation behind the scenes, it was to be a political show trial. Medieval law was invoked to frame watertight charges, and ancient rules of evidence were cast aside to ensure convictions. As each prisoner was brought before the court – and before a word of evidence was heard – the public hangman came and stood beside him holding a noose.[1] The public entered into the sense of theatre. When the elderly cleric Hugh Peters stood trial and invoked the name of God, the crowd shrieked with laughter – hardly normal behaviour in a religious and superstitious age.

In one respect, the regicides were not the only ones to be tried: many of those who sat in judgment were also on trial, or at least their loyalty was on trial. Men like George Monck sat on the judges' bench to condemn their former colleagues to a slow and agonising death, thereby proving to their new king that they were now royalists through and through.

Of those regicides appearing on the death list finally agreed by the Houses of Parliament and excluded from pardon, sixteen avoided being sent for trial thanks to a good word from well-placed allies, or by having shown themselves to be amenable to the new regime. The death list was, of course, fleshed out with the names of some who were not actual regicides, including John Cook, the attorney-general, and Colonels Axtell and Hacker, who commanded the guard during the trial and execution. As we have seen, at one stage the king's masked executioners were added to the list even though their identity was at best uncertain.

In the midst of the excitement and expectation, the king grew silent. A Cavalier Parliament, watched over by the king's brothers and his parliamentary contacts, had drawn up the list of those to be tried. Charles's placemen had done their jobs in other ways, too; the highest lawyers in the land, all royal appointees, had designed the trials in such a way that there could only be one possible outcome. Yet we have no record of what Charles thought as he watched these preparations. He must have recalled his father's death and his own reactive declaration of bloody retribution. But none of those who knew him well or had close contact with him chose to record the king's thoughts or feelings regarding this key event.

Among the few letters we have from Charles about this time are two written shortly before and after the trial to his Chancellor, Edward Hyde. The first tells Hyde he needs to have some letters prepared for signature by noon as the king is going to play tennis; the second asks him when affairs of state will allow Charles the time to visit his sister in Tonbridge.[2] Prior to the trial, Charles did have one very serious matter to attend to – the secret marriage of his brother James to Anne Hyde, Edward's pregnant daughter, thus taking the duke out of the running for any suitable royal marriage that might cement or strengthen an alliance. The marriage was a great surprise to many – including the king – for James was known to be every bit as much a womaniser as his elder brother. Although the duke and his friends dreamed up many scandalous stories about the girl in their endeavours to get him out of the marriage, Charles declared that his brother had made his marital bed and would have to lie in it – which was more than he would ever do himself.

His brother's problems apart, everything went well for Charles II in the run-up to the trial. His anxiety to expedite the Indemnity Bill had reflected his need to clear the Parliamentary way for two other crucial matters to be settled, and now they were settled. The first was the dismantling of the New Model Army, and its replacement by a Cavalier-officered militia. The army numbered some forty thousand men and, despite George Monck's regimental purges, it remained the Cavaliers' nightmare, a hotbed of republicanism whose existence was a threat to the throne. A Bill to disband the army was tabled two days after the Indemnity Bill became law. A poll tax was to be levied to pay off the men and George Monck was earmarked to help oversee what could be an explosive process. The second matter which the King urgently wanted resolved was settled four days later – the royal stipend, the issue that had bedevilled so many monarchs, not least his father. This too went Charles's way. Parliament, still in that mood of heady generosity towards its young master, voted him £1.2 million a year, which was 50 per cent more than his estimated annual income under existing provisions.

As the trial opened, most of London had thoughts of little else. The king was often otherwise engaged; he was spending increasing amounts of time with his new mistress, the very beautiful and willing Barbara Villiers, with whom he was totally infatuated. It was said that their relationship 'did so disorder him that often he was not master of himself nor capable of minding business, which in so critical a time, required great application'.[3] Hyde, a fastidious man, found Charles's philandering a considerable irritation. He was also infuriated by the king's general lack of attention to matters of state; but Charles's inattentiveness and apparent laziness were traits developed over long years of exile and futility and were to prove fixed within his character.

Around the country, trials were being held to silence other dissident voices, though with all attention focused on events in London they went largely unremarked. In Bedford, the trial of an obscure Baptist preacher was held unnoticed by the weekly news sheets. The preacher was one of hundreds of nonconformists who resisted the legislation barring anyone except ordained Anglican ministers from preaching. His name was John Bunyan.

At his trial, Bunyan admitted he was a persistent offender, but said he intended to remain so. The judge urged him to stop preaching and so save himself from years in prison and his wife and family from penury. Bunyan refused and the judge sentenced him to six years, saying: 'I strongly suspect that we have heard the last we shall ever hear from Mr. John Bunyan.' He could not have been more wrong. After serving his six years, Bunyan continued preaching and received six more years. In prison, he sat down to write the book that became the best-selling work of fiction of the century. *The Pilgrim's Progress* has never been out of print since.[4]

The London trials began five weeks after Bunyan's first court appearance. Twenty-eight men were on trial. If found guilty, they faced death by the grisly form of torture known as hanging, drawing and quartering. The most important of these were twenty-four who had sat as judges at the king's trial. Most of them had played other key roles in bringing the king to trial. Sir Hardress Waller had participated in Pride's Purge before sitting in judgment. He signed the king's death warrant and helped organise the execution. Of Thomas Harrison we have already heard a good deal. Colonel Adrian Scroop was a member of the Oxfordshire gentry who also supported Pride's Purge. He helped organise the king's trial before sitting in judgment and signing the death warrant. Gilbert Millington was a wealthy barrister and one of the few senior lawyers willing to put aside personal interest for what he saw as the national good. He took part in the trial and voted for the king's death. In

1660, men like these represented a purely symbolic threat to the resurgent monarchy.* The purpose of the trial was revenge against the few, so that many others who had fought against the king could pretend they had always supported the House of Stuart. A truly vindictive arraignment was that of Hugh Peters, the Puritan preacher who had become a target because he publicly preached in favour of the king's trial and execution.

On 8 October, in the absence of the accused, the court sat for preliminary business at Clerkenwell in Hick's Hall, the session house of the county of Middlesex. We are lucky today to know anything of what occurred during the trial. In contrast to the trial of the king, it appears no clerks were employed to keep a verbatim record. According to the Oxford antiquary Anthony Wood, the court record was kept by the prosecutor Sir Heneage Finch, and later edited by Sir Orlando Bridgeman. This might explain how both men come over so well in the published report.[5] Although the accuracy of this account cannot be entirely relied upon, it contains a remarkable amount of detail and dialogue that rings true. The account was supplemented by reports in the news sheets and pamphlets as well as a contemporary compendium of speeches by the regicides.[6]

Bridgeman presided over ten other judges and thirty-four commissioners or non-judicial members. These included Edward Hyde (whose brother was one of the judges), the Duke of Somerset, the Duke of Albemarle (the former George Monck), several earls, including Southampton, Manchester, Lindsey and Dorset, other aristocrats including Viscount Saye and Sele, and a handful of leading parliamentarians including Denzil Holles and Arthur

---

* The others were: Sir Hardress Waller, Thomas Harrison, William Heveningham, Isaac Pennington, Henry Marten, Gilbert Millington, Robert Tichborne, Owen Rowe, Robert Lilburne, Adrian Scroop, John Carew, John Jones, Henry Smith, Gregory Clement, Edmund Harvey, Thomas Scot, John Downes, Vincent Potter, Augustine Garland, George Fleetwood, Simon Meyne, James Temple, Peter Temple and Thomas Waite.

Annesley. Several of these commissioners had once fought on the parliamentary side against the king and now sat in judgment of their former comrades.

The accused were to be tried under a three-hundred-year-old Act. The Treason Act of 1351 had come into being during the reign of Edward III, its purpose to define and limit the number of offences classed as treason. It sill exists today. The last person to be tried under it was William Joyce, Lord Haw-Haw, the pro-Nazi propagandist, tried for breaking a citizen's allegiance to the crown and hanged.*

The 1351 Act defines treason as: 'where a man doth compass or imagine the death of our said Lord the King in his realm, or be adherent to the enemies of our Lord the King in his realm, giving to them aid or support in his realm or elsewhere . . .'[7] This definition cast the net wide enough to encompass not only those who took part in the king's trial, but also those who only thought about it or gave encouragement. It also included 'levying of war against the king'. At this, some of the judges should have felt very uncomfortable. What had the Earl of Manchester, commander of one of Parliament's armies, done if not wage war against the king? What about General Monck, now elevated by a grateful king to Duke of Albemarle – had he not waged war against the king? And what of Lord Saye and Sele, a member of Parliament's Committee of Safety during the first Civil War – had he too not waged war against the king? Even Denzil Holles, arch-enemy of Oliver Cromwell, had fought against the king in the first Civil War. Edmund Ludlow estimated that no fewer than fifteen of the thirty-four commissioners and eleven judges had 'engaged for parliament against the late king, either as members of parliament, judges or members of their army'.[8]

No matter; such men were safe now that they were set on destroying their former allies.

---

* While William Joyce was undoubtedly a despicable individual, he should not have been tried under the 1351 Act for, as an Irish national, he was not strictly committing treason against the British crown.

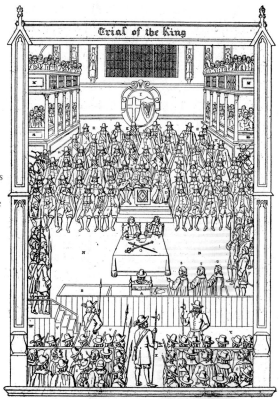

The trial of Charles I in Westminster Hall in January 1649. The king sits facing two clerks at a table, with his back to the viewer. Behind the clerks sit the ranks of the commissioners, or judges, who would become known as 'regicides'.

INTERFOTO/Sammlung Rauch/MEPL

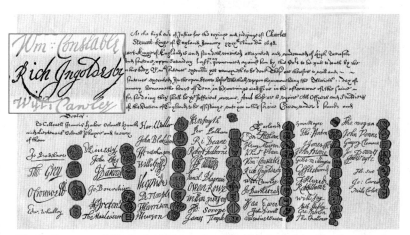

The death warrant of Charles I, which was signed by fifty-nine judges. The signature of Richard Ingoldsby (inset) is particularly clear and assured, despite his later claim that Oliver Cromwell held his hand and made him sign. INTERFOTO/Sammlung Rauch/MEPL

A contemporary woodcut of the execution of Charles I on 30 January 1649. The illustration was far from accurate – not unusual for the time. The executioner wore a mask and a false beard, and he had an assistant, also disguised. British Museum

CAROLVS SECVNDVS
D.G. MAGNÆ BRITANNIÆ,
FRANCIÆ, ET HIBERNIÆ REX

This engraving by Wenceslaus Hollar is of a brooding Charles II, the year after his father was executed. The text asserts his claim to the thrones of Great Britain, France and Ireland, even though he was living in exile on the charity of others.

University of Toronto

The frontispiece of *Eikon Basilike* ('The King's Image'), a royalist propaganda publication, which appeared within days of Charles I's execution. Here Charles is portrayed as a holy martyr, envisaging a heavenly crown. His temporal crown is lying abandoned at his feet. British Library 077713

Above left: A contemporary portrait of John Milton by Wenceslaus Hollar. Milton was an active opponent of the monarchy. After the restoration, his life was in jeopardy. Authors' collection

Above right: Radical lawyer John Cook led the prosecution of Charles I. Following the restoration, he was charged with high treason in a notorious show trial, despite protesting that he had only done his legal duty. NPG

George Monck, the enigmatic general whom republican leaders saw as their saviour. The former royalist had other plans, however, and was later rewarded with a dukedom. Authors' collection

John Lambert, the republicans' last hope, led his troops against Monck and was humiliated. Authors' collection

Charles II was crowned king of Scotland by the Marquis of Argyll at Scone in 1651. Charles promised to make Argyll a duke but ten years later consigned the great Covenanter to the gallows. Private collection/Bridgeman Art Library

This group portrait depicts eleven prominent regicides, with Oliver Cromwell in the centre. In fact, only eight sat in judgment on the king. Two, Daniel Axtell and Francis Hacker, were merely officers of the guard, while a third, Hugh Peters, was a Puritan cleric who preached to the court. Their lowly station did not save them from Charles II's revenge. British Museum

Sir George Downing, the arch-turncoat, who entrapped old comrades and sent them to the brutal deaths reserved for traitors.
Private collection/London Library

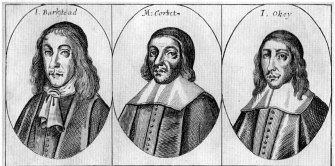

The exhumed head of Oliver Cromwell was displayed on a spike for Londoners to gape at.
Pennant's London

John Barkstead, Miles Corbet and John Okey, the fugitive regicides, who were kidnapped by Downing and dispatched to London to be hanged, drawn and quartered. Cromwell Museum

The posthumous 'execution' of Oliver Cromwell, John Bradshaw and Henry Ireton. Their heads can be seen on the roof of the Banqueting House.
Private collection/Bridgeman Art Library

This contemporary woodcut depicts the butchering of three of the regicides: John Jones, Gregory Clement and Adrian Scroop. A horse-drawn sledge brings two other condemned men to the gallows. British Museum

Right: Edmund Ludlow, the republican general, blamed by royalists for every plot against Charles II. MEPL

Far right: When parliamentary grandee John Lisle fled abroad, he unwittingly placed himself in the sights of a royalist assassination squad. NPG

The brutal spectre of hanging, drawing and quartering became counterproductive thanks to the powerful speeches by the leading regicides on reaching the scaffold. MEPL

The story of the Angel of Hadley became an American legend. The angel was widely thought to be the regicide general William Goffe, who escaped to America.

The political theorist Algernon Sidney was at first opposed to Charles I's treason trial but later changed his mind. He spent his later years in exile, pursued by royalist assassination squads across Europe.

Aphra Behn, famous as a novelist and dramatist, was also a royalist spy. She successfully inveigled a former lover into becoming a double agent for the royalist cause. NPG

After selecting and swearing in a hand-picked jury, the prosecution then lowered the bar for the amount of evidence necessary to convict. Traditionally, in a treason trial, a minimum of two witnesses was required to prove guilt. Bridgeman announced that one witness would now be sufficient.

The next day, 9 October, the trial began in earnest. Bridgeman explained to the jury that they were called to serve by the Act of Free and General Pardon, Indemnity and Oblivion, under which there were several exceptions: 'You will find in that act there is an exception for several persons, who (for their execrable treason for sentencing to death and signing the warrant for taking away the life of our said sovereign) are left to be proceeded against as traitors according to the laws of England . . .'

Of course, this seemed to preclude men like Axtell, but Bridgeman pointed out the clause in the Treason Act of 1351 declaring it treasonable 'to levy war against the king'. By this clause men like Axtell were swept up.

Bridgeman took up the old matter of whether or not the king was above the law and quoted a statute from Edward III – 'the king can do no wrong.' Finally, he made sure the jury knew where their duty lay: 'To conclude, you are now to enquire of blood, of royal blood, of sacred blood, of blood like that of saints under the altar . . . This blood cries for vengeance and it will not be appeased without a bloody sacrifice.'

The indictment for high treason was then read out against the twenty-eight who were waiting in the Tower to be brought to trial – plus three more who were absent. These were three who had fled to Holland – John Barkstead, John Okey and Miles Corbet. For some reason, the names of many more who had fled all over Europe and to North America were omitted. Perhaps it simply might not have looked good to have declared so many runaways beyond the reach of the court.

At six o'clock in the morning on 10 October, the prisoners were taken from their cells in the Tower and gathered in a courtyard.

Under the supervision of the Lieutenant of the Tower, Sir John Robinson, they were shepherded on to several wagons. With Sir John in the lead and surrounded by both cavalry and foot soldiers, a wagon train set off for Newgate Prison, situated next to the Old Bailey. The prisoners were herded into Newgate, which made a good holding point during the trial. When the call came at nine o'clock that the judges were ready, the Sheriff of London brought the prisoners to stand before them at the Sessions House in the Old Bailey. According to Ludlow, the trial had taken so long to organise because the authorities had had to wait some months for the retirement of the previous sheriff, who would not have gone along with a rigged hearing.[9]

In the seventeenth century, the Sessions House was designed so that the courtroom was partially under cover and partially in the open air. The judges and officials sat on a raised dais at one end of the room. Facing them at the other end was a large archway open to the elements. In this way, one whole wall of the court was open, allowing the proceedings to be visible to passers-by. In front of the judges was a railing, known as the bar, at which the accused stood while being tried. Down some steps and out into the open air was a boxed area in which the accused were kept under guard until called up to the bar. Beyond that were further boxed-in areas for the public. The trial of the regicides was such a draw that the entire street around the Sessions House was packed with thousands of spectators.

The court's first task was to bring the prisoners to the bar in batches and ask them how they pleaded. The first batch consisted of Sir Hardress Waller, Thomas Harrison and William Heveningham. Almost immediately, Harrison said, 'My Lord, if you please, I will speak a word.' It was an uncomfortable echo of the opening of the king's trial. Sir Orlando would have none of it and told Harrison he would be heard in due course. Harrison capitulated and the clerk read out the indictment, stating that the three men at the bar, 'instigated by the devil, traitorously compassed and imagined to take away the life of Charles Stuart, late King of England; and in pursuance of that intent and design, assembled and sat upon, judged, tried, and condemned, his said late Majesty of blessed memory, and also signed a warrant for killing and executing him'.

The first to be asked how he pleaded was Waller. According to Ludlow, this was because he was a man known to be liable to say anything to save his life. The clerk asked, 'How sayest thou, Sir Hardress Waller; art thou guilty of the treason whereof thou standest indicted, or not guilty?'

The once decisive military leader shilly-shallied around the question. 'My Lords, I dare not say "not guilty" but since that in a business of this nature we have no counsel or advice and being not able to speak to a matter of law . . .'

In his ineffectual way, Waller was trying to introduce important issues that could affect whether or not he received a fair trial. The prisoners had been kept in solitary confinement without access to legal advice and had only been informed of the trial the night before it began. Bridgeman cut sharply across Waller, saying in a sarcastic tone, 'I am loath to interrupt you, but this is the course . . . you must plead guilty or not guilty. There is no medium. Guilty or not guilty?'

After some verbal exchanges, Sir Hardress replied, 'Insomuch as I said I dare not say not guilty, I must say guilty.'

The clerk sought to conclude the affair. 'You admit the indictment?' he asked.

Beaten down, Sir Hardress answered feebly, 'Yes.' He was told to stand down.

The court had bludgeoned the first defendant into pleading to charges he had only just heard, charges he had been allowed no time either to consider or to consult a lawyer about. When Sir Hardress and his colleagues had put Charles I on trial, the king had been able to plan his defence in advance and had then been given several chances to enter a plea spread over several days.

After that sad spectacle, the court called to the bar an altogether tougher defendant – General Thomas Harrison. The clerk asked him if he was guilty of the treason he stood indicted for, or not guilty.

Harrison answered, 'My Lords, have I liberty to speak?'

The judges realised it was going to be a long day. Harrison was instructed that he could say no more than 'guilty' or 'not guilty'. But Harrison was not to be bullied. He succeeded in making the complaint that Sir Hardress had stumbled over. He had, he said, been held in prison for three months in solitary confinement without access to a lawyer. He had only heard the charge against him at nine o'clock the night before, and he wanted to discuss with the court the law on what he termed 'this special case'.

The fact that Harrison and Waller sought to raise similar issues indicated that they had been schooled, probably in haste, by John Cook. Cook was the best qualified among the accused to put together some kind of defence. After all, he had written the charge against Charles I. Now he created a legal defence for the regicides based on similar legal arguments to those he had used to claim the legitimacy of the Rump Parliament's trial of the king.

Cook's labours were in vain. The court refused to budge an inch. Seeing this, Harrison accepted the rules and pleaded not guilty.

As the contests between the court and the previous two defendants worked their way to their conclusion, William Heveningham had stood by and taken note of all that had happened. When it was his turn to stand at the bar and plead, he did so immediately, pleading not guilty in the correct manner and saying he would be tried by God and country. Once that was done, the court allowed Sir Hardress Waller to present a written petition, entitled 'To the King's majesty and the Parliament'. The document was laid aside, unread. Waller and his fellow prisoners were led from the court.

No doubt relieved to have finished with the first batch of defendants, the court called the next group. This comprised six men: Isaac Pennington, Harry Marten, Gilbert Millington, Robert Tichborne, Owen Rowe and Robert Lilburne. Pennington was the first to be called. He held up his hand in answer and pleaded swiftly not guilty. He was followed by Harry Marten, who attempted to say he was not excepted from the Act of Pardon, because the name that appeared was Henry Marten, not Harry Marten. The individual named in the Act, he argued, was some other person.[10] This novel defence was beaten down by Sir Heneage Finch, the solicitor-general.

The rest of the prisoners all pleaded not guilty, except for General George Fleetwood, who said, 'I must confess I am guilty.' He then presented a petition addressed to the king. Fleetwood claimed he had been pressed by Oliver Cromwell into signing the king's death warrant. Monck interceded for him and his sentence was commuted to imprisonment. He was later sentenced to transportation to Tangiers, though it is not known whether he actually went. Some accounts say he died there in 1672, while others say he was released and went to America.[11]

When all had pleaded, the process was adjourned, for evidence to commence in the morning. Samuel Pepys recorded his reaction to the day. Although a senior government official and a royalist, he was not entirely happy with the selection of a few men to stand trial when so many had opposed the king:

> At night comes Mr. Moore, and staid late with me to tell me how Sir Hards. [Hardress] Waller, Scott, Coke, Peters, Harrison, &c. were this day arraigned at the bar at the Sessions House ... They all seem to be dismayed, and will all be condemned without question. In Sir Orlando Bridgman's charge, he did wholly rip up the unjustness of the war against the King from the beginning, and so it much reflects upon all the Long Parliament, though the King had pardoned them, yet they must hereby confess that the King do look upon them as traitors. To-morrow they are to plead what they have to say. At night to bed.[12]

On 11 October, the trial began in earnest. John Evelyn recorded the event tersely: 'The regicides who sat on the life of our late king, were brought to trial in the Old Bailey, before a Commission of oyer and terminer.'[13] As a fervent royalist, Evelyn would not be so abrupt when he came to describing the suffering on the scaffold. Six defendants were called to account: Thomas Harrison, Adrian Scroop, John Carew, John Jones, Gregory Clement and Thomas Scot.[14] They were considered the most hard-line of the republicans; all of them had signed the king's death warrant, and so were excepted from the Act of Oblivion to be executed.

Sir Heneage Finch opened the prosecution with a lesson on the divine right of kings and their sanctity throughout history: 'We bring before your Lordships into judgment this day the murderers of a King. A man would think the laws of God and men had so fully secured these sacred persons that the sons of violence should never approach to hurt them. For, my Lord, the very thought of such an attempt hath ever been presented by all laws, in all ages, in all nations, as a most unpardonable treason.'

Had Isaac Dorislaus been alive he might have sought to put Sir Heneage right on a few points, chiefly by explaining that the killing of kings and tyrants had an ancient pedigree. Milton, if he had been able, might have pointed out that kings were anything but sacred. Despite his uncertain history, there was nothing shaky about Sir Heneage's legal acumen. Homing in on the key aspects of the charge necessary to find the defendants guilty, he informed the jury that the indictment was for 'compassing the death of the king' – in other words, for devising and bringing about the execution, though not actually carrying it out in person. This was a key point, as Sir Heneage explained:

'The rest of the indictment … the assembling, sitting, judging, and killing of the King, are but so many several *overt acts* to prove the intention of the heart … as the encouraging of the soldiers to cry out, "Justice, Justice!" … this may be given in evidence to prove the compassing and imagining the King's death.'

Even though the verdict was a foregone conclusion, Sir Heneage employed all his rhetorical skills for the jury, describing the king as 'blessed' and sacred: 'My Lords, when they had thus proceeded to . . . try, sentence, condemn, and kill, I had almost said crucify, him, whom they could not but know to be their King.'

Next, the prosecutor set out the background to the numbers of defendants selected to stand before the court. 'The judges, officers, and other immediate actors in this pretended court, were about fourscore: of these some four or five and twenty are dead, and gone to their own place. Some six or seven of them, who were thought to have sinned with less malice, have their lives spared indeed, but are like to be brought to a severe repentance by future penalties.'

During his successful career as an attorney, Sir Heneage had gained a reputation for oratory. He demonstrated his old skills now: 'Some eighteen or nineteen have fled from justice, and wander to and fro about the world with the mark of Cain upon them, and per-petual trembling, lest every eye that sees, and every hand that meets them, should fall upon them.'

Thomas Harrison was brought to stand at the bar. Turning directly to him, Sir Heneage proclaimed, 'The first that is brought is the prisoner at the bar, and he deserves to be the first; for if any person now left alive ought to be styled the conductor, leader, and captain of this work, that is the man. He, my Lord, brought the King up a prisoner from Windsor. He sat upon him, sentenced him.'

It says much for the butcher's boy from Newcastle that he was chosen to be first. Everything about him marked him out: his style and confidence, his Fifth Monarchist beliefs, his role in escorting Charles I to London and his part in the trial, and – perhaps most unforgettably – his place in history as the man who called Charles a 'man of blood'.

Four witnesses were called to testify that they had seen Harrison stand in court to indicate his agreement with the king's death sen-tence. Among them was MP James Nutley, who had been elected to the Protectorate Parliament in 1659. Nutley's improbable testimony could not have been more fortunate for the prosecution.

He testified that, thanks to his friendship with the court clerk Phelps, he had been admitted to a private committee hearing. When he slipped into the Painted Chamber he heard Harrison discussing his conversation with the king over supper in Fareham on his way to Windsor. According to Nutley, Harrison said that when the king had asked, 'What do they intend to do with me – whether to murder me or no?' he had replied, 'The Lord hath reserved you for a public example of justice.'

Next to come under scrutiny were Harrison's actions when they stopped at Lord Newburgh's house for lunch. Newburgh gave evidence of the plan he had hatched to free the king by giving him a swift horse on which to speed off. He claimed that, sniffing a plot, Harrison had posted guards at all the doors of Newburgh's house and had commanded his soldiers to ride 'close' to the king when they set off towards Windsor. According to the prosecution, these actions constituted imprisonment of the king and amounted to treason. Next, the court was shown two documents: the first had been drawn up to convene the High Court of Justice to try the king; the second was the king's death sentence. Harrison asked to see the documents and agreed that his signatures were on them.

The evidence quickly completed, Harrison was allowed to speak. He said he was proud of his actions and that the trial of the king had 'not been done in a corner' – meaning it was no clandestine or underhand thing, but was carried out in the full light of day and before the public. He then tried to raise the changed allegiances of many of the judges: 'Divers of those that sit upon the bench were formerly as active ...'

Bridgeman cut him short: 'Pray, Mr Harrison, do not thus reflect on the court. This is not the business.'

Harrison was not easily deflected. He continued that he now loathed many who had once been the apple of his eye but had changed their allegiance: 'Rather than turn as many did, that did put their hand to this plough [meaning the restoration], I chose rather to be separated from my wife and family.'

Harrison turned to make a defence based on the argument that he had acted constitutionally: 'this that hath been done was done by a parliament of England, by the Commons of England assembled in parliament; and this being so, whatever was done by their commands or their authority is not questionable by your lordships . . .'

Harrison then found himself under an onslaught from three judges. Bridgeman, Holles and Annesley castigated him for daring to claim that the Rump Parliament constituted a legal authority. Harrison would have liked to have had a barrister to argue that his actions were ordered by the de facto supreme law of the land – Parliament. The court ruled that since the Rump Parliament was not truly the supreme authority – lacking the completeness of the full Commons and the House of Lords – the argument was void.

When Harrison tried to raise the point that both the Commons *and* the Lords had decided to go to war against the king in 1642, he was prevented from continuing. Soon he discovered that he had no arguments left. 'The things that have been done,' he concluded, 'have been done upon the stage, in the sight of the sun.'

'The matter itself is treason upon treason,' said Sir Heneage. 'Therefore we pray direction to the jury.'

The clerk said, 'Gentlemen of the jury, look upon the prisoner. How say ye? Is he guilty of the treason he standing indicted and hath been arraigned, or not guilty?'

The foreman of the jury replied, 'Guilty.'

The jailers stepped forward and put chains on Harrison's hands and feet. Sir Orlando passed sentence: 'That you be led back to the place from whence you came, and from thence upon a hurdle to the place of execution; and there you shall be hanged by the neck, and being alive shall be cut down, and your privy members shall be cut off, your entrails to be taken out of your body, and you, living, the same to be burnt before your eyes, and your head to be cut off, and your body to be divided into four quarters, and head and quarters to be disposed of at the pleasure of the king's majesty, and the lord have mercy on your soul.'

The court was adjourned until seven o'clock the following morning. Harrison would have to wait two days before his sentence was carried out.

On 12 October, the first defendant of the day was Adrian Scroop, pardoned under the Act of Oblivion having handed himself in only to find his faith betrayed. Like so many of the regicides, he had been schooled at one of the Oxford colleges and subsequently had learned the law at one of the Inns of Court. According to Ludlow, Scroop came from an ancient family and had a considerable estate. When the first Civil War broke out, he raised a troop of cavalry at his own expense.

During Scroop's trial, several of the same witnesses who had testified that Harrison had been one of the king's judges, likewise testified to Scroop's presence. Being a shrewd individual, Scroop asked each of them where he sat among the other judges and received the same answer from each; they could remember he was there but not where he sat. This line of questioning indicated that the witnesses may have been schooled to give the same evidence.

However, the evidence given by Richard Browne, the Lord Mayor elect of London, proved decisive. Browne was a wealthy Presbyterian timber merchant and MP, whose initially strong support for the New Model Army had been undermined by the seizure of the king at Holmby House in 1647. Browne was ejected during Pride's Purge and disgracefully imprisoned without charge for five years. He subsequently led the triumphant procession of Charles II into London and was knighted by the king.

Browne recounted to the court his conversation with Scroop some time after the new king had returned to England from The Hague, when Scroop had replied, 'Some are of one opinion and some are of another', an answer Browne took to mean that Scroop was in favour of killing the king. Scroop denied he meant any such thing. Like Harrison, he asked for legal representation to argue he had acted as an agent of the government of the land. This was denied. Summing up, Bridgeman told the jury that it hardly needed to retire to consider its verdict. After conferring for a few moments, the jury found Scroop guilty. He was sentenced to be hanged, drawn and quartered.

Scroop's trial was followed immediately by that of the Cornish MP and friend of Thomas Harrison, John Carew. Sir Edward Turner, for the prosecution, said that Carew had been seduced by the devil into imagining and compassing the death of the king. Once more, the witnesses who had already given evidence that Harrison and Scroop were present at the king's trial, gave testimony against Carew. They need hardly have bothered, for Carew admitted signing the king's death warrant. When he tried to justify himself, arguing he had acted in obedience to God's laws, the public galleries broke out in a loud humming to drown out his testimony, as if to say that they wanted to hear no more and he should be condemned. It was known as the 'Death Hum'.

Bridgeman silenced the public, saying, 'He stands for his life, let him have liberty.'

To defend his actions, Carew brought up the matter of the Grand Remonstrance of 1641, which had spelled out the shortcomings of the reign of Charles I, and had been passed by not one but both Houses of Parliament. The court moved quickly to shut him up. He was found guilty and again sentenced to be hanged, drawn and quartered.

Carew was taken away in chains. He was replaced at the bar by luckless Thomas Scot, the ardent republican MP and former spy chief to the Commonwealth. Scot faced the usual witnesses, who testified that he had sat in judgment upon the king and had signed the death warrant. An unexpected witness was William Lenthall, who had been Speaker of the House of Commons when Charles I entered at the head of a troop of soldiers and tried to arrest five members. With his reply that he 'had neither eyes to see, nor tongue to speak, but as the house is pleased to direct me', Lenthall entered history.[15] He gave evidence that Scot had told him he wished his role in the death of the king to be engraved upon his tombstone.

Scot argued that such comments should be subject to parliamentary privilege and not trotted out in a court of law. He went on to

claim that there were instances when the Commons alone constituted the supreme authority in the land. The court asked him to cite
an example and Scot said it was the case in the age of the Saxons.
This was too much for Bridgeman. In vain, Scot next attempted to
argue that his case came within the scope of the king's pardon. Like
Scroop, Scot had turned himself in and so should have been eligible
for pardon. The court overruled him. Bridgeman told him he should
have argued this before entering his plea. But, of course, Bridgeman
had refused to allow any legal arguments before the defendants
pleaded. It was another cruel and cynical ploy by the court. Scot was
sentenced to death.

Next, Gregory Clement and Colonel John Jones were together
called to the bar. Clement, the former MP notorious for being
expelled from Parliament having been discovered in bed with a
maid, was a merchant who had become rich trading with the new
American colonies and by buying and selling expropriated land
during the Commonwealth and Protectorate. Clement had confessed that he was guilty of sitting in judgment on the king, so the
court produced no witnesses. But before sentencing him, the court
tried the other defendant.

The fearless Welsh merchant John Jones, standing next to
Clement at the bar, had risen to become a colonel of a cavalry regiment, an MP and an important participant in the various
administrations during the Commonwealth and Protectorate. In the
eyes of the court, Jones was an especially good catch, for he was
Oliver Cromwell's brother-in-law. His wife, Katherine Cromwell,
was interesting in her own right, having been suspected of harbouring secret royalist sympathies.[16]

Jones had watched while the court crushed his co-defendant's
legal arguments. Perceiving that he would never be allowed to raise
any legal justifications for his actions, he decided to confess his role
in the trial of the king. Witnesses were shown the death warrant and
pointed out Jones's signature. Together, Jones and Clement were
sentenced to death.

While the high drama was unfolding at the Old Bailey, a related event went largely unnoticed in Hick's Hall in Clerkenwell. Based on the hearsay evidence that he had been one of Charles's masked executioners, a charge of treason was entered against the veteran soldier William Hulet. His name was added to the list for immediate trial – and what therefore seemed like his inevitable execution.

At the Old Bailey the court adjourned until seven o'clock the following morning, 13 October. It was to be a momentous day. The first execution would take place – and the court would try two men who had not sat in judgment on the king.

13

DAMNED IF YOU DO,
DAMNED IF YOU DON'T

13–19 October 1660

Having dealt with the men who sentenced Charles I to death, the show trial turned its attention to those who had the misfortune to have acted in an official capacity at Charles's trial. The first to be brought to the bar was Daniel Axtell, commander of the guard. The former Hertfordshire grocer was no ordinary Roundhead. Having been, in April 1660, one of the few senior officers to rally to John Lambert's side in an attempt to prevent Charles II being installed as king,[1] he was now to make a similarly spirited last-ditch defence in the face of a cynical onslaught from a publicly partisan court.

The evidence of the first witness repeated the claim that during the king's trial, Axtell had threatened to have his men shoot the mysterious woman in one of the public galleries believed to have been Lady Fairfax. According to the witness, this anonymous woman had taken exception to the charge against the king and shouted out that Cromwell was 'a rogue and a traitor'.[2] This particular outburst appears neither in the record taken by Phelps nor in the official record taken by the parliamentary stenographers. It seems that it was made up by the witness, one Holland Simpson. The robust reaction by the captain of the guard to an interruption in court hardly amounted to treason, but its retelling was a useful tool by the prosecution to blacken the prisoner's name.

The next witness was one of Axtell's former colleagues, Colonel Hercules Huncks, who had commanded the halberdiers at the king's trial. The court record does not tell us how Axtell reacted to seeing him. Huncks came from a royalist family in Warwickshire but had joined the New Model Army to fight for Parliament. Upon the installation of Charles II he had handily realised that the rest of his family had been right all along. In return for giving evidence against Axtell, Huncks was awarded a pardon.[3]

Huncks said that he had been present in Whitehall Palace together with Cromwell, Ireton, Harrison, and Colonels Phayre and Hacker on the morning of the king's execution. Cromwell had asked him to sign the warrant for the executioners. When Huncks refused, Axtell – who had been standing at the door – admonished him, saying, 'Colonel Huncks, I am ashamed of you. The ship is now coming into the harbour and will you strike sail before we come to anchor?'[4]

Axtell denied that he had met Huncks on that day. 'I know nothing of it, if I were to die at this bar presently,' he said.

Significantly, no other witness was called to corroborate Huncks's version of events. Several more had been called to say they saw Axtell commanding the guard at the trial, that he ordered his men to point their guns towards the woman who cried out, and that he also ordered his men to shout 'Justice! Justice!' and 'Execute!'*

One witness, who said he had been a soldier under Axtell's command, gave evidence that the colonel had commanded a troop of men to go to the house of the common hangman, Richard Brandon, and bring him back to execute the king. This testimony was directly contradicted by that of the next witness, who gave hearsay evidence

---

* There is no reference in any of the contemporary shorthand court accounts to soldiers shouting 'Execute.'

that he had been told the men who killed the king were called Hulet and Walker.

When this parade of witnesses ceased, Axtell told the court that his case did not fall under the law of high treason from the time of Edward III for the simple reason that he was a soldier obeying orders which came down from the houses of Lords and Commons acting together to raise an army. The Parliament that did so was held to be the lawful force in the land, even by foreign kingdoms. Axtell himself was bound by his commission to obey his senior officers and they had ordered him to Westminster during the king's trial. 'I conceive,' said Axtell, 'I am no more guilty than the Earl of Essex, Fairfax or Lord Manchester.'

The court had heard this defence before, of course, from Thomas Harrison and others. Axtell enlarged on the theme: 'I am no more guilty than his excellency the Lord Monck, who acted by the same authority, and all the people in the three nations.'

At this, Lord Annesley interjected to say that the role of soldier did not protect Axtell, for the army had not heeded the call by the people for peace when there was a treaty (i.e. the Treaty of Newport) that would have brought peace. Of course, by the court's reasoning, Axtell's commanding officer, Sir Thomas Fairfax, was also guilty of treason. But Fairfax, like Manchester and Essex, was not on trial thanks to his social rank and his willingness to forsake his former comrades.

The court realised it had to get Fairfax off the hook. As a seasoned court practitioner, Bridgeman undertook this task himself. He asked Axtell who had given him his orders. Axtell replied that his orders came from Fairfax. Bridgeman then asked if they came directly from Fairfax. Axtell replied that they came through the major-generals, Ireton and Cromwell. When asked how he knew the orders had come from Fairfax, Axtell answered that he knew because Cromwell and Ireton had told him they came from Fairfax. Fortunately for the court, Cromwell and Ireton were dead and could not be called as witnesses. Fairfax was now absolved from all possible crimes.

After this charade, Axtell argued that he was in a double-bind: if he had not done as he was ordered, he would have been shot for insubordination, but by doing as ordered he was to die anyhow. He was damned if he did and damned if he didn't. He then rebutted all the points made against him: he did not order that the woman who shouted should be shot, he did not order his men to call out 'Justice! Justice!', and so on. All in vain. After reminding the court of the rule which had formerly required two witnesses to events, he said, 'I leave the matter to the jury, in whose hands I and my little ones and family are left . . . I leave my case, my life, my all, in your hands.'[5] The jury took his life in their hands and crushed it.

After Axtell's conviction, it was a matter of formality for the court to convict Colonel Francis Hacker, one of those who signed the warrant for the king's execution. Hacker's case was unique in that the main evidence against him had been given by his wife, who had provided the court with the king's death warrant. If this was not torment enough, another turncoat was produced to give evidence against him. In return for his life, Colonel Tomlinson testified that Hacker had commanded the guard that took the king to and from Westminster Hall and subsequently to the scaffold.

A surprise witness was produced. In a breathtaking act of bias, the court called one of its own commissioners to testify for the prosecution. Lord Annesley stepped down from the bench and was sworn in. He testified that when Colonel Huncks was captive in the Tower, he had interrogated him. According to Annesley, Huncks told him he had witnessed Hacker sign the execution warrant. Seeing how the dice were loaded against him, Hacker said little more in his defence. He was quickly found guilty.

One colleague of these soldiers was absent from the trials. Colonel Robert Phayre had been arrested in Ireland and transported to England to stand trial for his role in organising the execution of the king. Although he was on duty during the trial and at the execution, Phayre had refused to sign the execution warrant. More significantly, he was married to the daughter of Sir Thomas Herbert, the faithful

companion to Charles I during his captivity, who was able to intercede on behalf of his son-in-law. Hence, Phayre was not among those
arraigned for high treason.[6]

Following the trials of the two colonels came the most peculiar of
all the cases: that of Captain William Hulet, charged with being
one of the king's executioners.

The case against Hulet was essentially that made against him
upon his arrest: on the day of the king's death, he had been one of a
large number of sergeants in Hewson's regiment who were asked to
assist the common hangman in return for £100 and promotion. All
reportedly refused, though it was suspected by some of his comrades
that Hulet had secretly agreed to the job. The two executioners
appeared on the scaffold heavily disguised, wearing hoods and false
beards, one of which was black, the other grey. Several witnesses gave
uninspiring testimony that the executioner with the grey beard was
Hulet, based on guesswork, hearsay and circumstantial evidence.

One prosecution witness managed to cast still more doubt on
Hulet's guilt. Walter Davis testified that, two years before the current
trial, he and Hulet had met at an inn in Dublin and had shared two
pints of wine. Davis had asked Hulet, 'I pray, resolve me in this one
question: it is reported that you took up the king's head and said,
"behold the head of a traitor."'

According to Davis, Hulet replied that it was a question 'I never
resolved any man, though often demanded. Yet, whosoever said it
then it matters not. I say it now: it was the head of a traitor.'

What is interesting here is that in contemporary descriptions of
the trial, it is recorded that the executioner who held up the king's
head said nothing. If Hulet had been on the scaffold, he would have
known this, but he answered the question without correcting Davis's
erroneous description of the event. There is no reason to suspect that
Davis asked a trick question, nor is there any reason to think that
Hulet would have considered it to be so. Hulet's reply might only
have been to acknowledge his feelings about the dead king. On the
face of it, the exchange seemed to offer slender evidence either way.

One piece of evidence was more compelling – the testimony about Hulet's voice. A man called Richard Gittins, a sergeant in the same regiment as Hulet who had been one of those who turned down £100, gave evidence that he was standing by the Banqueting House window leading onto the scaffold when the king was executed. When the executioner with the false grey beard asked the king for his forgiveness, he unmistakably recognised his voice as that of William Hulet. Gittins repeated the claim that Hulet had been made a captain-lieutenant shortly after the execution and added that Colonel Hewson often called him 'Old Father Gray-beard'.

Hulet said he could not have been on the scaffold because on the day of the execution he was imprisoned in the Tower for refusing to participate in the execution. He suggested the court call the various commanders of the guard present that day to confirm this. The court did not take up his suggestion. In an effort finally to nail Hulet, the court called Colonel Tomlinson, who said he thought the fatal blow was struck by the executioner with the grey beard, but he could not quite remember. The evidence against Hulet remained inconclusive. Despite this, the jury found him guilty, as they knew they should. Hulet now faced the same grisly death as his fellow defendants. The judges, however, remained uneasy about the proof of Hulet's role in the affair. Showing contempt for their own packed jury, they pardoned Hulet, possibly saving the life of a man who did assist in the death of the king.

William Hulet's unsatisfactory trial did not completely answer the question of the identity of one of the two heavily disguised men on the scaffold – but it did solve the question of the identity of the chief executioner. Ever since the morning of 30 January 1649, when Colonel Axtell had sent a detachment of troops to fetch Richard Brandon, the common hangman, from his home, rumours had circulated about whether or not it was Brandon who had actually cut off the king's head.

Of course, the court could have simply asked Colonel Axtell, who was languishing only a few hundred yards away in Newgate awaiting execution. He was one of the few people alive who knew with certainty the identities of both the disguised men (indeed, Hulet had suggested to the court that they should call Axtell). This could have put the court in a difficult situation. Having convicted Axtell for signing the execution warrant, to have then asked for his evidence would have placed him in a similar category to Tomlinson and Huncks, both of whose lives had been spared for helping the prosecution.

Making do without Axtell, the court called possibly its first witnesses to be truly independent. Abraham Smith was a boatman who had walked up Whitehall to see the execution. Shortly after the king was killed, a troop of musketeers had instructed him to take the hangman downriver. Smith was told, 'Waterman, away with him, be gone quickly.'[7]

When Brandon got into his boat, he gave one of the soldiers half a crown. A previous witness, employed by the sheriff's office, had testified that Brandon had been paid in half-crowns, which fitted the story of how he paid the soldiers for helping him escape safely from a potentially hostile crowd.

Once he was rowing downriver, Smith asked his passenger if he was the man who had cut off the king's head. Brandon replied that he was not. He said he had taken him to Whitehall where he had been held prisoner while his instruments – his axe and the block – had been taken away. According to Smith, Brandon was shaking uncontrollably.

It is hardly surprising that Brandon should deny his role – he could not have known whether Smith was for or against the king. Perhaps the best evidence that Brandon was the executioner was the professionalism of the man who had tucked a wisp of hair away from the neck and struck a clean blow to sever the head.[8] The next two witnesses both testified that they subsequently heard Brandon admit he had killed the king. Taken with the anonymously published confessions that appeared later in the year after he had died, it seems safe to conclude that the man who wielded the axe that cut off the king's head was indeed Richard Brandon, the common hangman.

While the trial continued, the first execution took place. On the morning of 13 October Thomas Harrison climbed the scaffold at Charing Cross. According to a contemporary account anonymously published as *The Speeches and Prayers of the Regicides*, Harrison was an imposing figure. When the noose was put around his neck he told the crowd, 'By God I have leaped over a wall, by God I have run through a troop, and by my God I will go through this death, and He will make it easy for me.' As he concluded by committing his spirit to Jesus, the hangman cast him off into space. He was cut down, still conscious, and the hangman set about cutting open his abdomen to remove his entrails. At this, Harrison is reported to have summoned up a final spasm of strength and boxed his executioner on the ear.

Among those who watched the spectacle was Samuel Pepys who that evening wrote that Harrison looked 'as cheerful as any man could do in that condition'. Two days later, Harrison's fellow Fifth Monarchist John Carew was taken to the scaffold, where he conducted himself with similar bravery. He prayed for some time before loudly addressing friends and colleagues in the crowd with, 'Farewell, my friends, farewell!'

Having been summarily tried themselves, on the evening of 15 October, Hugh Peters and John Cook made what preparations they could before their executions in the morning. Peters remained in a state of dread and anguish. He told the others that he was unprepared for death and feared he would not face his suffering on the scaffold with courage. Cook tried to comfort him, saying, 'Brother Peters, we shall be in heaven tomorrow in bliss and glory.' After midnight, neither man was sleeping (Cook had slept for only an hour and a half). Cook again comforted Peters, saying, 'Come brother Peters, let us knock at heaven-Gates this morning. God will open the doors of eternity to us before twelve of the clock.'[9]

On the morning of Tuesday 16 October, Cook took leave of his wife, saying, 'Farewell my dear lamb, I am now going to the souls under the altar that cry, "How long, O Lord holy and true? Dost thou not judge and avenge our blood on them that dwell on earth?" And when I am gone my blood will cry and do them more harm than if I had lived.'

Cook's wife embraced him and wept. He said, 'Why weepest thou? Let them weep who part and shall never meet again, but I am confident we shall have a glorious meeting in heaven.'

When the sheriff came to take him away, his wife clung fiercely to his arm, crying bitterly as she pulled him back. Cook gently chided her for preventing him from going to meet Jesus Christ. He eased his arm away from her grasp and went out to the yard where a wooden sledge of the type used to carry condemned prisoners to Tyburn awaited him. He was greeted by the head of Thomas Harrison, strapped to the sledge so that it faced him as he lay down and was tied on. As the horses started up and the sledge jerked forward, Cook shouted out, 'This is the easiest chariot that ever I rid in all my life.'

On the scaffold, Cook said he had no malice towards anyone and forgave everyone. He had no hard thoughts regarding the king, whose throne he prayed would be upheld by truth and mercy. For those who put him and his colleagues on trial, he had less forgiving words: 'But I must needs say that poor we have been bought and sold by our brethren, as Joseph was. Brother hath betrayed brother to death.' When he said he wished the king could show some mercy, the sheriff interrupted, saying that the king 'hath clemency enough for all but his father's murderers'.

Cook went on to talk about his hopes for a better judicial system 'good for both king and people', but the sheriff interrupted him again. Cook replied sternly, 'It hath not been the manner of Englishmen to insult over a dying man – nor in other countries among Turks or galley slaves.'

Interrupted by the sheriff a third time, Cook retorted, 'Sir, I pray take notice of it: I think I am the first man that ever was hanged for demanding justice, therefore I hope you will not interrupt me.'

He turned to the friends who had accompanied the sledge from Newgate and asked them to look after his wife and child, and that the king and Parliament would not take all the property from either them or the other attainted men. Finally he prayed that no more might suffer and said, 'Blessed Father, I come into the bosom of thy love.'

Cook was cast off the ladder and swayed above the crowd. Among those who watched his torture was Hugh Peters, who had been cruelly brought from the prison to observe what awaited him. He was brought up to the scaffold when Cook was being quartered. The hangman came over to him and, rubbing his bloodied hands together, said, 'Come, how do you like this, Mr Peters, how do you like this work?'

Peters gathered up what spirit he could and replied, 'I am not, thank God, terrified. You may do your worst.'[10]

When Cook's entrails were cut from his body and burned, the smell was reported to be overpowering. Many people turned away, covering their noses. After what remained of him was dragged away on the sledge, Hugh Peters was put on the scaffold. He spotted a man he knew in the crowd and gave him a golden coin, asking for it to be given to his daughter as a token from him. Before the coin came into her hands, Peters said, he would be with God.

Despite his fears that he would let himself and his fellow prisoners down, Peters met his death with bravery. Speaking to the crowd, he said, 'Oh, this is a good day. He is come that I have long looked for and I shall be with him in glory.'[11] His last words were drowned out by jeering and booing from the crowd.

The day continued at the Old Bailey with the trial of Charles I's remaining judges. This group of sixteen were in a different category from those who had been tried before. Though potentially facing the death penalty, it had been stipulated that they could only be sentenced to death by a further Act of Parliament. Therefore, they faced life imprisonment or loss of property or both. Some were more distinguished than others, some had been more active in the court or in the Rump Parliament. All but three had signed the death warrant. They were John Downes, Augustine Garland, Edmund Harvey, William Heveningham, Robert Lilburne, Henry Marten, Simon Meyne, Gilbert Millington, Sir Isaac Pennington, Vincent Potter,

Owen Rowe, Henry Smith, James Temple, Peter Temple, Robert Tichborne and Thomas Waite.

Among them, one man's name stood out. Henry Marten's strong republican sentiments were well known to the House of Stuart. Although friendly with Sir Edward Hyde, Marten had consistently called for the Stuarts to be swept away. Charles I had called him 'an ugly rascal and a whore-master'.[12] Marten repaid the compliment by playing a central role in setting up the High Court that tried the king. Given all this, it was remarkable that he had not been included in the primary death list. His omission seems to have been due only to sheer weight of numbers. Even he and the others on the secondary list, of course, were not entirely secure for their lives.

In his defence, Marten said that he was not guilty according to the wording of the charge, namely that he 'maliciously, murderously and traitorously' conspired to kill the king, for there was no malice in his actions. Hence, while not denying what he had done, he did deny he was guilty under the Act. Among his accomplishments, Marten was a lawyer and this was a good point. The bench must have collectively groaned.

But the prosecution was up for the fight and sought to prove that Marten had on the contrary acted maliciously. Heneage Finch recalled the moment in Whitehall Palace when Cromwell and Marten marked one another's faces with ink before signing the king's death warrant:

Finch: We shall prove against the prisoner at the bar (because he would wipe off malice), he did this very merrily, and was great sport at the time of the signing of the warrant for the king's execution.

Marten: That does not imply malice.[13]

After this, Marten based his defence solely on the fact that he had acted on instruction from the Parliament that existed at the time. In the same spirit, he would obey any Parliament; he would thus obey the present Parliament that had invited Charles II back and hence would be obedient to the king.

On the court's stated position that the Rump was not a real Parliament, Finch asked the jury to find Marten guilty 'out of his own mouth'.

The two men among the remaining prisoners who had not been signatories to the death warrant were Edmund Harvey and Sir Isaac Pennington. Harvey told the court he had not signed the warrant because he was against killing the king and had done all he could to argue against it. This was a reasonable argument. Pennington pleaded stupidity for sitting in the court in the first place, saying, 'I knew not what I did.' It was a wretched defence by a thoroughly wretched man.

Among the rest of the unhappy crew, Gilbert Millington changed his plea to guilty and asked for forgiveness, saying he had been 'awed' by the previous Parliament and court. Robert Tichborne did much the same, changing his plea to explain he had been led astray 'by want of years' (he was thirty-eight at the time). Owen Rowe pleaded ignorance, as did Robert Lilburne. Henry Smith claimed he couldn't remember what he had signed.

Edmund Ludlow, who must have received the published court record in Switzerland, summed it all up well: 'Some of them pleaded simply guilty; but others, though they acknowledged the guilt, denied the malice; and some confessing the fact, denied the guilt.'[14]

The court chose to ignore the fact that men like Marten had given themselves up under the king's promise of clemency. Bridgeman recapped the evidence and, following a short discussion, the jury found all of the men guilty. They were returned to Newgate until the court decided what sentence awaited them. Ludlow said of the court's decision, with particular reference to his friend Henry Marten: 'the sentence of condemnation was passed against him; the convention making no provision for securing the lives either of him or the rest of the gentlemen that had been decoyed into the surrender of their persons, though they had implicitly promised them favour.'

The court finished its deliberations by considering the fate of the remaining members of the group: Augustine Garland, William Heveningham, Simon Meyne, Vincent Potter, James Temple, Peter Temple and Thomas Waite. They all resorted to similar arguments: that they now pleaded guilty but had been under duress or had misunderstood what they were involved in. All were declared guilty by the jury.

It was evening now. All that remained was the sentencing. The clerk ordered the sheriff's officer to bring Sir Hardress Waller back to the bar. Waller had admitted his guilt on the very first day of the hearings, six days before. He was accompanied by George Fleetwood, the major-general who also had pleaded guilty. They were joined by all the others previously found guilty but not yet sentenced: Axtell, Hacker, Harvey, Hulet, Lilburne, Marten, Millington, Pennington, Rowe, Smith, Tichborne and Heveningham.

In an extraordinary last-minute development, Heveningham, the wealthy MP and religious radical, was told he should stand aside from the others, away from the bar. He was evidently not about to be sentenced. Heveningham was one of those who pleaded that he had been duped into participating in the trial and had not signed the king's death warrant. The court had heard all this before. There was one possible reason why the case was suddenly set aside – the influence of Heveningham's father-in-law, the wealthy and influential Earl of Dover. The earl seems to have let his son-in-law sweat before putting in a word.

With the light fading fast, Bridgeman made his speech to the guilty. He told them they belonged to three distinct categories. For the first group, the death penalty would be suspended until a further Act of Parliament; for the second, comprising Axtell and Hacker, there could be no mercy. The third category included only one member, William Heveningham, and here Bridgeman's speech swerved from his usual direct and decisive manner. He became evasive. 'I presume some time will be given to him to consider something relating to him before any order will be given for his execution,' he offered.[15] It was a clumsy cover-up. Bridgeman, who edited the court reports, did not even bother to insert a better choice of words for posterity.

Squinting to read his prepared text, Bridgeman complained about the light before sentencing all to death by hanging, drawing and quartering. In total, ten were actually executed. Harrison, Carew, Cook and Peters had already been disembowelled, leaving six still to be attended to. The next day, 17 October, John Evelyn recorded in his diary that the regicides died 'in sight of the place where they put to death their natural prince, and in the presence of the king, his son, whom they also sought to kill'.[16]

So, if we can believe Evelyn, Charles was present and watched the executions. According to Evelyn – who had very good connections at the royal court – curiosity proved too much for Charles and he watched some of those who passed sentence on his father meet their terrible deaths. If this is the case, why did the courtiers not record this interesting fact? It is impossible to say why a courtier such as Hyde might not have known about it and therefore recorded it, except out of fealty to Charles. Others might not have known of the presence of the king: perhaps he watched from the gallery in the Holbein Arch, which overlooked Charing Cross, or from an unmarked coach on the edge of the crowd. Either way, it was only natural that the king should wish to see those who had held the monarchy in such contempt pay with their lives.

Charles would not have cared much for the nuance that most of the men he now watched tortured to death did not detest the monarchy itself but had run out of patience with a duplicitous and obdurate king. Indeed, Cromwell and Ireton had once seen the younger Charles, when still Prince of Wales, as a substitute for his father. That had all ended with the second Civil War and the realisation by Cromwell and others that the king could never be trusted.

Now the men who had judged him to have been guilty of treason were paying dearly. Evelyn said of it: 'I saw not their execution, but met their quarters, mangled and cut and reeking as they were brought from the gallows in baskets on the hurdle.'

The noxious smells from the gruesome executions led to petitions from local residents asking the king to remove the scaffold from Charing Cross. Perhaps, having witnessed the stench at first hand, Charles was more than receptive. Whatever the reason, the scaffold was moved more than a mile north-west to Tyburn, a traditional site of executions, situated at what is today Marble Arch.

On Friday, 19 October, ten days after the trial began, Colonel Axtell was hanged, drawn and quartered. The smell would not have reached Whitehall. His colleague Colonel Hacker was hanged. Though this form of execution was dreadful enough – the victim was left to dangle on a rope until he asphyxiated, rather than the modern technique of being dropped sharply to break his neck – he was spared the torture of disembowelling and castration. This may have been due to the loyalty of his brothers to the crown.

The entire series of trials and executions lasted ten days. Thirty-two men were indicted and ten were executed; one was released thanks to his connections at the royal court; another was released because the judges felt the conviction was unsound. This left seventeen waiting to know their fate, and three who had already fled abroad and so were left untried.

The state was not done with those who had escaped its grasp. Spies and secret agents would spread across Europe to fetch them back. At home, a search began to discover the identity of those who had dared to publish the last speeches of the regicides. The reign of Charles II had begun in a vile spectacle of gore, but the desire for vengeance was by no means sated.

14

DISINTERRED

November 1660—April 1661

After the heads of the dead had been impaled for display on the end of poles around the capital, the executions stopped for a time. It would later be claimed that Charles called a halt to the butchery because he was so sickened by what he witnessed. However, another theory was that the condemned men were dying too well. Most of the executed men had exhibited 'such firmness and piety', wrote Gilbert Burnet, Bishop of Salisbury and nephew of Lord Wariston, 'that the odiousness of the crime grew at last to be so much flatten'd ... the King was advised not to proceed farther'.[1]

Attention was given instead to the twenty regicides who had vanished abroad. Shortly before the October bloodletting, the authorities made their first tentative move to secure foreign help to track them down. A Catholic priest named O'Neill is reported to have been sent to the Netherlands to negotiate the surrender of the regicides there. He found the Dutch authorities unhelpful. They had a proud tradition of offering sanctuary and had no reason to go against it for the Stuarts. 'Nothing could be done against the liberties of the state,' Lord Clarendon noted sourly. It could hardly have helped that O'Neill had evidently been given little or no briefing before his mission. When the Dutch Stadtholder Johan de Witt asked for the names of the wanted men, O'Neill did not have them. It would take six months before a more effective agent was deployed.[2]

The New England authorities would prove at least as difficult as the Dutch when London became aware that Whalley and Goffe were in America and ordered action against them. That was nearly four months after their arrival on the *Prudent Mary*. Since then they had wandered freely, not bothering to disguise themselves. Such a way of life began to look unwise in November after a warrant for their arrest was produced in Boston and a £100 reward for them dead or alive was posted. But as we shall see, New England was in no mood yet to give them up to the Stuarts. Even after details of the Act of Oblivion arrived, and with them grisly details of the first executions, the two fugitives seemed to have nothing to fear.

In London, vengeance quickly resumed full flow. Before the stink of disembowelment had time to clear around Tyburn's triple tree, moves were afoot for a new form of retribution there. On 6 November a parliamentary Bill was introduced that would lead to the posthumous dismemberment at Tyburn of the rotting corpses of three dead regicides, first and foremost that of Cromwell himself.

The Lord Protector had been dead for twenty-six months. His monumental tomb lay in Westminster Abbey. It stood in the Henry VII chapel, the glittering gothic masterpiece erected six generations earlier at the end of the Wars of the Roses. The remains of most of the Tudors, the victorious dynasty in that earlier English bloodletting, were housed in the chapel. It was also the resting place of the first Stuart to sit on the English throne, James I, and of his mother Mary Queen of Scots. Cromwell's tomb, set by the western wall of the chapel, represented him too as royalty, as the monarch that he had reluctantly refused to be in life. The tomb, which is believed to have been of marble and alabaster, was surmounted by an effigy of him reclining, dressed in royal robes, a sceptre in one hand, a globe in the other, and a crown on the head.

One can imagine Charles and his two brothers exploring the

abbey after their delirious welcome back to London six months earlier, perhaps looking for their grandfather's tomb, only to be brought
to a juddering halt by the monument to Cromwell, the man most
blamed for the ruin of their father. After a pause the young trio might
then have drawn each other's attention to other newish memorials in
the abbey. More than a dozen luminaries of the Commonwealth
who had died after the king were interred there too. They included
men who almost rivalled Cromwell in the pantheon of royalist hate –
Henry Ireton, Thomas Pride and John Bradshaw, the stony-faced
lawyer who had presided over the king's trial.

Not surprisingly, the dead regicides' tenure in the abbey did not
last. The Bill introduced to Parliament in November ordered them
removed: 'That the carcasses of Oliver Cromwell, Henry Ireton,
John Bradshaw, and Thomas Pride, whether buried in Westminster
Abbey, or elsewhere, be, with all expedition, taken up, and drawn
upon a hurdle to Tyburn, and there hanged up in their coffins for
some time; and after that buried under the said Gallows'.[3]

This grisly idea came direct from the court, if not from the king
himself. The proposer of the measure, Silius Titus, was one of
Charles's most trusted aides, who had claimed authorship of *Killing
No Murder* and had been the agent sent to help Miles Sindercombe
in the attempts to assassinate Cromwell. He was also a key inter-
mediary during preparations for the restoration. Here in the
Convention Parliament, he vied with William Prynne in eagerness
to punish. Titus acted as teller for the attempt to except Sir Arthur
Haselrig from pardon, and he was partly responsible for Adrian
Scroop's execution, calling on his former commanding officer,
Richard Browne, to repeat to the House the words which brought
Scroop to the block. Titus introduced the disinterment proposal as
an addition to a larger Bill codifying the attainder for treason of all
regicides, alive or dead, so their property could be seized. He said
that his addition aimed to provide that 'execution did not leave traitors at their graves, but followed them beyond it.' A few days after
tabling the amendment, Titus was awarded £2000 for 'signal services

for the Royal family', a sum subsequently raised to £3000, though he had difficulty obtaining all of it. Later Charles granted him a pension of £500. All of which leads to the assumption that if the posthumous punishment was not Charles II's own idea, he certainly approved of it.[4]

The date set by Titus's Bill for the disinterments was 30 January, the anniversary of Charles I's execution. Parliament decreed that the date was to be a holy day in perpetuity, a day of 'fasting and humiliation'. It was one more step towards the sanctification of the little monarch.

News of the posthumous punishments to come left a bad taste in some mouths. Samuel Pepys, in his youth an admirer of the Lord Protector but now a convinced royalist, recoiled at the news. 'It ... doth trouble me that a man of so great courage as he should have that dishonour though otherwise he might deserve it,' he noted in his diary on hearing of the decision to take revenge on Cromwell's corpse.[5]

Titus's next step was to join Prynne in the attempt to hurry more to the execution block. On 7 December Prynne reminded the House that it was twelve years to the day since the trial of the king had been agreed and he moved an amendment to the new Bill of Attainder to secure further executions. Titus seconded him. Two of the judges who had surrendered themselves within the fourteen-day deadline were targeted for immediate execution, Sir Hardress Waller and Augustine Garland. Titus characterised Waller as a royal pensioner who had voted for his benefactor's death. 'The Turks would not eat the bread of any man they meant to betray, and a Roman soldier who betrayed his master, though for the public good, was executed.'[6] The executions didn't go through. Waller's life was saved by the lobbying of his cousin, the royalist general Sir William Waller, but he never regained his liberty. Similarly with Garland, who was incarcerated first in the Tower and then, it is thought, in Tangiers.

The weeks before the disinterments were full of argument, rumour and twitching nerves in government. Ministers shrieked in alarm at an earnest pamphlet questioning the constitutional status of the existing Parliament. Sir Heneage Finch told Parliament that he 'could not think of anything more dangerous than writing this book at such a time ... It blew up this Parliament totally and damned the Act of Oblivion.' The author, he said, was 'the greatest incendiary that could be'.[7] In fact the writer, William Drake, claimed to be a royalist. That didn't help him. He was dragged before Parliament and impeached. His pamphlet, *The Long Parliament Revived*, was ritually burnt.

Drake's impeachment came during a brief moment of calm after the excitements in the Strand. On 5 November the Venetian resident reported:

> nothing of consequence has happened this week. The regicides are executed, the disbanding of the army proceeds apace and most of the men are already paid off. When Parliament meets the most interesting question will be the affair of the duke of York and the chancellor's daughter. It becomes increasingly clear that though the father is trying to hush the matter up, parliament means to deal with it, especially as the duke persists in denying the marriage.*

The personal problems of the royal family did indeed command centre stage for a while. Apart from the scandal of the pregnant Anne Hyde and her hasty marriage to the heir to the throne, the king's youngest brother, the Duke of Gloucester, had died of smallpox in September, followed by his sister who succumbed to the same disease two months later. The Queen Mother, Henrietta Maria, decided not to stay in England and made plans to depart for the Continent. Anti-monarchists, of course, saw the deaths as God's retribution for the martyrs of Charing Cross.

---

* The Venetian resident's dispatches are available on the parliamentary website at British History Online: www.british-history.ac.uk

Talk of plots was now in the air. The 'White Plot' seemed the most serious. News of it surfaced in mid-December after a Major Thomas White was arrested trying to bribe a porter in Whitehall. A search of his chambers led to the discovery of lists of radicals, the arrests of forty or fifty men and the discovery of an alleged plan to assassinate George Monck. On 17 December the usual precautions were taken, with a proclamation banning all former soldiers from within twenty miles of London. Ripples of apprehension spread across the country. There were reports of conspiracies in Lincoln, York, Hull, Wiltshire, Essex and Leicester.[8]

The Convention Parliament was finally dissolved on 29 December, providing an occasion for the king to enjoy even more gushing adulation than usual. One historian dubbed the loyal address by the Speaker, Sir Harbottle Grimston, as 'eastern' in its adulation. The king who had been rescued from a hopeless exile by Parliament was told that it was the country that owed him endless thanks. 'Royal Sir,' Grimston began, 'you have denied us nothing we have asked this Parliament, indeed you have outdone your Parliament by doing much more for us than we could agree amongst ourselves to ask and therefore must needs be a happy Parliament. This is a healing Parliament, a reconciling, peacemaking Parliament, a blessed Parliament.'

Lord Clarendon, the Lord Chancellor, then treated Parliament to a hair-raising account both of the White Plot and of an earlier one which was said to involve seizing the Tower and Windsor Castle, freeing the regicides and killing the king. The Chancellor blamed the plotting on reaction to the execution of the regicides and he made much of rumours about the involvement of Ludlow and Lambert. Ludlow, he asserted, was expected 'to lead the fanatics'.[9] Ludlow had already fled to Europe and was at that moment a distant spectator of events in England, but as we will see his name would be attached to a host of alleged plots over subsequent years. He would become the Stuarts' bogey man.[10]

Before he was finished, Clarendon joined in the gushing praise of the king. Charles, he revealed, had attended the questioning of suspects and proved the master interrogator. 'His Majesty hath spent many hours himself in the examination of this business; and some of the principal officers, who, before they came to His Majesty's presence, could not be brought to acknowledge any thing, after the king himself had spoken to them, confessed, that their spirits were insensibly prevailed upon and subdued, and that it was not in their power to conceal their guilt from him.' This was not to be the last time Charles II made the river trip to the Tower to interrogate men accused of wanting to kill him.

A week after the dissolution of Parliament, Sir Arthur Haselrig died in the Tower, aged about fifty-nine. It is not known whether a rapprochement was effected between him and his former ally, Sir Harry Vane, who was also in the Tower.

But Sir Arthur's death was overshadowed by a violent eruption by the Fifth Monarchists in response to the regicide executions. It occurred when the king and his brother were two days away from London, in Portsmouth, seeing their mother off to France. Thomas Venner, a wine cooper, had assumed the leadership of the movement after the execution of Thomas Harrison. On 6 January 1661 Venner led a group of up to fifty armed followers who broke into St Paul's Cathedral shouting 'King Jesus and the heads upon the gates' and demanded of passers-by whom they supported. One man was shot dead when he answered, 'God and King Charles.' It was said that one of their aims was to rescue the head of Thomas Harrison, which had been rotting on a spike on London Bridge for three months. The group never managed that, but over the next four days they were to conduct an astonishingly effective guerrilla war in the city. Well armed and well trained, they appeared and disappeared 'like wildfire', rampaging fearlessly through the city, beating back all comers. Samuel Pepys' reaction was almost admiring: 'these fanatiques that have ... routed all the trainbands that they met with, put the king's life guards to the run, killed about twenty men, broke through the City gates twice; and all this in the day-time, when all the City was in arms'. He thought there had to be five hundred of them and was astonished to hear there were nearer thirty. 'A thing that never was heard of, that so few men should dare and do so much mischief.'[11]

Charles dispatched his brother James back to London to join Monck in suppressing the outbreak. It took four days to subdue Venner and his men. All or most of them were too badly wounded to fight on. Charles himself returned from the coast to see Venner and two others hanged, drawn and quartered at Tyburn and nine more hanged. It is not known if he interrogated them too.

Venner posed no real threat, and his death and those of his followers appear to have inspired none of the sympathy shown to the executed regicides. Instead they were condemned. But Venner's uprising, as it would be called, provided the excuse for a clampdown. The government filled the Gatehouse, Newgate and Counters prisons with suspected Fifth Monarchists, Quakers and Baptists, and all meetings of these sects were banned. Some four hundred Baptists were arrested in London alone. It was the beginning of the end of that other promise in the Declaration of Breda – 'freedom for tender consciences'. Within four months the old Anglican straitjacket was being reimposed. The Corporation Act required all persons holding office in the towns where the Puritans were most numerous to renounce the Presbyterian Solemn League and Covenant,* to declare that opposition to the king was treason, and to take the sacrament according to the rites of the Anglican Church. The following year the Uniformity Act required every clergyman to use the Book of Common Prayer, under penalty of losing his position. Two years after that the Conventicle Act forbade all meeting for purposes of worship not prescribed by the Church of England.

Two days after the Venner executions, work began on digging up the corpses chosen for posthumous punishment. Three were buried

---

* This Anglo-Scottish pact signed in 1643 saw England officially adopt the Presbyterian form of church government operating in Scotland.

in the abbey: Cromwell, Henry Ireton and John Bradshaw. The last resting place of Thomas Pride, the fourth on the list, was at Nonsuch, the site of a demolished royal palace in Surrey. In the event he was left there to rest in peace. Work on disinterring his three comrades began on 26 January, four days before the anniversary of the king's death. The bodies of Cromwell and Ireton were dug out first. There would have been particular trepidation about handling the Lord Protector's corpse. According to contemporaries, his burial had been a messy, hurried affair with nauseating consequences. Bishop Burnet described the washing, examination and embalming of the corpse, and then how things had gone wrong. Cromwell's body was wrapped in six double layers of sere cloth and a sheet of lead, then enclosed in 'an elegant coffin of the choicest wood'. But then the body 'swelled and bursted, from whence came such filth, that raised such a deadly and noisome stink, that it was found prudent to bury him immediately'.[12]

Cromwell's vault abutted that of Henry VII, sited centrally under the middle aisle. At the disinterment the vault was broken into and the elaborate coffin located by the sergeant-at-arms, James Norton. The body inside, wrapped in lead and sere cloth as described by Bishop Burnet, was identified by a silver gilt medallion hanging round his neck; on one side were engraved the arms of England entwined with those of Cromwell's, and on the reverse the words *Oliverius Protector Republicae Angliae, Scotiae & Hiberniae Natus 25 April 1599. Inauguratus 15 Dec ris 1653. Mortuus 3 Sep ris 1658. Hic situs est.**[13] People paid sixpence a head to glimpse the body, with abbey officials and others jostling for a view. 'The people crowded very much to see him.'[14]

Next a shrouded corpse identified as that of Henry Ireton was unearthed, followed by that of John Bradshaw. The latter had been buried only fourteen months earlier and the men who broke open

---

* Oliver, Protector of the English, Scottish and Irish Republic. Born 25 April 1599, inaugurated 15 December 1653, died 3 September 1658. Here he rests.

his coffin were nearly overpowered by the smell. His body 'was green . . . and stank'.[15] From the abbey the corpses were taken by cart to the Red Lion in Holborn, from where they would process west to the 'tripple tree' at Tyburn.

The corpses were conveyed to Tyburn early in the morning on 30 January. The odour of John Bradshaw's corpse accompanied them. 'All the way the universal outcry and curses of the people went along with them', reported *Mercurius Publicus* dutifully. 'When these three carcasses arrived at Tyburn, they were pulled out of their coffins, and hanged at the several angles of that triple tree, where they hung till the sun was set; after which they were taken down, their heads cut off; and their loathsome trunks thrown into a deep hole under the gallows.' As usual with high-profile executions at Tyburn, a crowd of boys fought to get under the gallows to cut off the corpses' toes and sell them as keepsakes.

Those who had not been present to relish the spectacle were told by *Mercurius Publicus*: 'The heads of those three notorious regicides, Oliver Cromwell, John Bradshaw, and Ireton are set upon poles on the top of Westminster Hall by the common hangman.' And there the Protector's head remained for at least a century.

Charles's coronation was set for 23 April. London prepared for the most lavish week of celebrations. The ceremony was not without its dangers. The authorities were concerned that 'fanatics' might use the distraction it provided to strike a blow against the king. With this in mind, Sir Edward Nicholas sent word to Sir William Davidson, a Scottish merchant based in Amsterdam who also acted as a royalist agent, to watch for coronation plots. Sir Edward would not have been reassured by a report that regular émigré meetings involving John Desborough were taking place in Sedan, where the talk was of taking revenge 'for the blood of God's servants' by the overthrow of the king.

Ten days before coronation day, Nicholas took precautions. A dozen ex-officers were arrested and all former soldiers were ordered to keep twenty miles from London until May. If there had been a threat, it vanished now. A week of fabulous celebration went ahead undisturbed.

The celebrations began with the making of knights and other ceremonial in Windsor, where the display had the Venetian ambassador drooling over the 'pomp and magnificence' of it all. Those events were inevitably outmatched by the coronation a few days later. A two-day affair, this began with a vast ceremonial procession from the Tower of London that clattered along the ancient route through the City and on to Whitehall. It had been raining steadily for a month, wrote the royalist James Heath, 'but on this and the next day it pleased God that not one drop fell on the king's triumph'.[16]

The City had been unstinting with the decorations. Oriental carpets disguised ramshackle houses, flowers and gravel covered filthy streets and on every corner was a tableau or display saluting monarchy, all to the sound of trumpets or beat of drum. The procession was magnificent. It was headed by the king's law officers, the masters of chancery and judges; next were sixty-eight Knights of the Bath in crimson robes, followed by the great aristocrats and other lords according to their rank; then crowds of dignitaries in bejewelled finery, each outdoing the last in opulent display.

Unsubtle but stirring images of royalist propaganda dotted the route. Four triumphal arches, designed around large allegorical paintings depicting Charles directly or showing him taking vengeance on his father's killers, had been constructed. One had him as the emperor Augustus exacting vengeance on Caesar's assassins. Another portrayed 'usurpation' as a many-headed Gorgon with Cromwell's as one of the heads. Yet another featured a collection of severed regicides' heads stuck high in the air on the end of long poles. When, next day, Charles was crowned, he must have been a happy man.

Other heads would soon be going up on poles, this time in Edinburgh. The next high-profile targets of the king's revenge were the Presbyterians who had forced him to accept the Covenant as the price of crowning him king of Scotland in January 1651. Their leader

'King' Campbell, the formidable Marquis of Argyll, who had placed the crown on Charles's head a decade earlier, was now in prison awaiting trial in Edinburgh for treason.

He went on trial before the Scottish Parliament at the end of February 1661. It was a protracted, bitter affair which lasted nearly three months. The book was thrown at him by the royalists. Among the charges were complicity in the king's death and allegations that he had betrayed Scotland to the English. Argyll's defence was so persuasive that acquittal seemed a real possibility – until Argyll himself was betrayed by no less than the Duke of Albemarle, George Monck. Argyll and Monck had worked well together when the Englishman was in command in Scotland and there was considerable correspondence between them. As the trial neared its conclusion in May 1661, Monck sent a selection of Argyll's letters to Edinburgh. They revealed Argyll collaborating with the English against Scots royalists, thus shattering Argyll's defence. The great Campbell was duly convicted of treason. Bishop Burnet called Monck's intervention an act of 'inexcusable baseness'.

Argyll was on his knees as the sentence of death was pronounced. He rose to his feet and said, 'I had the honour to place the crown on the King's head and now he hastens me to a better crown than he owns.'[17] On 27 May, just forty-eight hours after the verdict, Argyll was beheaded at Edinburgh's Mercat Cross. His most prominent ally, James Guthrie, was executed in the same place four days later, along with a Captain William Govan who had deserted the Scottish army and joined Cromwell and who some suspected of being on the scaffold in January 1649. Argyll's head, stuck on top of the city gate known as the Netherbow Port, greeted visitors to Edinburgh for the next four years.

15

BLOODHOUNDS

May–September 1661

The spring of 1661 was significant not only for the crowning of the king or for the Marquis of Argyll's execution. Hitherto Charles had paid little attention to the capture of regicides abroad, but that was about to change. As carpenters sweated over the erection of those magnificent coronation arches with their dual themes of royal triumph and revenge, Charles unleashed his bloodhounds in America and Europe. Two royalists set out from Boston to lead a hunt across New England for Whalley and Goffe, and the most ruthless operator in the king's service was drafted in to spearhead a search across Europe for Ludlow and the other nineteen regicides who had escaped in 1660.

The American manhunt was launched on 6 May by John Endecott, governor of Massachusetts. Endecott had received an arrest order from the king which, dispensing with flowery courtesies, had been brutally curt:

Trusty and well-beloved,
  We greet you well. We being given to understand that Colonel Whalley and Colonel Goffe, who stand here convicted for the execrable murder of our Royal Father, of glorious

memory, are lately arrived at New England, where they hope to shroud themselves securely from the justice of our laws; our will and pleasure is, and we do hereby expressly require and command you forthwith upon the receipt of these our letters, to cause both the said persons to be apprehended, and with the first opportunity sent over hither under a strict care, to receive according to their demerits. We are confident of your readiness and diligence to perform your duty; and so bid you farewell.[1]

The abrupt tone reflected Charles's fury at the welcoming reception accorded the regicides in America. Their unchallenged presence was not only an insult but a danger that threatened to undermine still further Britain's fragile hold on the colony. The two men were openly enjoying their freedom, sometimes challenged by the odd royalist, but admired and welcomed by the majority Puritans. In London the Council of Foreign Plantations was told that the two were holding public meetings, praying and preaching and justifying the killing of the king. Whalley was quoted as saying that 'if what he had done against the King were to be done again, he would do it again.'[2]

All changed after May 1661. Having received the menacing royal command, John Endecott had to be seen to respond decisively. He commissioned two ardent royalists to conduct a manhunt right across the territory. The two men – a young Boston merchant called Thomas Kirk and Thomas Kelland, an English sea captain – were furnished with the governor's authority to impress all the men and horse they needed and with letters requesting help to the governors of other English colonies. There was also one for Peter Stuyvesant, the governor of the neighbouring Dutch colony of New Amsterdam, a bolt-hole for people fleeing the English colonies. The search party set off on 25 May, launching a hue and cry that would fade then sound again for years.[3]

The hunters had the outward support of the most senior colonial officials like Endecott. But it was a reluctant backing, and they could scarcely have known when they set out the depth of the opposition they would encounter.

They had a good idea of their quarry's whereabouts when they left Boston. On receipt of Endecott's commission, they secured warrants from the governor of Connecticut and made directly for New Haven. Their target was the house of the millennialist pastor John Davenport, founder of the New Haven colony. Since their arrival on the *Prudent Mary* the previous summer, Davenport had become perhaps the fugitives' greatest ally. A man with a mesmerising personality, Davenport had been followed by five hundred Puritans when he left London in the 1630s to establish his ministry in the New World. He built there a fiercely independent bastion of Calvinist zealotry.[4] In New Haven, Mosaic law held sway – only church members judged predestined to be saved by God could vote, own land or hold office. Quakers and other outsiders were turned away at the colony's borders (even at the beginning of the nineteenth century Jews and Catholics were barred from setting foot on New Haven green). There was no argument when Whalley and Goffe came knocking in the early months of 1661. They were greeted as 'Godly' people and allowed in.[5]

Whalley was put up in Davenport's house while a neighbour, Thomas Jones, offered his home to Goffe. Jones had more reason than most to sympathise with the two men, for he was the son of regicide John Jones. Young Thomas had been a fellow passenger with the two fugitives on the *Prudent Mary* the previous summer. Three months after they disembarked on the Boston quayside, the older Jones had been hanged, drawn and quartered in the Strand. Of course, anyone aiding Whalley and Goffe in New England faced the same. A proclamation outlawing the regicides warned that none 'should presume to harbour or conceal any [of] the persons aforesaid under pain of misprision of high treason'.

Kirk and Kelland pushed south through New England's rugged highlands and reached Guildford, the capital of the New Haven colony, in three days. This put them a mere eighteen miles from the town of New Haven and their target. There was time enough that day to reach their men, but they needed warrants from William Leete, the colony's governor. It was here that their problems began, for Leete smoothly sabotaged their mission.

An account of what transpired was later sent to Endecott by the two royalists. They arrived in Guildford on a Saturday and Leete received them courteously enough. Then things began to go wrong. To their great discomfort, the governor insisted on reading the king's proclamation aloud while locals clustered around, so ruining the royalists' hopes of surprising the fugitives. Leete then asserted that the two colonels had left New Haven nine weeks before. This was untrue, as Kirk suspected after questioning locals. Several claimed that the regicides were still in New Haven and named the Reverend Davenport as their protector. Probing further, Kirk heard that Leete was well aware of this.

The royalists went back to the governor, demanding warrants to search and arrest and fresh horses to get them to Davenport's home. Much delay and evasion ensued. The horses were provided but Leete apologetically refused any search and arrest warrant. Before he could issue the document he would have to consult the New Haven magistrates. This, unfortunately, couldn't be done quickly because the next day was Sunday, and nothing was allowed to move in New Haven on the Sabbath. On Monday the magistrates did convene, but they came to no decision. After agonising for much of the day, they announced that the freemen of the colony would have to be summoned. That would take another four days, the increasingly angry royalists learned.

Needless to say, the birds had long flown. On the day that Kirk and Kelland led their search party into Guildford, a Native American rode through the night to warn Davenport, Jones and their guests. The two colonels were quietly shifted to a secure, if uncomfortable, hiding place not far away, though well hidden from inquisitive eyes. This was a cave halfway up a rocky escarpment a few miles beyond

New Haven. It is said that on that Sunday the Reverend Davenport's sermon drew from the book of Isaiah and his favourite proverb: 'Hide the outcasts, betray not him that wandereth. Let mine outcasts dwell with thee.'[6]

The royalists heard about the night ride of the Native American and demanded to interview him or that Leete question him. The governor refused, insisting there were no grounds to do so. They then asked him to authorise raids on the homes of Davenport and Jones. In the absence of a decision by the freemen, this was also refused.

Searches were at last conducted and Davenport was reported to have been 'very ill used' when they got to his house. The searches were of course fruitless. However, all kinds of stories have been handed down through the generations suggesting prolonged searching during which the royalists came very near to their prey. One story has a search party coming through the front door while Whalley and Goffe ran out of the back. Another has them almost cornered and hiding under a bridge as their pursuers thundered over it. Yet another has them deciding to surrender in order to save Davenport from arrest but being dissuaded by their friends. According to one tale, Governor Leete hid them in his own cellar, which invites one to wonder whether they were there, listening even as their whereabouts were being discussed upstairs by their host and the two frustrated royalists.

After weeks of frustration, Kirk and Kelland switched their attention to the south, disappearing across the border into New Amsterdam, presumably after another tip-off. There they secured the co-operation of the Dutch governor Peter Stuyvesant, but to no avail. They returned some weeks later bitter and vengeful. Their report to Massachusetts' Governor Endecott called the New Haven authorities 'obstinate and pertinacious in their contempt of his Majesty'.

To buy off the two royalists, the Massachusetts authorities presented each with a juicy land grant. At the same time Edward

Rawson, secretary of the colony's council, warned Governor Leete that his own future and that of New England was imperilled:

> I am required to signify to you ... that the non-attendance, with diligence to execute the King's warrant, for the apprehending of Colonels Goffe and Whalley, will much hazard the present state of these colonies, and your own particularly, if not some of your persons ... there remains no way to expiate the offence, and preserve yourselves from the danger and hazard, but by apprehending the said persons, who, as we are informed, are yet remaining in the colony, and not above a fortnight since were seen there: all which will be against you.[7]

In the event, Leete survived unscathed, and so did John Davenport. Having preached so bravely from Isaiah, he sent Secretary of State Sir William Morrice a grovelling denial that he or his colony had ever aided the two fugitives. The colonists had 'wanted neither will nor industry to have served His Majesty in apprehending them, but were prevented and hindered by God's overruling providence ... The two Colonels, who only stayed two days in the Colony, went away before they could be apprehended, no man knowing how or whither.'

Another attempt to catch the two was promised. Thomas Temple, a future governor of Nova Scotia, let London know that the fugitives were in the south of New England and pledged to uproot them. A note in the archives says of him: 'Has joined himself in a secret design with one Pinchin, and Capt. Lord, two of the most considerable persons living in those parts, resolving to use their uttermost endeavour to apprehend and secure those Colonels, and has great hopes to effect it if they are in those parts. Will hazard his life and fortune in his Majesty's service.'[8]

Nothing came of Temple's pledge. Judging from the archive there was a feeling in London that the two men were no longer on the other side of the Atlantic. There were reports of them being seen with Ludlow and in the Netherlands. Apparently they were amused to see other reports that they'd been killed.

Whalley and Goffe stayed in the cave during the summer of 1661. When the hullabaloo died down, they were quietly moved to Milford, another Puritan settlement eight miles away. This time their hiding place was a cellar and they would spend the next two years 'in utter seclusion without so much as going into the orchard'. Not until 1664 was there another threat to them.

On the other side of the Atlantic, things would not prove so easy for the regicides in 1661. As Kelland and his partner were being thrown off the scent in New England, a man of far more menacing and astute calibre was being appointed to lead the European hunt. This was a former Roundhead, Sir George Downing, who had been posted as envoy extraordinary to the Netherlands in 1661. Over the next year this burly, quick-witted man would serve the ends of his royal master Charles II so well that he would be granted a baronetcy, huge monetary reward and the plot of land next to Whitehall Palace that forever commemorates him – Downing Street. He would also gain a reputation as an odious, treacherous turncoat: Andrew Marvell likened him to Judas; his former clerk, Samuel Pepys, labelled Downing a 'perfidious rogue'; and in his native New England 'an arrant George Downing' became an epithet for anyone betraying a trust.

Until a year earlier, Downing could have been counted as a convinced republican. He was born to a God-fearing family of Puritans in Dublin who settled in New England in the 1630s. Like the Puritans of New Haven, the Downings had opted for the New World to escape the Anglican straitjacket which Charles I wanted to impose. Their son George, it seems, flourished there. He became one of the first students to gain a degree at Harvard, the recently established college in Boston, and after that began to make his mark as a preacher. Then came news of the Civil War in England. Like many other young Puritans, Downing was drawn to it, taking ship to

England and joining a parliamentary regiment of dragoons as chaplain. Downing's commanding officer was the dour, radical Puritan
Colonel John Okey; he became the chaplain's mentor, enthusiastically pushing his career. That career was meteoric, but not as a
preacher. Downing gave up his chaplaincy during the first Civil War
and became an expert in intelligence gathering for the parliamentary
armies. So good at this was he that at the age of twenty-six he was
appointed 'scoutmaster general' – the chief field intelligence officer – of Oliver Cromwell's all-conquering army in Scotland. It was
the equivalent to being a major-general. Come peacetime, Downing
breathlessly maintained his success, accumulating sinecures from
Cromwell's government, marrying a beautiful moneyed aristocrat
from the Howard family and being elected to Parliament. The clever
young parvenu from Massachusetts personified the confident, new,
and supposedly godly world of republican England. Yet it could be
argued that deep down he believed in monarchy – Downing, always
a sycophant to the right people, led the clamour in Parliament for
Cromwell to take the crown.[9]

In 1656, Downing was appointed special emissary to the
Netherlands, where one of England's principal concerns was the
threat from royalist exiles. Large numbers of them were clustered
there, mostly around the great ports of Amsterdam and Rotterdam,
existing in various states of desperation and hope, dreaming and
plotting Cromwell's downfall. The Netherlands was 'the nursery of
Cavalierism', declared Secretary of State John Thurloe, who directed
Downing to set up a spy network there. The former chaplain was a
huge success in the dark arts of espionage and his network eventually
spread beyond Europe and into England. A study of intelligence in
this period paints a picture of Downing's blithe ruthlessness: 'He
was engaged in entrapment, hiring spies, harassing exiles as well as
the bribery and chicanery to which he appears to have been well
suited.'[10] The study judges that most of Downing's 'talents as a spymaster' emerged in this earlier period, but that 'one or two
refinements were to be added after 1660 such as more scope for

assassination attempts, kidnappings and even suggestions of grave robbery'.

The royalists were terrified of Downing – 'that fearful gentleman', one called him – and he himself claimed that he was a target for royalist assassins. A Major Whitford, one of the royalists suspected of killing the regicide Isaac Dorislaus, was seen with others lurking around Downing's house. The emissary called on the Dutch to provide him with protection.

All in all, this feared spy chief and dyed-in-the-wool Cromwellian would seem to have much to fear from a return of the Stuarts. Yet, at the restoration, far from being thrown into prison or worse, George Downing was knighted by Charles II in the very month that the king returned. What was behind this astonishing turn of fortune? One story, possibly apocryphal, might explain it. During his frustrating years of exile in France, Charles had several times slipped over the border into Dutch territory, either on a secret visit to his sister, the wife of William of Orange, or to rendezvous with exiled supporters. The story goes that, very shortly before the restoration, Charles made one of these visits and an 'old reverend like man in a long grey beard and ordinary grey clothes' succeeded in forcing his way into his presence. The old man then pulled off his beard to reveal himself as the feared George Downing, come to warn the king that the Dutch planned to arrest him and hand him over to the English. Charles promptly terminated his visit. Downing had saved his life.[11]

Whatever the truth, we do know that on the eve of the restoration Downing set out to worm his way into royal favour. He used an intermediary, Thomas Howard, a brother of the Earl of Suffolk and a close intimate of Charles and his sister, the Princess of Orange. Howard had been one of Downing's informants since 1658, after making the mistake of entrusting potentially damaging private papers to the keeping of a mistress and then falling out with her. Downing somehow acquired the papers and blackmailed the young aristocrat – or, as he put it, 'gained' him. 'I think I can hardly pitch for one better instrument than Tom Howard, he being the master of the horse to the Princess Royal', Downing boasted in a report to London. From then on Howard was his creature, passing on every titbit about the Stuarts.[12]

Two years on, in April 1660, when General Monck's army was in London and astute men were changing allegiances, Downing summoned Tom Howard and instructed him to tell the still exiled king that he now desired 'to promote His Majesty's service'. To prove his new allegiance Downing showed Howard intelligence material that he wanted communicated to the king. This included a letter in cipher from Secretary Thurloe reporting feeling in the army and among the general populace. Downing begged for a royal pardon and promised that if he got it, he would 'work secretly on the army in which he has considerable influence'. As for his own past as a Roundhead, Downing told Howard to relay his repentance for taking up arms against Charles I. He wanted it understood that he had been misled as a youth in New England, where he had 'sucked in principles that since his reason had made him see were erroneous'.[13]

As Downing awaited the king's reply, his good friend John Milton was publishing two anti-monarchist tracts which three months later would be ritually burned by the common executioner, and would see the poet jailed and in danger of joining the regicides on the scaffold. A kinder future was in store for George Downing. In the second week of June the reply came back from the king that he was forgiven. Howard conveyed that Charles would forget past 'deviations' and would accept 'the overtures he [Downing] makes of returning to his duty'. Three weeks afterwards, the new monarch knighted Downing and paid him £1000.

On his reappointment to The Hague, the man who had wished Oliver Cromwell king now oozed loyalty to Charles. He vowed to the king's chief minister, Lord Clarendon, that on pursuing the regicides he would do 'as much as if my life lay at stake'. Indeed, 'if my father were in the way I would not avoid him for my loyalty.'

Downing's first task was to locate the regicides' bolt-holes, 'that I may know where they are and what they do' – far from easy in a country flooded with English fugitives. 'It is not to be credited what numbers of disaffected persons come daily out of England into this country', he reported in his first dispatch, describing the new arrivals from across the Channel as 'well funded and confident . . . [they] do hire the best houses and have great bills of exchange come over from England for them'.

In prising out the regicides from among these exiles, Sir George knew he could expect little co-operation from the Dutch. During his previous incarnation in the Netherlands he had been the agent of a fellow republic and, to an extent, approved of. As the agent of a king, particularly one engaged in the execution of republicans, he was now in hostile country. Decades of bloody war with the Spanish monarchy for control of the Low Countries had left the Dutch more wholeheartedly republican than any people in Europe except perhaps the Swiss. A guide to the Netherlands published in England in 1662 warned: 'The country is a democracy . . . Tell them of a King and they cut your throat in earnest. The very name carries servitude in it and they hate it more than a Jew doth images, a woman old age and a nonconformist a surplice.'

Anti-royalism ran in the veins of the Dutch authorities. Father O'Neill, the Catholic priest dispatched to the Netherlands in the autumn of 1660 to sound out officials about extradition, had got nowhere. Clarendon complained at the Dutch refusal to co-operate, only to receive a lecture from Johan de Witt, the ruling hand in the United Provinces, on his country's tradition of sanctuary. 'Nothing could be done against the liberties of the state', he was told. Dutch resolve was then put to the test by royalist agent Sir William Davidson. In December 1660 Davidson asked the aid of the burgomaster in Amsterdam to apprehend English fugitives there. The burgomaster's response was an order forbidding local police to offer any help at all.

At this early stage we do not know who Downing used as agents to discover the regicides, but presumably many old informants were still present in Holland and Germany and there were potentially many more among new refugees. By no means were all of these as well funded as Downing suggested. Some exiles were in dire financial straits and a few guilders bought their loyalty. Others were suborned and blackmailed into spying while still in England, then sent abroad to mix in exile circles.

Downing would ultimately accumulate a rich mix of informants. Along with the unpredictable adventurer Joseph Bampfield, who had once rescued Charles's younger brother James from the Roundheads dressed as a girl before switching sides to spy for the same Roundheads, and then switching sides again, they included an Irish cutthroat called James Cotter who gloried in his reputation as an assassin. And there was also the bewitching Mata Hari figure of Aphra Behn.

A memorable picture of the efficiency of Downing's agents was later made by his former clerk, Samuel Pepys. Downing had boasted to Pepys of his intelligence coups in the mid-1660s, during the second Anglo-Dutch war. Pepys' diary for 27 December 1668 records:

> Met with Sir G. Downing, and walked with him an hour talking of business, and how the late war was managed, there being nobody to take care of it; and he telling, when he was in Holland ... that he had so good spies, that he hath had the keys taken out of de Witte's pocket when he was abed, and his closet opened and papers brought to him and left in his hands for an hour, and carried back and laid in the place again, and the keys put into his pocket again. He says he hath always had their most private debates, that have been but between two or three of the chief of them, brought to him in an hour after, and an hour after that hath sent word thereof to the king.

In June 1661 Downing's informants reported sightings of five fugitives, some in the Netherlands and others in Germany – George

'Cornet' Joyce, Edward Dendy, John Barkstead, John Hewson and John Okey.[14] Of the five only Barkstead, Hewson and Okey had been among the king's judges, but the other two were each considered sufficiently implicated in Charles's fate to deserve a traitor's death.

Joyce, the young officer responsible for seizing Charles I from custody at Holmby House, thus arguably setting off the chain of events that led to the king's trial and execution, had fled to Rotterdam in the summer of 1660. He was living there with his wife and children when spotted by Downing's men.[15]

Like Joyce, Edward Dendy was not among the king's judges. His part in Charles I's death was as master of ceremonies. He was the House of Commons sergeant-at-arms in 1649 who proclaimed the indictment against Charles with much pomp. Unlike some other servants of the republican cause, he appears to have received little reward for his unique service. In the 1650s he was granted some land in Ireland plus part of the profits from the sale of royal forests. He was also made governor of the Marshalsea prison, which housed government prisoners, who had to pay him for their keep. At other times and in other prisons governors made fortunes from prisoners' fees. Dendy claimed that he didn't. He complained that he received only £80 over two and a half years because the government sent its richest prisoners not to him but to the Tower.[16]

The keeper of the Tower at the time, and a far richer man, was John Barkstead, the second fugitive spotted in Europe by Downing's spies. Barkstead was said to have made a colossal £2000 a year from fees. A contemporary complained that his exactments were so extortionate that 'it stinks in the nostrils of both good and bad'. Barkstead was one of the king's judges and had signed the death warrant in a strong, decisive hand. The son of a goldsmith, he took up arms for Parliament at the outset of the Civil War and rose from the rank of captain to become a major-general and governor of several strategic towns. According to Edmund Ludlow, Barkstead joined the struggle because of 'the invasions which had been made upon the liberties of the nation'. That meant political liberties, certainly not behavioural liberties. Barkstead was one of the major-generals appointed in 1655–7 to give 'Godly rule' to England and he strove enthusiastically to do so, personifying the grim, killjoy Puritan. His bailiwick was Westminster, Middlesex and London. In what was a whirlpool of ungodliness, Barkstead tried to banish not only the more barbarous pleasures but the more innocent too. Shakespeare's Globe Theatre was pulled down. Prostitutes were arrested, with some shipped to America into virtual slavery. The bear garden in Bankside was closed. The horses of those caught riding on Sundays were confiscated. Cock-fighting and cock-throwing (stoning a cockerel tied to a stake) were banned. Maypoles were cut down. Under Puritan jurisdiction a woman caught in adultery faced death. The wealthy, money-grabbing, misery Barkstead was not a popular figure. Wisely, Barkstead had joined the exodus in the summer of 1660 and was now living in the prosperous Prussian town of Hanau, twenty-five kilometres from Frankfurt, becoming a burgess of the town and thus securing some measure of protection.

One-eyed John Hewson was if anything an even more unpopular figure, a man particularly hated in Ireland and in London too. Never allowed to forget his humble origins as a shoemaker, Hewson had proved an outstanding soldier in the Civil Wars. He was also a ruthless bigot. In Ireland, where he lost an eye in battle, he took a leading part in the terrible sack of Drogheda in which at least two thousand royalist and Catholic troops were killed after refusing to surrender. Like Cromwell, Hewson justified the massacre as God's will. He warned after Drogheda that if the Irish did not submit, 'the Lord by his power shall break them in pieces like a potter's vessel.' When Cromwell appointed Hewson to the peerage, royalists sneered at the idea of a former cobbler sitting in the House of Lords. It was claimed that the Earl of Warwick, the senior peer on Parliament's side, was so affronted at the appointment of one of such low blood that he refused to take his seat. As for the hatred that Londoners bore for him, this stemmed from that incident in December 1659 when he ordered troops to fire on rioting apprentices and there were a number of deaths. The apprentices had used old shoes as ammunition to throw at Hewson's soldiers. Now in frail health, Hewson was living in Rotterdam.

The fifth exile to have been sighted in Europe by Downing's informants was John Okey, his old commanding officer. An altogether more attractive figure than Barkstead or Hewson, Okey's record suggests him to have been heroic both in battle and in politics, but inconsistent and a poor disciplinarian. A brilliant cavalry leader, like most of the regicides Okey was an ardent Puritan, sometimes too much so for his men. He attempted to sack a captain suspected of holding the anarchistic views of the Ranters, who rejected all authority, believing God to be in every living thing. Okey charged the officer with singing bawdy songs. However, the captain was backed by his men and Cromwell himself had to be brought in to resolve the matter, which he did by persuading the officer to resign.

Okey had not only served as a judge at the king's trial, he also supervised security at the execution and so was doubly damned in royalist eyes. To the end he would justify his role in 1649, insisting that he had borne no malice towards the king. His subsequent career showed him to be as strong a republican as he was a Puritan. He helped Cromwell to crush the Levellers but when the future Lord Protector began to assume a monarch's mantle, Okey opposed him every step of the way. His opposition saw him line up with his old Leveller enemy at one point, then tried for his life at another. Having later openly challenged George Monck and finally joined John Lambert's force in the doomed effort to stop the restoration by force of arms, Okey unlike Lambert had avoided capture when his troops surrendered at Daventry. Subsequently making his escape, like Barkstead he had found a haven in Hanau.

There is no record of Downing's personal attitude to the five fugitives. But he must have known all of them well. He had served under Okey, who according to some contemporaries had been his friend

and mentor. He had sat as an MP and would have regularly seen
Hewson, who sat in the upper house. As a government intelligencer
it is inconceivable that Downing had not been closely acquainted
with Barkstead. No one was better placed to smell out the next conspiracy than the keeper of the Tower of London, with its gossipy
population of political prisoners. Cromwell said of England's grand-
est prison: 'There never was any design on foot but we could hear of
it out of the Tower.' The Marshalsea too held men jailed for their politics, and Dendy as its keeper would also have been a magnet for
Downing.

The question of how to bring these men back to England and to
the scaffold occupied Downing and Secretary Clarendon for much
of the summer of 1661. They eventually decided to make Edward
Dendy in Rotterdam their first target, but first they needed to
square the Dutch to his abduction. The opportunity to do so came
with the opening in The Hague of negotiations over a trade treaty
with the Dutch. Downing led the English delegation and pressed
for the inclusion of an extradition clause in the treaty. Initially
Johan de Witt was uninterested, but, after days of wrangling, he
gave Downing what he wanted, agreeing to a clause that entitled
the English to extradite regicides automatically with no right of
appeal and – according to Downing – giving a secret promise that
if any regicides were caught before the treaty came into force,
they too would be extradited. De Witt agreed with Downing that
the extradition should be swift because of the uproar it would
unleash.[17]

Few details survive of the subsequent plan to abduct Dendy. All
we can deduce from the archives is that some time in August 1661,
a kidnap team was assembled in Rotterdam ready to snatch him,
and that the royal yacht was moored in the port ready for a quick
getaway. Come the appointed day, all that was needed was a warrant for the arrest and extradition. Downing wanted the names of
his targets left out of the warrant so nobody could warn them.
Then, with everything in place, de Witt refused to issue a warrant

without the names. Furious, George Downing scrabbled around for someone in the States-General who could rescue the situation, eventually persuading Admiral Jacob van Wassenaer Obdam to authorise a warrant. But the States-General baulked at giving Downing a blank warrant and the name of Dendy had to be revealed. Before it could be served, Dendy had been alerted and he fled the country.

Dendy's narrow escape alerted all the regicides. Some vanished from sight, others became extra cautious. Downing ruefully reported that the exiles were 'perpetually changing their abode else that way we agreed [would have] taken them. For the murderers nothing protects them here but their continual removings from place to place, never being two nights in a place.'[18]

Another disappointment followed the Dendy failure. Death put John Hewson out of reach. The 'child of wrath' died of ill health in Rotterdam early in September. Hewson's life history described a perfect arc, from obscurity as a cobbler to Civil War colonel, to regicide, to the House of Lords (though only briefly in 1658) and back to obscurity. Sir William Davidson conveyed the news to Downing and made a suggestion, perhaps in jest but possibly serious: 'That rogue Hewson ... Seeing we could not get him apprehended in his lifetime ... you might get him taken out of his grave and send him for England.'[19] In the event Hewson's body stayed where it was.

Death by natural causes deprived the hunters of several other quarry that autumn, including one of Oliver Cromwell's brothers-in-law, Valentine Walton. Inevitably high on the list of wanted men, Walton had fled in 1660. He too settled in Hanau but eventually quit Germany in fear of royalist killers, finally going to ground in Flanders where he scraped a meagre living as a gardener. He kept his identity secret until he was on his death bed.

Reviewing the difficulties involved in kidnapping the regicides, Downing casually suggested murdering them. In a dispatch to the Earl of Clarendon in the autumn of 1661, he wrote: 'what if the king should authorize some trusty persons to kill them ... let me have the king's serious thoughts about this business.' If Charles did give the idea some thought, nothing was put down on paper, and the secretary of state moved quickly to disassociate himself and the king from the idea. Charles would never countenance murder, he insisted.

The breakthrough Downing needed came in September when he found the weak link in the chain of friends protecting the exiles in Germany. An English merchant living in the city of Delft was revealed as the front man for some of the exiles. His name was Abraham Kicke and he acted as the regicides' post box. Much of their correspondence with wives back in England appears to have gone through him, as did the odd bundle of money sent to keep them going. Little is known about Kicke except that he had the regicides' trust. Barkstead called him 'my real friend'. That would prove a fatal misjudgment. Kicke turned out to be weak, equal to anyone in treachery and as money-grabbing as Barkstead himself.

An acute judge of human weakness, George Downing took the measure of Kicke after a single meeting, divining that money and threats would overcome whatever loyalty the merchant felt for the regicides, and quickly proved it. Kicke was given a choice by Downing: a reward of £200 per head for every regicide he helped to snare or the ruin of his business if he didn't co-operate. From that point on, the merchant was in the control of George Downing and a saga of betrayal began. It would climax in triumph for Downing and disaster for the regicides.

16

ON THE WORD OF A KING

September 1661–July 1663

As George Downing prepared to spring his trap in Holland, the baying for more blood rang out in England. Charles stirred the calls by ordering another clear-out of offending corpses from Westminster Abbey, and the newly elected House of Commons tried to pave the way for another round of mass executions.

The removal of corpses took place in September. Out came the remains of Isaac Dorislaus, the assassinated regicide; Admiral Robert Blake, the scourge of the Dutch and the French navies, and two other admirals; two colonels; several divines; a historian; Cromwell's beloved mother and sister; and John Pym MP, the parliamentary titan whom Charles I had come stamping into the Commons to arrest in 1642. The remains were dumped in a pit dug in the grounds of St Margaret's church, next door to the abbey.

The new House of Commons would turn out to be still more royalist than its predecessor and would quickly be known as the Cavalier Parliament. One of its first decisions was to instruct the common hangman to burn the 'treacherous' Act setting up the High Court that tried the king. It followed up by instructing the solicitor-general to prepare a Bill authorising the executions of regicides who had been condemned in the October 1660 show trials but were given hope by a decision to leave their fates to a future Parliament. The favourites to escape a repeat of the brutal deaths of October 1660 were those who had given themselves up by the deadline set out by Charles in his proclamation the previous June, assuming that he had given his word that they would not die. Eleven of them were hauled before the Commons in November and asked why they should escape execution. All had spent more than a year in the Tower or other prisons and they seem to have been cowed by their experience. Most made no attempt to justify their own action, instead throwing themselves on the king's mercy. One claimed he had been tricked by Cromwell into serving as a judge, and three that they had become involved in the trial in order to help the king. The big exception was Harry Marten. Typically he made a dangerous joke of it. The bon viveur of the Rump Parliament told MPs that he had never obeyed any proclamation before this, and hoped that he should not be hanged for taking the king's word now.[1]

In February 1662 the Bill authorising more executions had passed all its key stages and the hangman must have been preparing. Before the next batch of prisoners could be selected, George Downing provided other victims.

At the end of the previous year, two of the regicides in Germany had taken a decision that put them into Downing's hands. John Okey and John Barkstead agreed to venture out of Frankfurt and risk meeting their wives in Holland. Their intentions were set out in a letter written by Barkstead to his 'real friend', Abraham Kicke. The projected meeting place was to be Kicke's home in the town of Delft. Barkstead planned to collect money and a trunk of clothes to be brought by his wife. 'Myself and Mr Williamson [Okey] intend to be with you about the latter end of February or the beginning of March and hope there to meet our wives with you.' He added that the women had promised to be present. Kicke received the letter at the beginning of December and passed it on to a delighted George Downing.[2]

The ambassador knew that he could use the extradition clause in the new Anglo-Dutch treaty to snatch the two men legally and bundle them off to England. Anticipating an outraged reaction from the Dutch public and possible attempts at sabotage by the Dutch leadership – after the fiasco over Dendy he had little trust in Johan de Witt – he planned the timing of his moves so tightly no one would be able to stop him. He aimed to be on hand himself to supervise the capture.

Downing also hoped to net more than two of the judges. He suggested that Kicke get word of Okey and Barkstead's visit to Miles Corbet, a regicide living somewhere on the outskirts of Amsterdam, and invite him to supper with the two guests from Germany. Aged eighty-three, Corbet was the oldest of the fugitives. Unlike most of the others, he was no military man, but instead a lawyer who had been a member of the Long Parliament. Corbet's elegant lawyer's signature had been the fifty-ninth and last on Charles I's death warrant. He readily accepted the invitation.

Barkstead was evidently nervous, wanting reassurance before leaving Frankfurt and writing to Kicke asking what risks they would be running in the Netherlands. George Downing dictated the merchant's reply: there was no order to arrest or detain them, wrote Kicke, they 'might be as safe there as himself'.

Okey and Barkstead reached Delft on 4 March 1662, arriving at Abraham Kicke's house early that evening. The men were always prepared for trouble and, beneath their heavy greatcoats, were well armed. But once inside their friend's house they relaxed. Cloaks, greatcoats and arms were discarded and left in a room indicated by their host. At some time later in the evening Kicke slipped away from his guests and, unbeknown to them, locked the room that held the arms, retaining the key.

Timing was everything. Sir George wanted to avoid any repeat of the Dendy episode. With that in his mind, he needed to get the warrant issued and verified as late in the day as possible to lessen the chances of his targets being warned, but early enough so the three men could be seized before their supper party broke up and Corbet went home. He also wanted the trio in irons and safely en route for England before Holland woke up to what was afoot.

In a similar kidnap venture a few years later, the king's royal yacht would be sent ready to transport captives. This time a vessel called the *Blackamoor* had been provided, probably laid on by the Royal Africa Company. This new mercantile venture was largely owned by Charles's brother and heir, James, Duke of York, and their sister the Duchess of Orléans. The *Blackamoor* lay moored and waiting in Rotterdam.

There is no record of the talk that evening but there must have been much to catch up on. It was at least eighteen months since Corbet had seen his two fellow fugitives and in that time the world had turned upside down. Perhaps the three men mulled over the betrayal by General Monck, or Okey's attempts to stop him. Perhaps they read together some of the last speeches of their friends, the fellow regicides who had been executed and whom they regarded as martyrs. No doubt they speculated on the vulnerability of the Stuart regime and the chances now for the success of the Good Old Cause. Presumably there was also talk of hearth and home and some excitement at the arrival next day of two of their wives. Perhaps, too, they talked of Okey's old comrade Sir George Downing, and praised God that he and not some vengeful royalist was the ambassador here.

Accompanied by three English officers serving as mercenaries in Holland, along with some sailors, presumably from the *Blackamoor*, Downing was hidden in a house nearby. He had set the wheels in motion early that afternoon, arriving at Johan de Witt's home with a request for a warrant and informing the Dutch leader that he was presenting him with an opportunity to do the king of England a 'most acceptable kindness'. There were, as Downing expected, long delays. Not till early evening was the warrant ready and then it had to be rushed to Delft.

As the minutes went by, Kicke became worried. He told Downing

later that Miles Corbet ('the hunchback', he called him) was showing signs of leaving, which might mean only two regicides in the
net – and £200 less for himself. One imagines the old man getting up
from the fireside table and beginning to make his farewells when
there was a knock at the door. In his report to Clarendon, Downing
gloated over what happened next:

> Knocking at the door one of the house came to see who it was
> and the door being open, the under Scout and the whole com-
> pany rushed immediately into the house, and into the room
> where they were sitting by a fireside with a pipe of tobacco and
> a cup of beer. Immediately they started up to have got out at a
> back door but it was too late, the room was in a moment full.
> They made many excuses, the one to have got liberty to fetch
> his coat and another to go to the privy but all in vain.

No doubt the king was thrilled as Clarendon passed him Downing's
dispatch.

There was still hope for the three fugitives. The Delft authorities
had insisted on taking them into local custody and Downing's hopes
of a quick departure were thwarted. The following day news of the
Englishmen's seizure spread, a crowd gathered outside the Delft
prison and there was immediate pressure on the local magistrates to
release them. Amsterdam magistrates sent a message to their Delft
colleagues calling on them to 'Let the gates of the prison open', and
the chief bailiff at the prison warned that 'the common people will
force the gates'.

Another day passed before bribery and sheer opportunism won the
day for Downing. Two English merchants arrived offering payoffs to
the bailiffs to release the prisoners. Downing offered more and stationed one of his men in the cells to ensure they didn't vanish
overnight. Finally he fixed them legally. The Delft authorities offered
the three the chance to receive legal advice and on their behalf
found a friend to seek out the best advocate available. The 'friend'

was Abraham Kicke. Perhaps his dinner guests still did not realise that he had betrayed them, or perhaps the Dutch authorities asked him without consulting the three. On leaving the prison, Kicke went straight to the waiting Downing, and Downing – doubtless hugging himself – provided an advocate who could be trusted not only to fail but to ensure that no other lawyer was brought in. The three men were handed back to Downing.

On 16 March, *Mercurius Publicus* carried a report that the *Blackamoor* and her cargo was off Gravesend and His Majesty had ordered a barge 'with a sufficient guard of soldiers to receive and conduct them to the Tower where they are to be kept closed prisoner till further order. They are expected there by this night's tide.'

A month later, on 16 April, the three were brought to court, in order, in the words of the Lord Chief Justice, 'to offer what they could say for themselves, why execution should not be awarded upon them'. John Okey, saying 'I am ignorant of the law,' asked for access to a counsel. It was refused. Similarly with Barkstead and Corbet. The three were now told that they had only two options – either to plead for the king's mercy or to claim they were not the persons named in the indictment. Confused, and without legal advice, they each chose the second option and watched as witness after witness testified to seeing them sitting among the jurors who had condemned the king. One farsighted observer had attended the whole of the king's trial and noted down the names of jurors every day. Now, twelve years later, he produced his list and read out the names: Okey, Barkstead and Corbet. After another lengthy admonition on their 'horrible crime', they were taken away.

Three days later, Londoners turned out in their thousands to watch the condemned trio dragged on separate sledges from the Tower of London to Tyburn and the scaffold. Extra troops had been drafted in to control the crowds, with *Mercurius Publicus* reporting the mood as being so hostile to the condemned men that the guards barely prevented the people 'anticipating the executioners'.

A very different crowd – perhaps equally big, certainly too big for Charles's comfort – turned up at Okey's funeral. Previously none of the executed regicides had been allowed a Christian burial. After the ritual butchery their heads had been boiled and stuck on spikes in Westminster Hall or London Bridge, their quarters carted away. Okey's interment was to be different. Charles agreed that his body should be treated with respect and interred in the family vault in the East End parish of Stepney. No such concession was offered the families of his two comrades. On the appointed day, the remains were taken to Christ's Church, Stepney. There had been no publicity but the Puritan grapevine sufficed. People began to stream towards Stepney. The news quickly filtered through to Charles that hordes of 'fanatics' were on their way to pay tribute to this murderer of his father. The king – outraged, horrified or both – ordered it stopped. The Sheriff of London was dispatched to Stepney to end the ceremony. By the time he and his constables arrived, however, as many as twenty thousand people were assembled round the church. They were dispersed 'with much harshness and many bitter words', but appear to have gone home peacefully. To prevent another demonstration of solidarity with the 'Godly martyrs', Okey was buried where no crowds could gather – in an unmarked plot, somewhere in the grounds of the Tower of London.

The unexpected beneficiaries of this spectacle were the other regicides awaiting their own deaths. The Bills authorising more executions had reached their final reading but were dropped and up to twenty regicides were saved. Instead of Tyburn they were kept in the Tower or dispersed to strongholds in the furthest reaches of the realm. Why were no more of them executed? Charles's own dwindling blood lust was undoubtedly part of it. As early as the first batch of deaths he had written to Clarendon that he was 'weary' of the hangings. The new butchery can only have increased his distaste. Another factor was the propaganda bonus the 'fanatics' secured from the executions. The victims' heroic performances on the scaffold were retold in pamphlets and books like *Prayers and Speeches of the*

Regicides which were constantly reprinted and turned men who were supposed to be damned for martyring their king into martyrs themselves.

Admiration for the executed men spread beyond London, indeed beyond England. 'Every body here admireth the constancy and resolution of those men who were lately executed in England for having judged the late King', wrote a Paris-based correspondent. Naturally the authorities came down hard on the printers and booksellers. Four men involved in the trade were put on trial for publishing and selling seditious literature. Three were fined, pilloried and imprisoned. The crime of the fourth, a John Twyn, made the king overcome any distaste for spilling more blood. Having published a book entitled A *Treatise on the Execution of Justice*, calling for an end to the royal family, Twyn was sentenced to be hanged, drawn and quartered.

Another display of punishment, had been ordered a few months earlier, to mark the anniversary of the day when the death sentence was passed on the king. Three of his judges were roped to sledges, each with a halter round his neck, and dragged through the streets from the Tower to Tyburn – then back again. None of the three – Sir Henry Mildmay, Viscount Monson and Robert Wallop – had signed the death warrant or had been present when sentence was pronounced, so they didn't qualify as regicides. Indeed all three insisted that they agreed to act as judges in order to help the king. That cut no ice. The trio had all been ardent republicans and they were all sentenced to life and, on top of that, to the humiliating trip to Tyburn. According to Pepys it was to be an annual excursion.[3]

Though regicides like Sir Henry Mildmay and Harry Marten were saved from death, there were two heads which the Cavalier Parliament and the court still seemed determined to have. Neither Sir Harry Vane nor John Lambert was a regicide. But they were regarded as the most dangerous men in the realm: Lambert for his popularity among the thousands of discharged soldiers wandering the country, Vane because of his rhetorical power and appeal to the extremist Fifth Monarchists. Both had been prisoners since 1660, Vane in the castle of St Mary on the Scilly Isles, Lambert on Guernsey in the Channel Islands. The fresh intake of MPs was determined to execute them and circumvent the deal done to save their lives in 1660. That convoluted three-way arrangement had allowed the Lords to claim that it had condemned the two men to death while supposedly ensuring that a death sentence would never be carried out. It involved the two houses jointly excluding Vane and Lambert from pardon and the king pledging to save them if ever they were attainted and faced execution. A joint petition from Parliament embodying the deal went to the king on 5 September 1660. It read:

> That, Your Majesty having declared Your Gracious Pleasure to proceed only against the immediate Murderers of Your Royal Father, we Your Majesty's most humble Subjects, the Lords and Commons in Parliament assembled, not finding Sir Henry Vane or Colonel Lambert to be of that Number; Are humble Suitors to Your Majesty, That, if they shall be attainted, yet Execution as to their Lives may be remitted.[4]

The Lord Chancellor reported that the king had agreed: 'That he had presented the petition of both Houses to the King, concerning Sir Henry Vane and Colonel Lambert; and His Majesty grants the desires in the said petition.'[5] Apparently the two were safe. But, three days after the executions of John Okey and his friends, Vane and Lambert were 'delivered up' into the hands of Sir John Robinson, governor of the Tower of London, preparatory to trial. The Duke of York had dispatched ships to pick up Vane from the Scilly Isles and Lambert from the Channel Islands. The Venetian resident rubbed his hands in anticipation. 'It is believed that when they arrive parliament will make them pay with their lives for their crimes,' he told the Doge.[6]

As the trial approached, Charles was preoccupied with domestic matters. Two months earlier he had married. His queen was a buck-toothed but pretty Portuguese princess, Catherine of Braganza. After greeting his bride-to-be in Portsmouth, the thirty-two-year-old king had rhapsodised over her. 'She has as much agreeable in her looks as ever I saw and if I have any skill in physiognomy which I think that I have, she must be as a good a woman as ever was born,' he wrote to Clarendon. 'I cannot easily tell you how happy I think myself. I must be the worst man living (which I hope I am not) if I be not a good husband.'

He was still more captivated by his mistress Barbara Castlemaine, who made the king eat his words. Determined to assert her presence at court, Lady Castlemaine persuaded Charles to have her appointed first lady to the queen's bedchamber. The tearful and indignant Catherine resisted and Clarendon urged the king to back down. At this Charles exploded. In a letter worthy of a lovesick boy, he warned Clarendon:

> I wish I may be unhappy in this world as well as the world to come if I fail in the least degree of what I have resolved which is of making my lady Castlemaine of my wife's bedchamber. And whosoever I find using any endeavour to hinder this resolve of mine (except it be only myself) I will be his enemy to the last moment of my life.

The issue was still unresolved when Charles was forced to give attention to John Lambert and Harry Vane. On 6 June 1662 the two were charged in Westminster Hall, the scene of past triumphs for each of them. Neither was given advance notice of the indictment nor given a copy in court, and both must have been shocked when the charges were read out to them. They referred not to the 1640s but to 1659 and rested on the novel assertion that Charles II had been *de jure* king of England at the time, even though he was in fact a wandering exile. John Lambert, who had helped reinstate the Rump and led its troops into battle that year, was indicted for stirring up rebellion against the king. Sir Harry Vane, the politician, was accused of 'compassing and imagining the King's death', contriving 'to subvert the ancient Frame of Government' and preventing the king from 'the exercise of his regal authority'.

Predictably the proceedings that followed were as loaded against the defendants as the show trials of 1660 had been against their friends. Not only were they given no copy of the indictments, but counsel was denied them, the jury was packed with royalists, and they were allowed neither sufficient time to find their own witnesses nor the right to question those who did appear.

Cool but apologetic, Lambert made no challenge to the charges but stressed his loyalty. Described by a foreign observer of the trial as 'trying to excuse and justify the crimes of which he was accused', he was 'for all the world not upset about them and did not speak to deny his deeds, but tried all the time to make them appear less serious, and appealed to the King's Mercy, by which he won the judges' hearts'.[7] Lambert was nevertheless found guilty of treason and sentenced to be hanged, drawn and quartered.

Vane took the prosecution on and argued every point. Everything he had done was ordered by Parliament, he insisted, and Parliament, not the absent Charles, was sovereign at the time. It was not possible to commit treason against a king not in possession of the crown. The prosecution accused him of insolence, telling him that his own defence 'was a fresh charge against him, and the highest evidence of his inward guilt'.[8]

On the second day of the trial Charles decided to break his word and deny Vane a pardon. He wrote to Clarendon about Vane: 'He is too dangerous a man to let live, if we can honestly put him out of the way.' The king was reported to have been particularly incensed by Vane's insistence that he could not be regarded as de facto monarch when in exile. Sir Harry was duly found guilty and sentenced to the tortured death of a traitor. Charles refused the promised royal pardon and an equally tortured way was found to show that the king's honour was intact despite his broken word. Lord Chief Justice Foster announced that the gift of mercy did not abide with the king but with God, and God intended mercy only for the penitent. Vane, of course, remained thoroughly unrepentant.

Charles did, however, keep his promise to John Lambert. He was spared death and returned to Guernsey, initially to be held in close confinement, but later he was allowed to buy a house there and live with his wife Frances. Guards were told to shoot him if he was ever found colluding with enemies of the king.

In the end, Sir Harry Vane was spared a traitor's death. Charles, perhaps in recompense for his broken pledge, agreed to his being beheaded. On 14 June, Vane stood on the scaffold before a vast crowd on Tower Hill and began to deliver his last speech. The sheriff standing nearby attempted to snatch his notes but Vane evaded him and began to speak. Immediately a thunder of drums beneath his feet drowned out his words. An array of drummers and trumpeters were stationed under the scaffold. Since Thomas Harrison's unexpected oratory at Charing Cross, the authorities had learned new tricks about information management. Every time Sir Harry began a sentence the cacophony sounded.

Vane died unheard by most in the crowd but he died well. 'In all things,' wrote Pepys, 'he appeared the most resolved man that ever died in that manner.'[9] To the chagrin of the court, a copy of the speech which Vane had tried to give above the drumming and trumpeting was smuggled out. It was as impressive as the authorities feared.

While the captive regicides might now be spared death, that did not hold for the dozen or more fugitives abroad. Catching and killing them – or just killing them – remained a priority. In the next two years the hunters would score in France and Switzerland.

In France, they tracked down Archibald Johnston, Lord Wariston. After the Marquis of Argyll, Johnston was probably the Scot most hated by the supposedly forgiving Charles. He was the leading Covenanter, who had imposed humiliating terms on Charles when he sought support in 1650 and 1651. But that was not all. Wariston, the epitome of the stern Calvinist, is said to have been horrified at the unabashed licentiousness of the young king. In one incident Wariston upbraided Charles for reportedly forcing himself on a noblewoman. It is said that the alleged royal rapist never forgave Wariston for his temerity.[10]

Wariston was the one Covenanter leader to escape the dragnet ordered by Charles in July 1660 after Argyll's arrest. Wariston fled to France and then Germany, where he established himself in Hamburg. One year later, in May 1661, a decree of forfeiture and death was issued against him in Edinburgh. He was accused of high treason in accepting office from Cromwell, sitting in the upper house after having been appointed King's Advocate by Charles I, and of persecuting royalists.[11]

Wariston was finally traced after his name was mentioned during the panic over the so-called Tong Plot in the autumn of 1662. This was yet another alleged assassination plot against the king involving the seizure of Windsor Castle. Once again informants alleged that Edmund Ludlow was involved, Sir Ralph Verney reporting that Ludlow was to have led a rising on Lord Mayor's Day in London, 'about noon, when all were busy, or at night when all were drunk'. Hundreds were hauled in for questioning. The most talkative was an ex-halberdier in Oliver Cromwell's regiment who poured out names with blood-curdling examples of what fellow ex-soldiers were saying they would do to the king.[12] He accused in particular Captain Robert Johnston, another ex-halberdier. What he had to say prompted the authorities to arrest Johnston on suspicion of treason and led Charles himself to attend his interrogation.

This was not the king's first trip to the Tower to see alleged traitors face to face and quiz them himself, nor would it be his last. He had led the interrogations of the men entangled in the White Plot at the outset of his reign in 1660 and would continue to personally question men thought to threaten the throne. Among those he was to face in the future was the odious Titus Oates, author of the fictitious Popish Plot in 1678.

In the assessment of historian Alan Marshall, Charles was 'rather good at it', judging from his interrogation of Titus Oates more than a decade later. 'The King had the blend of wit and nastiness in his character that would have been valuable in such an area.'[13] It certainly appears to have worked on Johnston, who poured out the names of dissidents, among them that of Wariston. Johnston told Charles that the Covenanter leader was in Hamburg but had recently travelled to Holland. It is unclear what happened next, but papers in the National Archives show that within the month Johnston was acting as a government informer, though a deeply reluctant one.[14]

Johnston's reports reveal him homing in on Wariston's wife, who was in London. He appears either to have become, or already to have been, very close to her. Given that he shared a surname with the Waristons, the suspicion arises that he was a family member. He told his handler: 'Wrote her letters and knew all her secrets.' Through Lady Wariston he got to hear of her close circle of friends, which included the wives of other fugitive republicans, among them Frances Goffe and Mary Whalley. In one undated note he wrote: 'Mrs Cawley whose husband was one of the King's judges not yet discovered [found] lodges at her brother's in Red Cross Street [and] is intimate with the wives of Ludlow, Goffe and Whalley and might know where they live.' Another wife in the circle – now a widow – was Lady Vane.[15]

Late in 1662, Johnston discovered that Lady Wariston planned to meet her husband in Rouen. This risky trip was apparently undertaken following the king's rejection of a plea for clemency sent on Wariston's behalf. The couple hadn't seen each other for over two years and Wariston was an ill man. Evidently he was willing to take the risk of leaving the safety of Hamburg to see his wife. One Alexander Murray, commonly called Crooked Murray, was assigned to follow her. Unwittingly she led Murray straight to her husband in Rouen. Wariston had allowed 'a great bushy beard' to grow and wore a periwig as a disguise, but he was easily identified. Murray's men seized him while he was at prayer.

Unlike the Dutch republicans, the French under Louis XIV provided no impediment to the extradition of fugitives from the Stuarts. The king's council debated the case and thought of refusing extradition, but on Louis's orders allowed Murray to depart with his prisoner. Wariston was lodged in the Tower in January 1663 and held for six months, before being shipped to Edinburgh to hear in the Scottish Parliament the sentence passed on him in his absence.

Two and a half years on the run had left Wariston a wreck of a man who was now showing all the signs of dementia. But family pleas to stop his appearance because of his health were ignored and on 8 July he went before Parliament. He was 'so disordered both in body and mind, that it was a reproach to a government to proceed against him', wrote his nephew, Gilbert Burnet, Bishop of Salisbury. 'His memory was so gone that he did not know his own children ... It was apparent that age, hardship, and danger, had done their work effectually on his iron nerves, and the intrepid advocate of the covenant exhibited the mental imbecility of an idiot.'[16]

Wariston's family lobbied to save him and offered the usual bribes to those close to the king. It was futile. Bishop Burnet wrote, 'We solicited all the hungry courtiers. Many that had a great mind to our money tried what could be done but they all found it was a thing too big for them to meddle with.'[17]

Like Argyll two years before, Wariston was executed at Edinburgh's Mercat Cross. He had to be helped to haul himself up the ladder onto the scaffold but once there recovered his wits sufficiently to read out a speech denying all responsibility for Charles I's death. Royalists claimed he had faked senility in an attempt to save his life. Presbyterians referred to the notorious rape by the young king and claimed Wariston was a victim of Charles's vindictiveness. 'The real cause of his death', wrote James Aikman, was 'our king's personal hatred' following the dressing-down given to him by Wariston after the incident. 'This the king could never forgive'.[18]

17

THE TIGHTENING NET

1663–1665

The abduction and execution of Barkstead, Corbet and Okey filled the fugitive regicides with dread. Royalist spies were active across the Continent, making kidnapping or death a possibility at any time. Worse still, most of the regicides suspected – some were even certain – that royalist agents knew where they lived. The murders of Ascham and Dorislaus – though they had happened more than a decade before – were recalled with a shudder. The exiled regicides felt like hunted animals. It was no way to live, yet it was the only way to live.

The fugitives were keenly aware of the activity of royalist agents, with both sides' antennae twitching for reports of the other's movements. Despite the appeal of Holland and Germany, most of the fugitives chose Switzerland. The country had an attraction as a centre of the Protestant Reformation, with several cantons and cities – notably Zurich, Geneva, Bern and Basel – having been early adopters of the new theology. When the reformist priest John Calvin left France, he had moved first to Basel and then Geneva. Prior to the Civil Wars, several of the regicides had travelled to Geneva and had been enthusiastic about its democratic government, its Calvinist history and the present-day teachings of reformist theologians such as John Deodati, who had entranced John Milton and John Cook.

By the beginning of 1663, Switzerland was home to William Cawley, Cornelius Holland, John Lisle, Nicholas Love, William Say, Edward Dendy and the two unfortunate clerks to the Court of Justice, Andrew Broughton and John Phelps. The linchpin of the group became Edmund Ludlow, the man around whom so much hope was pinned for a counter-strike against Charles II. Ludlow was a relatively recent arrival in Switzerland, having spent the best part of two years travelling across Europe.

Basic survival was a major preoccupation for most of the run-aways. Few of them spoke any foreign languages. Some had more access to money than others, but even the wealthy found it difficult to extract funds from estates under threat of sequestration. Some would be forced to throw themselves on the charity of their foreign hosts. Others turned to trade. For magnates like William Cawley, finance was not a problem. During the first Civil War, he had been very active in his local county committee, charged with seizing and selling royalist property. In subsequent years he became a property speculator, opportunistically buying and selling former royalist estates, and grew immensely rich.

From his writings, we know something of how Ludlow managed. He had, he says, a supply of cash with him from England, and he had arranged for money to be available to him through European bankers. Not only did Ludlow have friends and contacts across northern Europe, he had a great ally at home in England. This was his wife, Elizabeth, an able and persuasive individual in her own right.[1] Elizabeth was undoubtedly Ludlow's main lifeline as he progressed through the Continent and into his new life, no doubt helping to maintain channels for funds as he went. Ludlow was so well organised that when he arrived in Geneva he received by post a bill of exchange allowing him to draw on more funds, even though he had no immediate need for them, having so much left over from his initial reserve.[2]

He travelled to Switzerland accompanied by another person, whom he doesn't name but may have been John Phelps. On the way through Europe, he occasionally received news sheets from home, keeping him up to date with events in England. Several times he learned he had been captured; *Mercurius Politicus* once claimed, 'we hear it from very good hands he is already in custody.'[3]

When Ludlow received the sobering news of the trial and execution of Harrison, Carew, Scot and the other regicides, it was a terrible blow. The deaths of friends such as John Cook hit hard, and so too did the betrayal of the Good Old Cause by men such as Denzil Holles, the Earl of Manchester and George Monck, now sitting in judgment and sentencing their old allies to die. When the trial ended, one of the judges, Sir Harbottle Grimston, had made a speech in which he railed against the regicides who had escaped. According to Grimston, there wasn't a plot afoot in England without Ludlow being at the head of it – in fact, Ludlow had recently been about to seize the Tower with a force of 2500 men.[4] (The previous year, the royalist spy Joseph Bampfield had claimed that Ludlow and Desborough were ready to lead a rebellion to coincide with the king's coronation.) It was another demonstration of how propaganda can foreshadow violent action. Royalist secret agents were already tracking the regicides in Europe.

Following the show trial and executions in London, the exiles in Geneva began to feel uneasy. The city lay in a most precarious geographical position, surrounded by French territory except for the wedge of Lake Geneva that sliced in from the north-east. The refugees' greatest fear was that Charles II might use his influence in Paris to persuade France to bring pressure on the small city state to give up its guests, just as Downing had successfully brought pressure to bear on the Netherlands.

As the group's natural leader, Ludlow took it upon himself to obtain assurances from Geneva's ruling councillors, known as syndics, regarding their safety. None of the refugees spoke French, so Ludlow asked his landlord to intercede with a senior councillor,

Monsieur Voisin, on their behalf. Ludlow's man did not come back with the cast-iron guarantees they had hoped for. Instead, he brought promises of help: 'if any letters should come into his hands concerning us, he would give us timely notice, but if such a thing would fall out in the night, he would cause the water-gate, of which he always kept the key, to be opened for our escape, and if we should be obliged to depart by day, we would have a safe passage through any of the city gates that we should choose ...'[5]

To these assurances, Voisin made one further promise: that when his fellow senior syndic Monsieur Dupain came back from a visit to Bern, they would discuss the exiles' safety. Ludlow thought their hosts were doing all they could in trying circumstances. Not all his colleagues agreed. Lisle saw things through a lawyer's eyes and wanted absolute guarantees. Cawley backed him up. As a result of their protestations, the regicides were advised to present their case in person before the entire body of syndics.

This was not at all what Ludlow wanted. As he expected, the presentation was a disaster. One of the syndics, a Monsieur Let, was owed money by Charles II and now saw his repayment put in jeopardy by the presence of English fugitives. The council told the Englishmen to withdraw their application, which was to be reconsidered once the fuss had died down. Ludlow and the rest were in a worse situation than before. They had no option but to find another city to take them.

By late spring in 1662, all three regicides, Ludlow, Lisle and Cawley, were in Lausanne, in the canton of Bern. They had not been there long before they received wretched news – Sir Harry Vane had been executed for treason following a trial that was all too similar in style to the great show trials of autumn 1660.* Ludlow

---

* Ludlow is unclear in his memoirs about just when he heard of Vane's death. He says he learned in a letter in July, two months after he had left Geneva for Lausanne, but he also says he learned when at Geneva. This seems impossible, for Vane died on 14 June.

said of Vane that he possessed 'the highest perfection, a quick and ready apprehension, a strong and tenacious memory, a profound and penetrating judgement, a just and noble eloquence, with an easy and graceful manner of speaking'. These sentiments were echoed by Edward Hyde, even though as Charles's Lord Chancellor he was Vane's political opponent: 'He was, indeed, a man of extraordinary parts; a pleasant wit, a great understanding, which pierced into and discerned the purpose of other men with wonderful sagacity.'[6] Charles's decision to order Vane's death despite all these attributes – or perhaps because of them, as he was 'too dangerous' to be allowed to live – was a sad example of cruel political expediency.

This repugnant act of revenge upon a man who had had nothing whatever to do with the death of Charles I had a profound effect upon the exiles. It demonstrated that Charles II and Parliament would stop at nothing to cut off political opposition, even if it meant manipulating the law to have an innocent man executed. Any lingering hope the Puritan exiles may have had that the royal desire for revenge would soon abate was dashed. Their chances of ever returning home receded far into the distant future.

Meanwhile, other threats against the monarchy were reported in the London press. According to one report, Ludlow was behind a scheme to kill both the king and George Monck, now the Duke of Albemarle. Several thousand unemployed soldiers of the old army were ready, it was said, to march on the City of London, the Tower and Whitehall. According to Ludlow, this was a plot organised by *agents provocateurs* – known at the time as 'trepanners' – as an excuse for rounding up Commonwealth sympathisers. The resultant clampdown led to yet more mass arrests and several executions. The chief organiser, a man named Bradley, was let off. He seems to have been in reality the chief trepanner. News sheets claimed that the authorities had been so close to seizing Ludlow that they had taken his cloak and slippers.

Despite the make-believe, Charles and his ministers had genuine concerns about possible uprisings. The reversal of his promise to allow freedom of conscience regarding religion had gone down badly and the new restrictions were openly defied in churches up and down the country. The execution of Harry Vane was poorly received, even by many royalists. Pepys said of the feeling against the king, 'they do much cry up the manner of Sir H Vane's death, and he [the king] deserves it.' To make matters worse, Charles had fallen out with his new wife Catherine of Braganza on their honeymoon, while the people had turned against her on seeing her attend her mother-in-law's old Catholic chapel, which had been done up and reopened. To the people, this did not reflect well on Charles, with rumours flying about his own religious affiliation.

In Lausanne, matters were taking a more serious turn. According to Ludlow's memoirs, a plot was hatched to assassinate him. As the memoirs tell it, the sum of 10,000 crowns was offered via the Duchess of Orléans to a 'person of quality' who lived in or around Lausanne for his murder. The duchess was Henrietta Anne, Charles's favourite sister, who had recorded her father's words to her on the eve of his execution, now married to the openly homosexual Philippe, brother to Charles XIV. It was unlikely that Henrietta, a cultured and flirtatious member of the French court, would have instigated such a plot unaided. Nor is there any way of knowing if the plot really existed; however, in the light of the events that followed, it is not impossible. If it did exist, it seems likely that it originated within the court of Charles II.[7]

In the autumn of 1662, the English group at Lausanne grew rapidly in numbers. Ludlow's stature was undoubtedly a draw to others, but more important was the knowledge that the Canton of Bern had offered official protection. During September and October, seven more exiles arrived.* With John Phelps probably

---

* This list, as near as we can make out, is: Slingsby Bethel, Andrew Broughton, Edward Dendy (fresh from his narrow escape in Rotterdam), Cornelius Holland, Nicholas Love, William Say and a Colonel John Bisco, who had sided with Lambert against Monck in the convulsions of 1660.

already in Lausanne, the total number of resident fugitives was now at least twelve.

Several of the new arrivals, including William Say, the lawyer and legislator, had passed through the city of Bern. There they made contact with the eminent English-speaking clergyman Johann Heinrich Hummel, who welcomed them and passed on the information that more of their group could be found at Lausanne; and so they travelled on. Once they had arrived in Lausanne and made contact with their fellow countrymen it was decided a letter of thanks should be sent to Hummel and the canton authorities. The reply they received was not what they expected. They were advised to relocate to Vevey, a pretty but relatively obscure town some twenty miles further east along the shores of Lake Geneva. The Bern authorities wanted to help but they didn't want it widely known that they were doing so.

Six of the exiles – Ludlow, Say, Lisle, Bethel, Cawley and Holland – elected to go to Vevey. Among those who decided to stay behind were Phelps and Colonel Bisco who, though not a regicide, felt he was under threat at home as he had taken up arms against Monck. Their reason for remaining sheds further light on the financial pressures the fugitives were under. According to Ludlow, these two had bought goods at Geneva and elsewhere and wished to see if they could sell those goods in Germany and Holland so as to 'improve the stock of money they had'.[8]

At Vevey, the magistrates and council greeted the exiles with great ceremony, praising them for their sufferings in the service of liberty. It seemed the exiles had finally found what they sought: political asylum. One of the members of the town council, a Monsieur Dubois, gave them a house in which to stay. It was on the edge of the town by the lake, beside the town walls; its slightly isolated position made the approach of any suspicious characters easier to spot. We know that Ludlow continued to reside in Dubois's house but, given the numbers of individuals involved, we must assume the regicides moved into a number of residences, though there is no record of their living arrangements.

In the autumn of 1663, Algernon Sidney came to call on Ludlow at his new home at 47 Rue du Lac. An aristocratic war hero who had been seriously wounded at the decisive battle of Marston Moor while leading a cavalry charge, Sidney was also a political theorist whose thinking underwent a profound change during the Commonwealth and Protectorate. Sidney had been appointed as one of the king's judges in 1649, but refused to serve, stating in one of his many famous phrases that 'first, the king could be tried by no man; secondly, that no man could be tried by that court.'[9] By 1659 he had changed his mind, calling the king's execution 'the justest and bravest act'.[10] As a republican, Sidney was an ardent foe of Oliver Cromwell. When Charles II gained the throne he was overseas on diplomatic duty. Given his republican views, he decided to stay away.

Sidney took up residence in Rome, a city he knew and whose culture he admired, though he distrusted the papal Church. While Charles's spies were tracking other republicans around northern Europe, Sidney must have thought Rome a most unlikely place from which to be suspected of launching plots or rebellions. He was received warmly by Roman society and the pope's nephew, Prince Pamphili, lent him a house. As so often, money was the worry. He was still owed money from his diplomatic work and was broke. He lived on a small allowance of five shillings a day from his father, the 2nd Earl of Leicester. With little money, Sidney threw himself into study and began to enjoy life in the city. His studious idyll did not last long. Even in Rome, assassins planned his death. The details are unknown but he was saved, he recorded, 'only by the charity of strangers'.[11]

Sidney left Rome to go to Brussels and Holland. En route, he stopped off to see the exiles in Vevey. In particular, he wished to see Ludlow. In the last days of the Commonwealth, Ludlow had suggested to Cromwell that Sidney should be made second-in-command of the army in Ireland. The appointment was never carried out; the support of the House of Stuart by some of Sidney's aristocratic relations put paid to that. Sidney and Say were also acquainted: they had been colleagues on the Commonwealth's foreign affairs committee prior to the imposition of the Protectorate.

We only know in the most general way what Sidney and the Vevey group talked about, but there is no doubting that it revolved around the possibility of unseating Charles Stuart – as Sidney might have put it in another of his oft-quoted sayings, 'God helps those who help themselves.' In his memoirs, *A Voyce from the Watchtower*, Ludlow described how the still-fragile state of the court of Charles II provided a background to Sidney's visit:

> The divisions of our enemies began to heighten ye hopes of friends touching ye approaching of our deliverance, in so much that Col. Algernon Sidney ... now thinks it seasonable to draw towards his native country, in expectation of an opportunity wherein he might be more active for their service; and in his way was pleased to favour us with a visit ...[12]

From this we know that conversation included discussion about how to restore the Commonwealth, for both men were ardent republicans. The persecution of Puritans roused Sidney to anger.[13] Due to several new Acts known, after the Earl of Clarendon, as the Clarendon Code, those who did not take the sacraments in a parish church (i.e. all Puritans, Baptists and other nonconformists) could not hold public office and all public worship by nonconformists was illegal. The effect upon Sidney and Ludlow of news of the religious clampdown in England cannot be overestimated; as Blair Worden's discoveries of manuscripts written by both men has shown us, religious enthusiasm coloured the glass through which they viewed the world.[14] To top it all, there came new rumours that the king was a Roman Catholic.

Sidney's stay in Vevey lasted three weeks. He left Ludlow with a present of a pair of pistols made by the most famous of Italian gunsmiths, Lazarino Cominazzo of Brescia. For the impecunious Sidney to bestow such an expensive present was deeply significant: he was hoping to entice Ludlow into leading an uprising to unseat Charles.

Leaving the cautious Ludlow to ponder his future, and that of the republican ideals both men believed in, Sidney headed on in search of his elusive victorious army. In the visitors' book of the Calvinist Academy in Geneva, he wrote in memory of Harry Vane, 'Let there be revenge for the blood of the just.'

In October 1663, an armed uprising took place in the north of England. It was largely inspired by the king's new policies, which forbade any cleric from preaching that had not been ordained by a bishop of the Church of England. The rebellion, which was small in scale, was led by a Congregationalist minister named Edward Richardson. Men gathered to join the rising in Yorkshire, Westmorland and Durham, but the numbers were low and the rebellion easily crushed. Richardson fled to the Netherlands. Ludlow's name was again raised in royalist propaganda as being behind it all. There was an uprising in Ireland, too. An attempt to seize Dublin Castle was led by Captain Thomas Blood, the Irish parliamentarian soldier who would later attempt to steal the crown jewels. The Dublin plot was betrayed and most of its participants executed. Captain Blood escaped.

In Vevey, there was cause for rejoicing: Ludlow and Cawley's wives arrived to join them. Cawley was by now quite sick with an illness from which he would never recover. He described this as a 'wide and incurable rupture in the intestines with a spice of the stone'.[15] The women's departure from England and arrival in Vevey was noted in London. For some time, the regicides' wives had been under scrutiny by Joseph Williamson's security apparatus. Their mail was read for clues about the actions and whereabouts of their husbands. Their support was also the fugitives' Achilles' heel.

Ludlow and some of the others decided to visit Bern to assure the authorities of their gratitude and so solidify their position. The syndic assured them that they remained honoured guests. No sooner had the Englishmen returned to Vevey than they received intelligence that a certain 'Riordo' was now in Turin and was on a mission to kill them.

'Riordo', also known as Major Germaine (or sometimes John) Riordane, was an Irish officer who had once served in the Duke of York's Regiment. Having left his commission and fallen on hard times, Riordane now sought, like many Irish soldiers, to find work where he could. For Riordane, this included the desperate world of espionage and murder. According to Ludlow, Riordane's real name was MacCarty and he had become a hired assassin for the English crown. Apart from information about MacCarty, the exiles also heard that Charles II had written to the authorities in Bern asking them to give up the English rebels. Although they hardly knew it yet, Ludlow and the rest of the group now had their backs to the wall.

From the fact that Riordane corresponded directly with Lord Arlington, secretary of state, spymaster and chief procurer of the king's mistresses, it was clear he was under the direction of Charles's government at the highest level. It is true that there is no paper evidence that Riordane was instructed by the authorities in London to do any more than seek out the regicides, but Arlington and his head of intelligence, Williamson, were far too wise to commit any base instruction to paper. However, as Ludlow discovered, Riordane was also in the employ of (or was at least paid by) the king's sister, Henrietta, the Duchess of Orléans, whom he often used to pass information to members of the French court, including Louis XIV himself.

The little group of exiles received intelligence of other death threats. As Ludlow recorded:

> Divers letters from Turin, Geneva, Lyons, and other places, which we and our friends at Vevey received, were full of advices from those parts, that so many, and such desperate persons had engaged against us, that it would be next to impossible to escape their hands. And one of my best friends, who was then at Geneva, sent a messenger express to me, with a letter to inform me, That he had received a billet from a person who knew our friendship, and desired not to be known, with these

expressions at the end, 'If you wish the preservation of the English General at Vevay, let him know, that he must remove from thence with speed, if he have any regard to his own safety.'[16]

Such frantic warnings placed the Ludlows and their companions in an awkward situation. They had promises of protection where they were, but if they moved, they might not be able to obtain the same level of protection. Ludlow received information that Riordane had been seen in the Pais de Vaux and Savoy. Alarmed by such reports, the Vevey group considered their options. Despite the dangers of remaining where they were, they decided they didn't want to play cat-and-mouse across Europe with men like Riordane. They concluded that with the protection in Vevey 'so frankly, publicly, and generously extended', the best option was to stay put. Meanwhile, Charles II's agents were closing in. Riordane reported to London that many of the king's murderers, including Ludlow, Lisle, Whalley and Goffe, were now in Vevey. While his intelligence was right on the first two, it was completely wrong on the others, for Whalley and Goffe were in a different continent. Riordane even suggested that one of Oliver Cromwell's sons was in Switzerland; he doesn't say which one, though it most likely would have been Richard.[17]

No sooner had they decided to remain in Vevey than a group of 'villains that had been employed to destroy us' arrived in the town.[18] On Saturday 14 November, Riordane, together with two other Irish soldiers and a group of locally hired thugs, crossed the lake from Savoy. They arrived in Vevey an hour after sunset. In total, there were ten in the group, plus two servants.[19] Riordane then split his group in two to lodge at different inns. They told anyone who asked that they were pilgrims on their way to a Catholic shrine further along the lake. The following morning, Ludlow's landlord, M. Dubois, went to church. At the quayside he saw a boat with four watermen sitting at their oars, ready to put off.

The ropes securing the town's boats had been cut to prevent pursuit. Nearby stood two men Dubois had never seen before, with their cloaks thrown over their shoulders and held closely around them. Dubois spotted the barrels of carbines sticking out from under the cloaks. Two more men were sitting under a tree with their cloaks held around them as if hiding something. Another two strangers were sitting a little way off.

Dubois reached the obvious conclusion – kidnappers or assassins had come for his guests. Abandoning his devotions, he retraced his steps. On the way back he met one of his neighbours, a Monsieur Binet, who informed him he had earlier seen two men loitering near his house and had spotted four more in the marketplace. These six had then moved down towards the lakeside. This information confirmed Dubois's suspicions and he hurried home to alert the Englishmen.

Ludlow reacted calmly. Knowing that the strangers no longer occupied the route to the church, he decided he would go to a later service, while taking the precaution of going armed and with other members of the group.

Riordane's men waited while the townsfolk left church to see if Ludlow would appear. When he failed to do so, the would-be assassins also left the church and were heard to say that their target had not shown up.'[20] The townsfolk then saw that the ropes of their boats had been cut. The only people whose boat had not been interfered with were the Savoyard boatmen hired by Riordane. A row broke out and the would-be assassins realised the game was up. They returned to the quayside and rowed off across the lake towards Savoy.

The exact intent of Riordane and his gang is not known. It has been speculated that their intent was to kidnap Ludlow rather than murder him. In the English state papers it is noted that following the foiled raid in Vevey, Riordane submitted a report setting out the case for a new raid in which all the regicides might be 'reclaimed'.[21] He envisaged a complex undertaking in which the king would write to

Bern, demanding that the exiles should be given up as 'parricides'. At the same time, the roads out of Vevey would be guarded (presumably by English agents). If the authorities in Bern refused to comply, the regicides would be taken by force to Savoy.

Riordane did not discuss the difficulties of transporting a group of political prisoners across Europe. The abduction gang would have had to convey their prisoners through France, where the government of Louis XIV would hardly have been pleased to have English political hostages on their soil. All things considered, it seems evident that murder was the sole motive the first time round, and the subsequent plan for a mass kidnapping was simply too difficult, both politically and logistically, to be implemented. Assassination remained the most effective weapon.

The thwarted attack sapped the exiles' morale. Here was indubitable evidence that their enemies knew where they were and had the ability to strike. Reports, accurate or otherwise, arrived from England that Riordane had been ordered to renew his efforts to murder them. In a bizarre twist, a relative of one of the French members of Riordane's gang told Ludlow he would try to warn him should his relation attempt anything more.

As 1663 drew to a close, the exiles felt cornered, but alternative places to run to were limited. The authorities in Vevey and Bern considered their options, weighing up whether it might be better for the English group to move to Lausanne or go north to Yverden on the shores of Lake Neuchatel. On the plus side, the choice of Vevey had been vindicated – the size of the town had made the presence of strangers more noticeable. In a larger city, assassins might not be spotted until it was too late.

When all was considered, the people of Vevey decided the fugitives could, if they wished, stay put. Extra precautions were taken. Ludlow's house stood by the town walls next to one of the gates. A rope was rigged up from a window to the bell above the gateway so that he could ring the bell in an emergency and summon the town militia.

In London, Arlington and Williamson did not give up. The interception of the fugitives' mail was proving to be difficult. London had a real need to find out whether plots were being hatched between the runaways and their friends at home. The method of discovery would be by the use of double-agents: 'by inducing some persons of those now in the islands by promise of reward to feign escape and fly to them'.[22] In January 1664 came news of the treatment of some of the regicides who had not been executed and who were incarcerated in the Tower. They were to be dispersed around the country for extra security; some were even to be transported overseas. The worst treatment was reserved for Sir Henry Mildmay, George Fleetwood and Augustine Garland (who was said, though he denied it, to have spat in the king's face as he was led from the court). All three were ordered to be transported to Tangiers. Mildmay was saved the horror of foreign slavery by dying en route at Antwerp. One report has Fleetwood's wife Hester successfully interceding for him, another has him dying in Tangiers. In the case of Garland, who was in his seventies, the sentence must be seen as a particularly cruel action by Charles.

As the winter of 1663–4 began to bite in Vevey, the English group could only trust to extra vigilance and bad weather for protection. At least one of them, John Lisle, was far from sure this was the best tactic. Lisle was a man with a facility to find difficulty where others saw strength. He found no solace in Ludlow's reasoning that they had survived attack and would do so again. Lisle felt their current base was compromised. He further reasoned that since the royalists' number one target was Ludlow, the biggest threat to the longevity of the others was their proximity to *him*. Lisle resolved to move to Lausanne. The decision would be the death of him.

With tension between Britain and the Dutch once more increasing, London was again concerned about possible alliances between the exiled republicans and the Dutch to plan and carry out an invasion. Shortly after Lisle left, Ludlow heard from his French source that a new plot had been hatched. This time, the assassins would not approach across the lake but would come less ostentatiously on foot, with horses held nearby on which to make a speedy getaway. Ludlow sent word to Lisle and the small group of other English exiles in Lausanne. Eight days after his intelligence, several well-armed men were encountered by one of Vevey's townsmen, a Monsieur du Moulin, near the lake between Vevey and Lausanne. However, once the group was discovered, nothing further transpired. On 21 July 1664, several Savoyards were spotted in Lausanne, standing by the door of the church attended by Lisle. When neither he nor any other English exiles came to the church, they were heard to curse and ride away.[23]

By now Lisle no longer thought he was better protected in Lausanne than he had been in Vevey. Royalist agents seemed to be everywhere. A few days after the agents were seen at the church, two suspicious characters lodged at a Vevey inn. The men made off once their presence was noted. As had been arranged under the town's new security measures, Ludlow was informed of their presence.

On the afternoon of 11 August, Ludlow received dreadful news from Lausanne: Lisle had been murdered. He had been shot on his way to church. From descriptions given by passers-by and those arriving for the service, the assassins were similar to those who had recently been seen at Vevey. They had taken up residence at a Lausanne inn after moving from Vevey about a week before. Their presence had become so noticeable that English émigrés in the town had been warned. In response, Lisle had sent his servants to try to ascertain who the men were but they returned with no firm information. While the strangers remained in town, Lisle was urged to stay at home. Saying his life was in the hands of God, he disregarded the warnings.

Lisle had been so sure of the security of his new billet that he had sent for his wife, Alice, to join him. Neither of them realised that Williamson had opened their mail and now knew exactly where his quarry lived. Of course, Lisle knew that having acted as a legal advisor and judge at the king's trial could make him a target. He took precautions and used the alias Mr Field – an action negated by his unfortunate habit of wearing his Lord Chancellor's cloak while walking around the town.[24] The ambition and vanity which had taken Lisle to the top had now helped pitch him into the abyss.

That morning, he had left his lodgings and walked to the church near the town gate to hear the morning sermon. It is thought that, due to his friends' urging, he may have been accompanied by bodyguards. Near the churchyard, several assassins were waiting. When Lisle appeared and walked towards the churchyard, one of them walked up to him and bid him good day, addressing him by name. Whether Lisle responded to the trick or not is unknown. He walked on into the churchyard. His assailant rushed up behind him, reached under his frock coat, pulled out a gun and shot him in the back at point-blank range and in full view of the congregation gathering to enter the church. The weapon the assassin used was a large-bore musketoon, or blunderbuss, designed to fire multiple shots like a shotgun. It was favoured for use at sea, particularly by pirates. Three pistol balls tore into Lisle's back. As he crumpled to the ground, the killer ran out of the churchyard to the town gate, where his accomplices waited with horses.

According to some sources, the killer's accomplices drew swords and briefly fought with Lisle's bodyguards, the engagement ending once it became clear Lisle had been fatally wounded. The assailants galloped off through the town gate, shouting, 'Vive le Roi!'[25] Official royalist versions claim that Lisle was first called on to surrender, and was shot only when his bodyguards drew their pistols. It is hard to reconcile this with the fact that Lisle was shot in the back. A musketoon was not a weapon to stick in a man's ribs, like a pistol, to persuade him to come quietly; it was a weapon with which to eviscerate him.

So died Sir John Lisle, aged fifty-four. Before his exile, he had been a senior barrister and an MP, had assisted in organising the trial of Charles I and had sat as a judge, though he did not sign the king's death warrant. He went on to be a Commissioner of the Great Seal, a member of the Council of State and a Commissioner of the Admiralty. His widow, Alice, already a pariah and known as 'the regicide's wife', lived on in the family home at Moyles Court in Hampshire on the edge of the New Forest. In old age she would face a scandalous trial for treason and be sentenced to death.

Ludlow wrote to his friends in England with the sad news of Lisle's death. His immediate version of events was understandably at variance with that which emerged later. For example, according to Ludlow, there were two assailants, not three. In London, there was great joy at the court when the news of Lisle's death arrived.

As with the attempt on the life of Ludlow, there is a tendency to claim that Lisle's murder was a kidnap attempt gone wrong. Again, it is hard to take this seriously. Even if he had been captured, quite how he would have been put on a horse against his will in a busy street and taken away in broad daylight is hard to comprehend.[26]

So who were the men who killed Lisle? There is little doubt they were Irish soldiers in the employ of the English crown: Germaine Riordane, or MacCarty, of whom we have already heard; Miles Crowley, or O'Croli, who also went by the name Thomas MacDonnell; and James Fitz Edmund Cotter, or Semus mac Emoin Mhic Choitir. It seems Crowley fired the shot that killed Lisle. Some accounts have it that Cotter, not Riordane, was in charge.

All three assassins were rewarded for their exploits, rather dispelling any view that Charles was against such thuggery (he had, after all, made that arch-promoter of political murder, Silius Titus, commander of the Cinque Ports). O'Croli was given a commission in the English army. Riordane already had a commission, although he was reported to have lost it in 1667 for being a Roman Catholic. In 1670, he surfaced to write to friends of Ludlow, saying he had changed his ways and now wished to serve the Good Old Cause. Ludlow was not impressed. Cotter received a commission in the English army, but ended up in prison on the West Indian island of St Christopher after a misjudged raid went wrong. Upon his release, he returned to England and was sent to spy once more on Ludlow in Vevey in the 1670s. For his pains he was paid a pension of £200, made Marshal of the Leeward Islands and retired to Ireland with a knighthood.

It has been suggested that the assailants were in the employ of the Duchess of Orléans, or that she at least paid for their hire. Although it is known that O'Riordane certainly received money from her, this does not mean the gang were directly controlled by the duchess, or that they received their orders solely from her. She is far more likely to have been the conduit for a policy conducted from London. The fact that Williamson knew via intercepted mail where Lisle and others were living, and that the assassins were afterwards rewarded with appointments and gifts by Charles's government, strongly indicates that while the action was perhaps controlled via Paris, the instigating orders came from London at the behest of the king. Such an arrangement would have had the added bonus of 'plausible deniability', the technique of disguised responsibility so beloved by the CIA and other security agencies in the twentieth and early twenty-first centuries. As Charles's childhood governor, the Earl of Newcastle, had instructed: *Plus ça change*.

At the time of Lisle's death, the search for Edward Whalley and William Goffe was revived on the other side of the Atlantic. Following previous frustrations and failures, the hunt had been largely abandoned since 1661. The fugitives continued to live in their cellar in Milford. Thomas Temple's promise to 'hazard his life' in pursuit of them had helped him become governor of Nova Scotia but it left the fugitives untroubled. Their old cave on Providence Hill lay abandoned to the bears and snakes.

That all changed in the summer of 1664. The king gave the order for an expeditionary force to be sent to New England. Its prime target was the Dutch colony of New Amsterdam on Long Island, which Charles wished to take over in order to create an unbroken wedge of British rule on the north-east seaboard. The force was led by four commissioners and commanded by Colonel Richard Nicholas. They had further orders 'to apprehend all persons who stand attainted of high treason, and to discover those who have entertained them since the restoration'. It was unnecessary to identify the traitors by name.

Four men-o'-war arrived, carrying four hundred troops and enough firearms and ammunition to equip several hundred more. Whalley and Goffe retired once more to their cave but remained there only for a week or two. One night, a panther screamed outside the entrance. More worryingly, a group of Native Americans chanced upon their hiding place and discovered their bedding, though they did not spot either of the men. Word spread around Milford about their presence. Their benefactors decided to move them to one of the most remote settlements in Massachusetts, an outpost called Hadley, some eighty miles to the north-west on the boundary of Indian territory and ninety miles from the coast. Goffe's sojourn here would become a legend, and inspire great storytellers on either side of the Atlantic.

Hadley in 1664 was a stockaded village of some fifty Puritan families. The settlers who built it in 1659 chose a site in the tranquil valley of the Connecticut river. It must have seemed to them that they had found the Promised Land. Their little satellite settlement was on an oxbow bend under the shadow of a richly forested mountain. They would discover that they were surrounded by the most fertile soils in New England. The great nineteenth-century landscape artist Thomas Cole would call it 'Arcadia' and immortalise the landscape in *The Oxbow*, an 1833 painting that became as famous in America as Constable's *Haywain* in England. After Niagara Falls, Hadley would develop into the most visited holiday site in America.

By pre-arrangement, the fugitives were received by the town's Puritan minister, John Russell. The Reverend Russell concealed them in an upstairs room. Since the Russells lived right in the middle of the settlement, this seemed an unnecessary risk; however, their luck held. Many decades later, a historian picked up folk memories of searchers from Boston and Redcoats from England arriving in Hadley around 1664, but there is no record that the Russell house ever came under suspicion.

Colonel Nicholas and his troops succeeded in their primary task of ejecting the Dutch, but they found it impossible to persuade the colonists of New England to aid the search for the regicides. Nicholas reported later that when he tried to set up a hearing of complaints in Boston and issued a summons for witnesses, a small mob-cum-delegation appeared and stopped him: 'The Government sent a herald and trumpeter and 100 people accompanying them to proclaim that the Commissioners should not act in that government nor any persons give obedience,' he reported, adding that 'the meeting was dissolved and nothing farther done.'[27]

The commission had secret instructions from Charles to tread gently with the Massachusetts Puritans. The colonial government had been slow to recognise Charles as king and the British strategy – unusually subtle – was to woo the colony gently back to full allegiance, prior to imposing a new charter. This might explain the failure to take tough action against people suspected of harbouring Whalley and Goffe.

Much of what we know about the fugitives' lives at this point comes from the researches nearly a century later of Thomas Harrison, then governor of Massachusetts. He acquired Goffe's papers – letters and a diary – while compiling a history of the colony published in 1764. The material revealed that the two were sometimes living 'in terror'. In letters between Goffe and his wife Frances the two tell each other to be careful of betrayal. Given that Frances' friend Lady Wariston was being betrayed by Robert Johnston, the warnings were timely.

Goffe's diary revealed that in February 1665, with Colonel Nicholas's men still in the area, they were joined by a third regicide. This was another military man, John Dixwell, formerly the governor of Dover Castle. Here was a man who took chances. In 1660 he was named as a regicide, but in order to sell as much of his property as possible before it was seized, he had hung on in England almost as long as Edmund Ludlow before fleeing abroad.

Dixwell went to Hanau in Germany and was one of the fugitives George Downing had in his sights in 1661. It is more than likely that he decided to quit Europe and make for America because of the callous betrayal of John Okey and his other friends, whose kidnapping was to have such a profound effect on some of the refugees. Dixwell remained in hiding in the Russell household with his two friends for perhaps two years before deciding to move on.

Whalley and Goffe were not completely hamstrung by their hermitic existence in Hadley. These two clever and energetic men may have lived in fear and have been constantly under cover, but through a front man they went very successfully into business. Their partner was the influential Daniel Gookin, a friend of the two since they had sailed to New England together on the *Prudent Mary* in May 1660. Copies of the Goffe letters show that he and his father-in-law eventually became sufficiently prosperous to send a message home to England asking their families not to send them any further remittances until they asked for more money. The pair went into stock raising and 'a little trade with the Indians'. By 1672 they 'had a stock in New England money of over one hundred pounds, all debts paid'.

In 1665, Colonel Nicholas discovered the connection between Gookin and the 'traitors' Whalley and Goffe. The regicides' whereabouts continued to mystify him. He issued an order to seize stock nominally owned by Gookin. Using the rights embodied in the colony's charter, Gookin blocked the seizure.

Dixwell moved to nearby New Haven and decided to dice with fate by living openly as a settler. He possibly calculated that the risk for him was low because the authorities in London had no idea where he had fled to. If so, he was correct. Under the alias James Davids, he married and, after his first wife died, married again. He raised a family and lived as a free man and a respected member of the community for another quarter of a century. Only on his death bed did he reveal his identity. He asked that no monument be erected at his grave 'lest his enemies might dishonour his ashes'. A simple gravestone was erected, inscribed with his initials – 'J. D. Esq.' – his age and the time of his death.

As for his friends in exile, one of them would become an American legend.

18

PLANS TO INVADE AND HOPES DASHED

1665–1692

Following the death of John Lisle, life for the exiles was filled with tension. Several decided to leave Switzerland for Germany; they included William Say, who tried to persuade Edmund Ludlow to go with him. Ludlow refused to budge, reasoning that there was no point in spending life on the run, always looking over one's shoulder. Meanwhile, Algernon Sidney was trying to stay at least one step ahead of the assassins on his trail. Although not excepted from the Act of Oblivion, it was clear that his remarks in favour of the trial of Charles I, together with his publicly stated antipathy to monarchy, placed him high on Charles II's list of enemies.

During the next few years, the government in London was to rank Sidney and Ludlow as the most dangerous fugitives at large in Europe. They continued to be prime targets for royalist assassination squads. Of the two, Sidney was the more actively threatening. At the end of 1664, he was moving fitfully through northern Europe in search of support for an invasion plan. Early the next year, he settled at Augsburg in Germany where once more an attempt was made on his life. In April, a group of assassins tracked him down and planned to kill him. The squad was led by Andrew White, one of three Irish brothers who had become soldiers of fortune before taking up the precarious trade of secret agent. Sidney avoided White's bullet or knife purely by chance – leaving for the Netherlands the day before the planned assassination. It was becoming clear to Sidney that his name was on a secret death list.

Sidney's invasion plans boiled down to gaining support in the Netherlands – both from the exile community there and from the government. The political climate in the Netherlands convinced many of the exiles that at long last the tide was turning in their favour. In 1665, skirmishing between England and the Dutch Republic had turned into outright war. For republicans like Sidney, this was a chance to get one of the few republics in Europe on their side to destroy the English monarchy. There even existed what might form the basis of an invasion force. The Dutch army had an English regiment, created from the remnants of English regiments that had served the Dutch until the outbreak of war in 1665.* The majority had returned home, but some were left behind who agreed to sign a pledge of allegiance to the Dutch Republic. With luck and persuasion, this Anglo-Dutch regiment might form the backbone of an army with which to invade England. William Say suggested the time had come to 'feel the pulse of ye Dutch, touching their uniting with ye honest party in England against Charles Stewart'.[1] He wrote to Sidney and they made for Holland, hoping to build up support for an Anglo-Dutch republican pact.

In The Hague, Sidney brought all his charm and persuasive powers to work on Johan de Witt, assuring him that English officers and men would rally to the venture. De Witt was ambivalent. Like Ludlow, he had a long memory and recalled the beatings the Dutch

---

* These regiments had come into existence when companies of English soldiers were raised to help the Dutch in their war with the Spanish (the Thirty Years' War). There were also several Scottish regiments.

fleet had taken at the hands of Admiral Blake and the Common-
wealth navy. De Witt worried that by helping to create a new English
Commonwealth he might be preparing the ground for the ruin of
Holland.

De Witt was unconvinced that the English exiles could deliver on
their promises. He saw Sidney as a whipper-up of intrigue but not a
man to lead an army. The man they needed was Ludlow. Ludlow
had attained something like mythical status – largely by dint of keeping his head down for several years and thereby becoming the object
of much speculation. From the moment he had left England, he was
the subject of lurid press reports naming him as the leader of just
about every plot, real or imaginary. From the shores of Lake Geneva,
Ludlow remained sceptical. He had mistrusted the Dutch ever since
de Witt had allowed George Downing to abduct three of his fellow
judges and make a mockery of the Netherlands' lauded policy of
political asylum.

Sidney wrote furious letters urging Ludlow to come to Holland.
William Say, Slingsby Bethel and John Phelps all wrote too. The
band of would-be rebels in Holland was growing. Even Cornet Joyce
was in Holland, having come over with his family in 1660. Although
not excluded from the Act of Oblivion, George Joyce knew his role
in taking Charles I into army captivity would never be forgiven. As a
lieutenant-colonel, he was just the sort of man a group of insurrectionists could do with in their ranks.

While the exiles were gathering and plotting in Europe, England
suffered a series of disasters. Bubonic plague took hold in London in
1665 and killed a hundred thousand people. This was followed by
the great fire that swept through the city and destroyed it. When the
fire took hold, Charles was swept up in the immediacy of the disaster.
His youthful love of action returned and he launched himself into
the fray. Abandoning his cosseted life, he engaged in the struggle to
deal with the fire. Together with his brother James, he directed
attempts to contain the blaze until it was too late. Only when all was
lost did he retreat from the stricken city. This was Charles at his best:

the fireman, the reactive man of action. Afterwards he relapsed into his more habitual mode of dreamer, excited by Christopher Wren's plans for rebuilding the city and St Paul's Cathedral. The notion of creating the sublime from disaster suited the king's mindset better than did the more difficult flux of political life.

With anti-monarchists still active on the Continent, the government felt it had to concoct some manner of dealing with the threat they posed. To make the best of a difficult task, it was decided that Charles would issue a form of amnesty with a threat attached: sixteen named revolutionaries and anti-monarchists should return to England immediately or suffer the penalty of being attainted for treason. Two key men on the list were former New Model Army hard men Thomas Kelsey and John Desborough. Kelsey was a Fifth Monarchist major-general strongly opposed to the Stuart monarchy, or any monarchy. Desborough, the former republican major-general who had shown his muscle in bullying Richard Cromwell out of office, had gone to Holland determined to lead an insurrection.

Also on the list were William Scot, the son of the executed regicide and Cromwellian spymaster Thomas Scot, and Dr Edward Richardson, the cleric and leader of the doomed Yorkshire uprising. Three names originally on the list were struck off after lobbying: Sir James Harrington, who had been a judge in the king's trial, Oliver St John, the lawyer and diplomat who had first risen to notice in 1640 urging Parliament to overturn Charles's ship money tax, and Algernon Sidney. Richard Cromwell's name was kept off the list by his wife who lobbied the court, saying that if her husband returned to England his creditors would bankrupt him.

Unsurprisingly, Ludlow was not on the list. The plotters continued to turn to him for the leadership he was loath to give. De Witt decided to make an offer to test the resolve of the English opposition. He would put up £10,000 to raise an army of four thousand men to launch an invasion which was to land at Newcastle. There was one condition – Ludlow had to lead the invasion. When Say wrote to

Ludlow telling him of this, the veteran general remained unconvinced.

Meanwhile, Charles II's spymaster set a honey trap aimed at one of the exiles. The chosen agent was the royalist spy and future celebrated writer Aphra Behn. Her target was William Scot, with whom Behn was reputed to have had an affair at an English sugar plantation in Suriname in 1663 when aged twenty-three.* Three years later, Behn was sent to Antwerp in an attempt to rekindle their affair and recruit Scot as an agent. In preparation for her mission, spymaster Joseph Williamson gave her the code name Astrea. In the time-honoured way of managing secret agents, Astrea was kept on a very tight financial rein.

In August 1666, she reported she had made contact with Scot, who was in an English regiment and based in Antwerp. Scot was given the code name Celadon. According to Behn, he agreed to spy for the English crown. 'Though at first shy, he became by arguments extremely willing to undertake the service ...'[2]

Scot was playing a dangerous game and may have been a double agent, working for both London and The Hague. Among the English living in Holland were royalist sympathisers who would be more than happy to kill a republican spy. Behn discovered that a Cavalier named Coney was threatening to murder Scot. She reported that Coney 'boasts as if he were the King's right hand' but spoke 'such rhodomontades' (vain boasting) she was unsure if he could be trusted.[3] Wisely, Scot moved from Antwerp to Rotterdam, the heartland of much of English republican activity.

Within a few weeks, Scot was proving a useful source. In mid-September he wrote to Behn that Sidney was 'in great esteem with De Witt' and that a parliamentarian captain named Thomas Woodman was offering to sink ships in the Thames to hinder the English fleet.[4] He next wrote to report that he had visited a Quaker exile and found several other renegades there including John Phelps,

---

* There is debate among Behn scholars about her trip to Suriname. On balance, it does appear to have taken place.

the former clerk to the regicide court. He judged that 'something is brewing.'

Scot next sent word to Charles's spymaster Joseph Williamson that the plan was to raise an army of twenty thousand men. Despite their fervour, the exiles' plans were making little progress. The problem was that Ludlow would not take part without cast-iron assurances from the Dutch that they would hold to their offer of support, while the Dutch would not make those assurances unless Ludlow was willing to lead.

Ludlow stubbornly refused to commit himself, saying: 'truly to me, the Lord by his providences speaks to his people rather fitter for suffering than action.'[5] Without Ludlow, the invasion plan from Holland was dead.

There was another blow to hopes of insurrection: Desborough took advantage of Charles's call to come home. He returned to England, was imprisoned in the Tower for a year and then allowed to retire, derided by royalists, despaired of by republicans and mocked in Samuel Butler's satire *Hudibras*.

A month after Desborough's return home, the government in London relaxed. Secretary of State William Arlington was told, 'There should be no great danger of uprisings now that the most dangerous men were secured.'[6]

William Scot revised his opinion of the threat from Holland. On 14 September 1666, he wrote to Aphra Behn that he thought 'the fanatics' need not be feared 'if due caution observed'.[7] Within a week, Scot learned that all his work had paid off: he had been pardoned. According to Behn, he was 'overjoyed'.

In spite of all her work, Aphra Behn was never paid. After a spell in debtors' prison, she took to writing to support herself. Her first book was *Oroonoko*, a novel about exotic lovers in exile.

The exiles now became further embroiled in the murky world of European power politics. Just as the Dutch had toyed with using the exiles in their war with the English, the French now tried to do the same. In January 1666, an officer in the service of the French had visited Ludlow in Vevey to propose an alliance between the English radicals and the French and Dutch. The idea behind this was obviously to explore combining their forces against the English crown. Substantial funds were reportedly available. Ludlow responded diplomatically: 'If any just and honourable way should be proposed for the restitution of the republic in England ... I would hazard my life in that service.'[8]

Ludlow learned that de Witt wanted him to go to Paris with Sidney to conclude a formal treaty with Louis XIV, to which Louis was said to have agreed in principle. Sidney travelled to Paris, where he hit a major snag: Ludlow refused to follow him. The indefatigable Sidney nevertheless managed to secure an audience with the Sun King. He asked Louis for 100,000 francs. Louis countered by offering 20,000 francs, with more to come when Ludlow was seen to be on board. Once Ludlow made it clear he would have nothing to do with the French, Sidney's English supporters fell away like leaves in autumn and the exiles' dreams of England slipped into eternal winter.

With all chance of their revolution ended, Ludlow, the leader who refused to lead, turned to writing what he called a 'history' that would be 'as true as the gospel'.[9] In disappointment, Sidney also turned from action to writing. His major works on republican theory, though a significant influence on the American founding fathers, would not be published in his lifetime.

As Charles's reign moved into its second decade, he continued to seek out new mistresses with which to divert himself. He had long enjoyed the theatre, both for its entertainment value and as a means to see new young actresses he might fancy. One actress he had often spent time with was Nell Gwyn, a former prostitute who had become a theatrical star by virtue of her intelligence, talent and wit. Though not a great beauty, she had a vivacity and style that captivated her audience and she became the most celebrated actress of her age. In 1669, the king made her his mistress. In comparison to the greed and scheming of more aristocratic mistresses such as Barbara Villiers, Nell Gwyn had the advantage of not requiring so much money to be expended upon her; nor was she involved in the poisonous intrigue at court. A bawdy rhyme summed up her appeal:

Hard by Pall Mall lives a wench called Nell
King Charles the Second he kept her.
She hath got a trick to handle his prick
But never lays hands on his sceptre.

Nell had one other advantage – she was genuinely fond of Charles and never asked him for anything. In turn, the king seems to have been fond of her and installed her in a mansion in Pall Mall so he could walk from the palace to her front door. Once he was safely behind Nell's door, the king could lower his guard. While plotting a risky secret treaty with France* in the hope of at last gaining from Louis XIV the independent income he craved, Charles was able to relax into a simpler world with the uneducated actress from Coal Yard Alley.

In America, the exiled regicides were to be hailed as apostles of liberty. Edward Whalley and William Goffe remained hidden with the Reverend Russell for another ten years, until Whalley's death around 1674 or '75. Goffe was to live on and become the centre of a hugely dramatic story – the legend of the Angel of Hadley, the white-haired stranger who in September 1675 appeared brandishing a sword, rallied the settlers, beat off an Algonquin attack and prevented a massacre, before disappearing as miraculously as he had come. The superstitious people of Hadley decided their saviour must have been a supernatural being. Ninety years after the incident, the president of Harvard, Ezra Stiles, wrote: 'The inhabitants

---

* The treaty was essentially a mutual-aid pact in which both parties agreed to help the other militarily – but it also included an agreement that Charles would convert to Catholicism whenever it was prudent to do so.

could not account for the phenomenon, but by considering that person as an Angel sent of God on that special occasion for their deliverance.'

By the nineteenth century the angel incident was presented as fact and so too was William Goffe's role as the angel. The story inspired many writers. The first to make use of the tale was Walter Scott, who based his novel *Peveril of the Peak* upon the legend of the Angel. He was followed by James Fenimore Cooper and Nathaniel Hawthorne. The cave that sheltered Goffe and Whalley is now a tourist attraction and bears a bronze plaque stating, 'Opposition to Tyrants is Obedience to God'.

In Whitehall, the question of the remaining fugitives ran like a secret river beneath the more pressing concerns of the kingdom's domestic and foreign policies, only occasionally bobbing up into the light of day. One of these moments occurred in 1670. Despite the years that had elapsed since the events of 1648–9, some names still had the power to rankle with the king. One was that of George Joyce, he who as a lowly Cromwellian cornet had taken Charles I into the custody of the army and who had since fled with his family to Holland. Apart from his role in securing the late king, there had also been a rumour spread by the ludicrous gossip and astrologer William Lilly that Joyce had been one of the king's executioners. Deciding it was best to remain abroad, Joyce had declined to accept London's invitation to Cromwellian exiles to return and be pardoned. From the fate of others who had 'come in', he guessed he would at best be imprisoned and at worst hanged, drawn and quartered.

Now, in 1670, the diplomat and politician Sir William Temple was dispatched on a secret mission to Holland, 'charged to seize and secure Cornet Joyce, the person that removed by force King Charles I from Holmby Castle, who lived in Rotterdam'.[10] The mission was clearly sanctioned by Charles himself for Sir William moved in the king's inner circles. Charles must have been very anxious for the success of Sir William's mission to abduct the fugitive, 'for the transporting of whom to England one of the King's yachts had been purposely sent to Holland'.

Although Sir William had the king's own ship lying ready to take his captive away, he was unsuccessful. On one occasion, he sat up through two consecutive nights keeping fruitless watch for Joyce. When he asked for the assistance of the Dutch authorities – as George Downing had done eight years before in the cases of Miles Corbet and his colleagues – help was unforthcoming. The Rotterdam magistrates declared that Joyce 'was a kind of mad, extravagant fellow that having long resided in their town, could be guilty of nothing against his majesty unless it were of words; and amounted not to a crime that was thought to deserve imprisonment'. The Dutch magistrates ruled that by vociferously denouncing the king Joyce was only exercising freedom of speech. This was not an argument that would have stood up well in the legal atmosphere in Restoration England, where courts ruled that words signalled intent and intent was enough to condemn a man for treason.

Sir William wrote to Charles's spy chief, Lord Arlington, that he had failed despite pursuing Joyce 'with all imaginable zeal and diligence'. Arlington, a confidant of the king (he was one of only two courtiers who knew of Charles's secret intention to convert to Roman Catholicism to secure a pact with France), replied that he suspected 'there was foul play as well as difficulty of form in the hindering' of Temple's mission. Having involved two such senior and trusted members of his circle in the task to capture Joyce, Charles would have been disappointed at their failure. Unfortunately for us, none of his courtiers thought to commit details of their king's true feelings to print. Samuel Pepys was sadly in orbit in a lower social circle, just below those who circled around Charles himself.

Following the Joyce debacle, attempts to capture or assassinate the fugitive regicides began to slip down the royal agenda. Pressing domestic issues included questions over the succession, for although

Charles had by now fathered many male children, none of them were the offspring of the queen. His heir was therefore his brother James, Duke of York, who was openly Catholic. If this were not enough, word leaked out of the king's secret pact with the ancient enemy, France. In 1677, partially to help quell public anxiety over his Protestant identity, Charles arranged the marriage of his niece Mary to William of Orange.

That same year, Algernon Sidney scented the political wind blowing from England and decided to end his exile. All would go well until six years after his return, when he was swept up in an extraordinary conspiracy which culminated in his death. A plot was hatched to ambush and kill Charles II and his brother James on their way home from the races. Among those arrested for alleged involvement were the most prominent of the king's political opponents. Through his friendship with one of them, Sidney was also arrested, and was tried for treason on very flimsy evidence – Sidney complained it came from only one witness. The prosecution's response was that it had another source – the manuscript of Sidney's unpublished republican writings.[11] The court argued that his words were an 'overt act' – putting Sidney in the bizarre situation of having become his own chief prosecution witness.[12] He was beheaded on 7 December 1683.

On 5 February 1685 the king had a seizure and died at the age of fifty-four. He was succeeded by his brother James, a Roman Catholic. Four months later, Charles's eldest illegitimate son, James Scott, the Duke of Monmouth, launched a rebellion. Scott was the son of Lucy Walter, Charles's first love. His rebellion was crushed at the Battle of Sedgemoor.

Following the uprising there was one last act of vengeance against a relative of one of the regicides. The widow of the assassinated regicide John Lisle was condemned to death for harbouring one of the Duke of Monmouth's supporters. The officer who led the search for the fugitive hidden by Lady Lisle had an axe to grind. His father,

John Penruddock, had been executed following a treason trial presided over by Lady Lisle's husband John in 1655. Alice Lisle was beheaded in Winchester on 2 September, so completing the tragic history of the Lisles, husband and wife. By the 1680s there were few of the regicides or of their pursuers left.

The regicide William Cawley died at Vevey in 1667, followed there is 1671 by fellow regicide Cornelius Holland and, three years later, by the former sergeant-at-arms Edward Dendy. By now, the little community in Vevey was becoming very small and its members very old. Nicholas Love had lived on until 1682, while Andrew Broughton succumbed to old age five years later.

Of the other runaways, Thomas Challoner, the fifty-fourth signatory to the king's death warrant, had escaped to Middelburg in the Netherlands, only to die there in August 1660. Valentine Walton escaped retribution to die in Hanau, Germany, in 1661. Sir Michael Livesey died in the Netherlands in 1665, where William Say died the following year. Daniel Blagrave died in Aachen in 1668. George Joyce was last heard of in the Netherlands with Sir William Temple's failed attempt to kidnap him. Perhaps he moved into deeper obscurity to avoid further attempts on his liberty.

In all, twenty regicides and their associates were executed. Many escaped that fate by the skin of their teeth. Edmund Ludlow and others had several close shaves in Switzerland, George Downing's agents narrowly missed capturing John Hewson and George Joyce in the Netherlands, and in America, Goffe, Whalley and Dixwell only evaded an exhaustive manhunt thanks to the help of Puritan settlers.

Of the regicides who remained in England, two evaded execution due to ill health. Sir John Bourchier was too ill in 1660 to be put on trial and died later that year, while Vincent Potter was sentenced to death but died before the sentence could be carried out. Many more were thrown in prison for the rest of their lives.

Some of the latter had been sentenced to death but reprieved. Sir

Hardress Waller escaped the scaffold thanks to the intercession of his cousin Sir William Waller, who changed sides after the wars to support the royalist faction during the Commonwealth and Protectorate. Sir Hardress died imprisoned on Jersey in 1666. Henry Smith, an ardent republican, was reprieved after pleading 'youthful ignorance' and sentenced to imprisonment for life, dying in Jersey around 1668. Robert Tichborne, a London merchant who helped organise the king's trial, was reprieved for having interceded to save the lives of Cavaliers condemned to death during the Protectorate. He died in the Tower in 1682.

Others who were sentenced to life imprisonment included Owen Rowe, who died in the Tower on Christmas Day 1661; Peter Temple, who died in the Tower two years later; Colonel John Hutchinson, who died in Sandown Castle in 1664; and Harry Marten, the republican *bon viveur* who was imprisoned in Chepstow Castle where, attended by the love of his life, Mary Ward, he died in 1680.

The most illustrious of the supporters of the regicides, John Milton, died peacefully at home in London in 1674. He continues to be one of the most lauded of poets and is considered to be as quintessentially English as the monarchy itself.

And what of the men who pursued the regicides? Charles II converted to Catholicism on his death bed in 1685, having left no legitimate male heir. Heneage Finch died the year before the king; William Prynne died in 1669; George Monck, the most eminent of the century's turncoats, died in 1670; George Downing, who turned a lesser though useful coat, in 1684; and Richard Ingoldsby, who turned his coat to save his skin, died in 1685. James II outlived them all. Having been deposed from the English throne by William of Orange in 1688, he died peacefully at his chateau at St-Germain-en-Laye near Paris fifteen years later.

While both enemies and friends dropped away, Edmund Ludlow lived on by the shore of Lake Geneva with his wife Elizabeth. In 1688, following the Glorious Revolution – a term he would have hated for being entirely erroneous – he felt it was at last safe to return home. Almost immediately, he was recognised and denounced as a regicide. A proposal was made in Parliament to have him arrested. So, at the age of seventy-two, Ludlow escaped once more and sailed away for the last time. Four years later, in 1692, with Elizabeth by his side, he died in his bed at 49 Rue du Lac – the last of the regicides.

All that now remains of the little group of Englishmen and women who once lived in the pretty town by Lake Geneva are their graves and some memorials in the church of St Martin, the very church to which Ludlow once walked while carrying a sword, in fear of a king's revenge.

19

EPILOGUE:
THE LEGACY OF THE REGICIDES

If Britain did have a 'Glorious Revolution', it took place not in 1688–9 but forty years earlier in 1649. On that date, the rule of an absolutist king was ended and the supremacy of Parliament was established. At the same time, the rule of law was confirmed and wider social freedoms than ever before granted, censorship lifted and relative freedom of worship assured. Despite a generally bad press, the regicides were men of principle who stood for many of the liberties that today we take for granted. The Glorious Revolution merely restored some of what the men who judged Charles I had achieved. Modern Britain has much to thank them for.

The trial of Charles I grew out of the exasperation of men who wanted his powers to be tempered by a representative Parliament that could make laws and raise taxes. This was the constitutional monarchy drawn up by John Lambert and Henry Ireton in 1647 and turned down flat by the king. Due to Charles's desire to raise taxes as he wished and to rule without Parliament ('Call no Parliaments', his father James I had advised), two bruising wars were fought between

1642 and 1648. Constitutional reform – rather than hatred of the king himself – was at the heart of the programme proposed by those who opposed the king. Finally, the conflicts led to Britain's first and only written constitution.

The king's judges were an odd coalition: hereditary landowners, parliamentarians, professional soldiers, lawyers, businessmen. Holding a broad sweep of political and religious views, from the conservative to the revolutionary, they ranged from those who, like Cromwell and his son-in-law Henry Ireton, tried to achieve a working relationship with Charles I to republicans like Edmund Ludlow and Harry Marten who sympathised with giving the vote to working men. Thanks to the intransigence of the king, England ended up with a republic even though what had been fought for was a monarchy with powers circumscribed by Parliament.

Whatever their individual views, the regicides as a body held that people had the right to worship as they chose (though, being sons of the Reformation, they were strongly opposed both to the papacy and bishops). They believed men had a duty to work together within society to improve the lot of mankind. An absolutist king clinging to notions of divine prerogative and an unreformed religion was seen as inimical to progress.

The regicides have bequeathed a series of reforms which underpin a good deal of the structure of Britain today. Thanks to John Lambert, we have the blueprint for today's political system. In 1653 he created Britain's only written constitution, in which the Lord Protector was advised by a Council of State and all legislation had to be passed by Parliament – how similar to today's parliamentary democracy with Cabinet government this is.

They had much to offer on the legal front. First, they reasserted the freedoms established under Magna Carta and common law. Through freedom of speech and the rule of law they ensured that the people had the sort of rights and freedoms that have developed into a modern liberal democracy.

At a more specific legal level, thanks to John Bradshaw and John

Cook, a defendant in court had the right not to incriminate himself – the right to silence. Cook proposed the 'cab rank' rule for barristers, by which advocates had the duty to take a case, and he proposed a scheme to fund cases for the poor – an early form of legal aid. Both these reforms survive today, ensuring that society's poorest can obtain legal representation. During the Commonwealth, English was made the language of the courts and of the law books. Cook also proposed reforms of a social nature, including the introduction of free health care for the poor.

On the wider political front, the writings of Algernon Sidney, that convert to the regicide cause, enthused John Adams and Thomas Jefferson and helped inspire the American Constitution. Though derided in their own land, in America the men who judged the king and found him wanting are lauded as apostles of liberty.

What would they make of modern Britain? They would marvel that the monarchy has been stripped of all active power but is kept on largely for ceremonial purposes. They would exult in the manner in which orderly elections are held and how defeated governments give way without violence. They would be astounded that women and even the unemployed have the vote. One would like to think that once they saw how well this broad enfranchisement appears to work, they would become reconciled to it.

Coming from an age of political fervour, they would be saddened at how few of the electorate bother to vote. At first they would be baffled by the common complaint that all the main political parties are somehow 'all the same'. On closer inspection, the regicides would notice there was something in this and wonder if it might be due to the fact that guiding moral principles now play so little part in politics.

One aspect of British public life would cause them immense concern – that there is hardly ever a mention of God. They would be dismayed to learn that the only avowedly religious prime minister of the late twentieth and early twenty-first centuries, Tony Blair, is a convert to Catholicism.

So, the seventeenth-century regicides, puritanical, often brutal, yet defiantly reformist, would find much to like and much to criticise. They would see that an excellent job has been made of building on the foundations they put down in the seventeenth century but notice there are still some flaws in the design. They would certainly like to make a few suggestions.

And what of the king's revenge? As British history is habitually told via the stories of kings and queens, tales of Charles II and his wonderfully corrupt and licentious court have unfairly obscured the histories of the men who killed a king in order to let freedom live. As John Cook wrote shortly before he was executed: 'We fought for the public good and would have enfranchised the people and secured the welfare of the whole groaning creation if the nation had not more delighted in servitude than in freedom.'

APPENDIX I: THE REGICIDES AND THEIR FATE

The following is a list of all fifty-nine signatories to the warrant ordering the execution of Charles I (popularly known as the death warrant) in the order their signatures appear. The absence of a date of birth indicates it is not known. Where no cause of death is indicated, it should be taken as natural causes.

John Bradshaw: bap. 1602, lawyer, President of the High Court of Justice, died 1659; following the restoration, his body was dug up for posthumous symbolic execution in 1661

Thomas Grey: Baron Grey of Groby, born 1622, died 1657

Oliver Cromwell: b. 1599, soldier, politician, Lord Protector (1653–8), died 1658; posthumous symbolic execution 1661

Edward Whalley: major-general; fled to New England and died in exile 1674/5

Sir Michael Livesey: b. 1614, politician; fled to Netherlands and died in exile 1665(?)

John Okey: bap. 1606, soldier; fled to Germany 1660; captured in the Netherlands by George Downing; forcibly returned to England in 1661 and executed 1662

Sir John Danvers: b. 1584/5, politician, died 1655

Sir John Bourchier: b. 1595, politician; declared too ill for trial, died 1660

Henry Ireton: bap. 1611, major-general and political theorist; died of fever on campaign in Ireland 1651; posthumous symbolic execution 1661

Sir Thomas Mauleverer: bap. 1599, politician, died 1655

Sir Hardress Waller: b. 1604, army officer; sentenced to death 1660; sentence commuted to life imprisonment; died Mount Orgueil Castle, Jersey, 1666

John Blakiston: bap. 1603, politician, died 1649

John Hutchinson: bap. 1615, army officer; pardoned 1660 but after being implicated in 1663 Yorkshire rebellion was imprisoned in Sandown Castle, Kent, where he died in 1664

William Goffe: major-general; fled to New England 1660 and died in exile 1679(?)

Thomas Pride: army officer, died 1658; marked for posthumous execution but body left undisturbed

Peter Temple: bap. 1599, soldier and politician, sentenced to death 1660; sentence commuted to life; died in the Tower 1663

Thomas Harrison: bap. 1616, army officer and Fifth Monarchist leader, executed 1660

John Hewson: shoemaker, army officer, governor of Dublin; fled to Amsterdam 1660 and died in exile 1661–2(?)

Henry Smith: b. 1619/20, politician, sentenced to death 1660; commuted to life imprisonment; died Gorey Castle, Jersey, in or after 1668

Sir Peregrine Pelham: bap. 1602, politician, died 1650

Richard Deane: bap. 1610, army and naval officer; killed in action during naval Battle of Solebay against the Dutch 1653; following the restoration his body was disinterred and buried in a communal pit

Robert Tichborne: b. 1610/11, politician, sentenced to death 1660; sentence commuted; died in the Tower 1682

Humphrey Edwards: b. 1582, politician, died 1658

Daniel Blagrave: bap. 1603, politician; fled to Aachen in 1660 and died in exile 1668(?)

Owen Rowe: b. 1592/3, merchant, sentenced to death; died in the Tower before sentence confirmed 1661.

William Purefoy: b. 1580(?), politician, died 1659

Adrian Scroop: b. 1601, army officer, executed 1660

James Temple: b. 1606, politician; sentenced to life imprisonment on Jersey, where he died 1674(?)

Augustine Garland: b. 1603, lawyer and politician; though sentenced to death in 1660, he was transported to Tangiers; it is not known if an order for him to be returned and imprisoned in Southsea Castle was carried out; died in or after 1677

Edmund Ludlow: b. 1616/17(?), army general and politician; escaped to the Continent 1660, died Vevey, Switzerland, 1692

Henry (Harry) Marten: b. 1601/2; politician; sentenced to life imprisonment and died Chepstow Castle, 1680

Vincent Potter: b. 1614, army officer; sentenced to death 1660; died in the Tower before sentence could be carried out, probably in 1661

Sir William Constable: bap. 1590, army officer, died 1655; disinterred after the restoration and his body thrown into a communal pit

*Richard Ingoldsby: bap. 1617, army officer, politician; was pardoned and made a Knight of the Bath by Charles II for his role in capturing parliamentarian general John Lambert in 1660; died 1685

William Cawley: bap. 1602, politician; escaped to Switzerland and died 1667

John Barkstead: escaped to Germany 1660; seized in the Netherlands, forcibly returned to England and executed 1662

Isaac Ewer: army officer, died 1650/1

John Dixwell: b. 1607, politician; escaped to Germany (Hanau), then America; died in New England, 1689

Valentine Walton: b. 1593/4, army officer; escaped to Germany (Hanau); moved to Flanders or the Netherlands; died 1661(?)

Simon Meyne: bap. 1612, politician; sentenced to death 1660; died in Tower before sentence could be carried out, 1661

Thomas Horton: bap. 1603, army officer, died 1649

John Jones: b. 1597(?) army officer, executed 1660

John Moore: b. 1599, army officer, died 1650

Gilbert Millington: b. 1598, lawyer, politician; death sentence commuted to life imprisonment; died Mount Orgueil Castle, Jersey, 1666

George Fleetwood: bap. 1623, major-general; sentenced to be transported to Tangiers in 1664; unknown whether he was transported; may have emigrated to North America; date of death unknown

John Alured: bap. 1607, army officer, died 1651

Robert Lilburne: bap. 1614, deputy major-general; death sentence commuted to life imprisonment; died in prison on St Nicholas Island in Plymouth Sound, 1665

William Say: b. 1604, politician; escaped to the Continent 1660; lived in Switzerland, Germany and Netherlands, where he probably died around 1666

Anthony Stapley: bap. 1590, politician, died 1655

Sir Gregory Norton: b. 1603, politician, died 1652

*Thomas Challoner (or Chaloner): b. 1595, fled to Netherlands 1660; died in Middelburg a few months later, in August 1660.

Thomas Wogan: b. 1620(?), army officer; imprisoned in York Castle; escaped to Netherlands 1664; died in or after 1667

John Venn: b. 1586, politician, died 1650

Gregory Clement: b. 1594, politician, executed 1660

John Downes: bap. 1609, politician; reprieved from execution and imprisoned for life; died in the Tower in or after 1666

Thomas Waite: army officer; sentenced to life imprisonment; died imprisoned on Jersey in or after 1668

Thomas Scot (or Scott): politician; fled to Flanders 1660; subsequently returned to England under disputed circumstances and executed 1660

John Carew: b. 1622, politician and religious activist, executed 1660

Miles Corbet: b. 1594/5, politician; escaped to Netherlands, seized by George Downing along with Barkstead and Okey; forcibly returned and executed 1662

*Richard Ingoldsby and Thomas Challoner were exceptional in not being present when the king was sentenced, though they later signed the death warrant

Commissioners present when judgment was passed on the king but who did not sign the death warrant; numbering ten in total:

Francis Allen: merchant and politician, died 1658

Thomas Andrews: London merchant and Lord Mayor of London, died 1659

Thomas Hammond: b. before 1605, army officer, died 1651

Edmund Harvey: b. 1603(?), merchant; found guilty of treason 1660 but his life was spared; imprisoned 1661; died in Pendennis Castle, Cornwall, 1673

William Heveningham: b. 1604; sentenced to death 1660, spared and sentenced to life imprisonment; died in Windsor Castle, 1678

Cornelius Holland: b. 1559, courtier and politician; fled to Continent; died Vevey, Switzerland, 1671

John Lisle: b. 1610(?), lawyer and politician; fled to Continent 1660; assassinated Lausanne, 1664

Nicholas Love: b. 1608, lawyer and politician; fled to Continent 1660; died in exile, Vevey, 1682

Isaac Pennington: b. 1584(?), merchant and Lord Mayor of London; sentenced to life imprisonment 1660; died in the Tower 1661

Matthew Tomlinson: b. 1617, army officer; given custody of the king during his trial and up to his execution; avoided trial for treason in 1660; died 1681

Significant associates of the regicides:

Anthony Ascham: bap. 1614, diplomat and pamphleteer; assassinated Madrid, 1650

Daniel Axtell: bap. 1622, an officer of the guard at the trial of Charles I; executed 1660

Andrew Broughton: b. 1602/3, clerk to the High Court of Justice; died 1687/8

John Cook: bap. 1608, lawyer, solicitor-general and chief prosecutor at the trial of Charles I; executed 1660

Edward Dendy: bap. 1613, sergeant-at-arms for the court; arrest ordered 1660; fled and died Switzerland, 1674

John Desborough: b. 1608, leading parliamentarian soldier and politician; died 1680

Dr Isaac Dorislaus: b. 1595, scholar and diplomat, prosecution counsel for the trial of Charles I; assassinated in The Hague, 1649

Francis Hacker: officer commanding halberdiers at the trial of Charles I; signed the king's execution order; executed 1660

Sir Arthur Haselrig: b. 1601, parliamentarian soldier and important Commonwealth politician; died 1661

George Joyce: b. 1618, army officer; arrest ordered in 1660; fled to Rotterdam with wife and family; last heard of on the Continent 1670

John Lambert: b. 1619 (?), politician and landed parliamentarian soldier; died 1684

Hugh Peters (or Peter): bap. 1598, Puritan preacher and polemicist; executed 1660

John Phelps: b. 1619 (?), clerk to the High Court of Justice; died 1666 (?)

Algernon Sidney: b. 1623, aristocratic republican and political theorist; executed 1683

Sir Harry (Henry) Vane the younger: b. 1613, patrician Puritan and parliamentarian; executed 1662

APPENDIX II: PEOPLE

(An (r) denotes a 'regicide' – i.e. a signatory to the king's death warrant or a judge in the trial who voted for the king's guilt)

House of Stuart
King Charles I: succeeded to throne 1625; beheaded 1649.
Queen Henrietta Maria: Charles's widow
King Charles II: Charles' eldest son, reigned 1660–85
James, Duke of York: second son, reigned as James II 1685–8
Henry, Duke of Gloucester: third son
Henrietta Anne, Duchess of Orléans: daughter of Charles I

Royalists
Sir Heneage Finch: solicitor-general after 1660
Sir John Grenville: royal emissary
Sir Edward Hyde: Charles II's Chancellor, later Earl of Clarendon
John Mordaunt: leading royalist agent in England 1658–60
Marchmont Needham: master propagandist for the Stuarts (and for the Cromwellians)
Sir Edward Nicholas: secretary of state for Charles I and Charles II
Arundel Penruddock: widow of leader of the Penruddock uprising
William Prynne: archivist/lawyer, former critic of the crown
Silius Titus: courtier
Barbara Villiers: royal mistress
Lucy Walter: royal mistress

Cromwellians

Oliver Cromwell: Lord General 1649, Lord Protector 1653–8 (r)

Richard Cromwell: Lord Protector 1658–9

Sir Charles Coote: Anglo-Irish magnate

Sir George Downing: army intelligence chief

William Goffe: major-general (r)

Richard Ingoldsby: colonel (r)

Henry Ireton: general, Lord Deputy in Ireland and Cromwell's son-in-law (r)

George Monck: commander-in-chief in Scotland and suspected royalist

Thomas Pride: colonel, notorious for 'Pride's Purge' (r)

John Thurloe: secretary of state and spymaster

Sir Edward Whalley: major-general (r)

Parliamentary soldiers

John Desborough: general

Sir Thomas Fairfax: Lord General in first Civil War

Charles Fleetwood: commander-in-chief 1659

John Lambert: general

Republicans

John Bradshaw: President of High Court of Justice (r)

Thomas Harrison: cavalry general and religious extremist (r)

Sir Arthur Haselrig: MP and dominant voice in Rump Parliament 1659–60

John Lisle: MP, barrister (r)

Edmund Ludlow: commander-in-chief, Ireland (r)

Elizabeth Ludlow: wife of Edmund

John Milton: poet, parliamentary advisor on foreign affairs

Hugh Peters: Puritan preacher

Thomas Scot: Secretary of Council of State 1659–60 (r)

Algernon Sidney: aristocratic republican and political theorist

Sir Harry Vane: MP, political and religious radical

Officers of the guard during the trial
Daniel Axtell
Francis Hacker
Matthew Tomlinson

Covenanters
Archibald Campbell, Marquis of Argyll
Archibald Johnston, Laird of Wariston

Officials and advisors
Richard Brandon: public executioner
John Cook: lawyer, prosecutor in king's trial
Edward Dendy: sergeant-at-arms
Isaac Dorislaus: legal academic
Sir Bulstrode Whitelocke: lawyer MP

Spies, plotters and assassins
Joseph Bampfield: mercenary colonel
Aphra Behn: novelist
Abraham Kicke: merchant
Germaine (or John) Riordane: assassin
William Scot: son of executed regicide, double agent
Edward Sexby: disillusioned Cromwellian and royalist plotter
Miles Sindercombe: renegade Roundhead and hired assassin

NOTES

1 The Watchtower

1 Public Record Office (hereafter PRO), SP 29/86.
2 Edmund Ludlow, *Memoirs*, printed Vevey, Switzerland, 1698.
3 Maurice Ashley, *Charles II: The Man and Statesman*, 1971
4 Edmund Ludlow, *A Voyce from the Watchtower*, Part 5, 1660–62, ed. Blair Worden, Royal Historical Society, 1978.
5 Ibid.
6 Ibid.
7 *Letters of King Charles II*, ed. Arthur Bryant, 1931.
8 *Memoires de Mlle. De Montpensier*, ed. A. Cheruel, 1889.
9 Margaret, Duchess of Newcastle, *Life of the Duke of Newcastle*, ed. C.H. Firth, 1886.
10 Ibid.
11 Ibid.
12 'The Parliaments' Commission to the Earl of Essex to be Captain-General of their Army', *Acts and Ordinances of the Interregnum, 1642–60*, 1911.
13 Isaiah 21, 6–9.
14 Ludlow, *A Voyce*.

2 'That Man of Blood'

1 'Heads of the Proposals', 1647. See S. R. Gardiner, *Constitutional Documents of the Puritan Revolution*, http://www.constitution.org/eng/conpuro71.htm.
2 Sir William Clarke Papers, PRO.

3　Sarah Poynting, 'Deciphering the King: Charles I's letters to Jane Whorwood', *The Seventeenth Century* (2006), vol. 21, no. 1.

4　Ludlow, *Memoirs*.

5　Bulstrode Whitelocke, *Memorials of the English Affairs, 1625–1660*, London, republished 1860, vol. 2.

6　A true copy of a petition promoted in the army, 1648

7　*The Diary of Sir Bulstrode Whitelocke, 1605–1675*, ed. Ruth Spalding, OUP, 1990.

8　Marcus Tullius Cicero, *De Legibus*, Book III.

9　'A Remonstrance of His Excellency Thomas Lord Fairfax and the Council of Officers', 1648, PRO, SP 116/531.

10　*The Letters and Speeches of Oliver Cromwell*, ed. T. B. Macauley, Methuen, 1904.

11　Ibid.

12　According to S. R. Gardiner in *History of the Great Civil War*, London, 1888–94, the order came from Fairfax, but we can see that Ireton and others were to a large extent directing his actions.

13　Sir Thomas Herbert, *Threnodia Carolina or Memoirs of the Last Two Years of the Reign of Charles I*, 1678, pub. 1701.

14　Ibid.

15　Mark Noble, *Lives of the English Regicides*, 1798.

16　Earl of Clarendon, *History of the Rebellion and Civil Wars in England*, 1717.

17　Herbert, *Memoirs*.

18　*Perfect Occurrences*, 23–30 December 1648.

19　James I, *Basilikon Doron*, Edinburgh, 1599; London, 1603.

20　Spalding (ed.), *Diary*.

21　Thomason Collection of Civil War Tracts, British Library (hereafter BL), E537.

3 A Wicked Design

1　Christopher Hill, *The English Revolution 1640*, Lawrence and Wishart, 1940.

2　Ronald Mellor, 'Tacitus, Academic Politics and Regicide in the Reign of Charles I: the tragedy of Dr Isaac Dorislaus', *International Journal of the Classical Tradition*, vol. 11, no. 2, 2004.

3　For this insight, the authors are indebted to the human rights lawyer Geoffrey Robertson, QC.

4 'A Remonstrance of Lord Fairfax and the Council of Officers'. See Libertyfund.org for complete text.

5 C. H. Firth, *Dictionary of National Biography* (hereafter *DNB*), 1889.

6 J. Nalson, *A True Copy of the Journal of the High Court of Justice for the Tryal of King Charles I*, 4 January 1683, reprinted 1731. Almost all the descriptions of the trial are taken from this source, except where the version of Nalson published in William Cobbett's *State Trials*, 1809, 1810, is used, or that given in the more partisan royalist version of events by Gilbert Mabbott, 'A Perfect Narrative of the Whole Proceedings of the High Court of Justice, in the Trial of the King', printed 23 January 1648, in *Lord Somers's Tracts*, vol. 5, ed. W. Scott, 1811.

7 *Mercurius Pragmaticus*, January 1648, BL.

8 Clarendon, *History of the Rebellion*, vol. XI.

9 Ibid.

10 Nalson, *A True Copy*.

11 C. V. Wedgwood, *The Trial of Charles I*, Collins, 1964.

12 Anon., *The King's Tryal*, in Thomason Tracts, BL.

13 James I, *Basilikon Doron*.

14 J. Cook, *The Poor Man's Case*, 1648.

15 *The Moderate Intelligencer*, 16–23 January 1649, BL

16 S. R. Gardiner, *Constitutional Documents of the Puritan Revolution, 1625–60*, Clarendon Press, 1906.

17 Mabbott, 'Perfect Narrative'.

18 Ibid.

19 J. Cook, 'King Charles, His Case', 1649, in *The Trial of King Charles the First*, ed. J. G. Muddiman, 1928.

20 Thomas Smith, *De Republica Anglorum, the Manner of Government or Policie of the Realme of England*, written 1562–3, published 1583.

21 Mabbott, 'Perfect Narrative'.

22 Cobbett, *State Trials*, vol. V.

23 Geoffrey Robertson, *The Tyrannicide Brief*, Chatto & Windus, 2005.

24 *State Trials*, ed., Cobbett. Augustine Garland states he signed on the last day of the trial. His signature is the twenty-ninth on the warrant.

25 Ibid.

26 A. W. McIntosh, *DNB*, 'The Numbers of the English Regicides', *History*, vol. 67, Issue 220, January 1982.

4 Execution

1 Herbert, *Threnodia Carolina*.
2 Ibid.
3 Letter from Charles Stuart to General Fairfax from The Hague, 23 January 1649, from *Letters of Charles II*, ed. Bryant.
4 Clarke Papers, PRO.
5 Ibid.
6 *The Confession of Richard Brandon, Hang-man*, London, 1649.
7 Clarendon, *History of the Rebellion*, XII.
8 'Sir Thomas Herbert's Narrative Concluded', in *Charles I in Captivity from Contemporary Sources*, ed. Gertrude Scott Stevenson, 1927.
9 Ibid.
10 Ibid.
11 'Sir Henry Halford's Report to the Prince Regent, in 1813, on the Discovery and Examination of the body of King Charles I', contained in *Charles I in Captivity*, ed. Stevenson.
12 Letter from Sir Thomas Herbert to Sir William Dugdale, 3 November 1681, quoted in *Memoirs of the Martyr King*, ed. Alan Fea, London, 1905.

5 Propaganda and Assassination

1 F. F. Madan, *A New Bibliography of the Eikon Basilike*, 1950.
2 L. Potter, *Secret Rites and Secret Writings: Royalist Literature 1640–1660*, Cambridge University Press, 1989.
3 Philip A. Knachel, ed., introduction to *Eikon Basilike*, Cornell University Press, 1966
4 Society of King Charles the Martyr, http://www.skcm.org/SCharles/Eikon_Basilike/eikon_basilike.html
5 A. Lacey, *The Cult of King Charles the Martyr*, Boydell Press, 2003.
6 Ibid.
7 John Milton, *The Tenure of Kings and Magistrates*, London, 1649.
8 Ibid.
9 Ibid. Here Milton is quoting Claude de Seyssel, *La Grande Monarchie de France*, 1519.
10 Thomas Hobbes, *De Cive*. Although this was released in limited form in 1642, it was not generally published until 1647.
11 Ibid.
12 Thomas Hobbes, *Leviathan*, 1651.

13 Bob Clarke, *From Grub Street to Fleet Street*, Ashgate, 2004.

14 C. V. Wedgwood, *The King's War*, Collins, 1958.

15 Francis Cheynell, *Aulicus, his dream, of the king's sudden coming*, 1644.

16 Clarke, *Grub Street to Fleet Street*.

17 *A Collection of the State Papers of John Thurloe*, 1742.

18 John Taylor, *Mercurius Melancholicus, Craftie Cromwell and His Murderous Crew, a Tragi-Comedie*, 1647.

19 Quoted in J. T. Peacey, 'Order and Disorder in Europe: Parliamentary Agents and Royalist Thugs 1649–1650', *The Historical Journal*, vol. 40, no. 4, 1997.

20 Ibid.

21 Related in *The Regicides and the Execution of Charles I*, ed. J. T. Peacey, Palgrave Macmillan, 2001.

22 *Perfect Diurnall*, no. 315, 6–13 August 1649.

23 Robert Chambers, *History of the Rebellions in Scotland under the Marquis of Montrose*, 1828.

24 George Wishart, *The Memoirs of James, Marquis of Montrose*, London, 1819.

25 Peacey, 'Order and Disorder'.

26 F. Peck, *Desiderata Curiosa*, 2 vols, London 1779; P. A. Maccioni and M. Mostert, 'Isaac Dorislaus', *Transactions of the Cambridge Bibliographical Society*, no. 8 (1981–4).

27 S. R. Gardiner, *History of the Commonwealth and Protectorate*, vol. 1, 1897.

28 Peacey, 'Order and Disorder'.

29 Ibid.

30 *DNB*.

31 A. Ascham, *A Discourse*, 1648 (revised 1649); *The Bounds and Bonds of Publique Obedience*, 1649.

32 Whitelocke, *Memorials of the English Affairs*.

33 Gardiner, *History of the Commonwealth*, vol. 1.

34 According to Whitelocke, writing not long after the events, he was employed by Hyde; according to Peacey's researches, by Cottington.

35 Peacey, 'Order and Disorder'.

36 John Evelyn, *Diaries*, vol. 2, Oxford, 1955.

37 For this disgraceful episode, see D. Jordan and M. Walsh, *White Cargo: The Forgotten History of Britain's White Slaves in America*, Mainstream, 2007.

38 The whole tale, so well known, is told in Gardiner, *History of the Commonwealth*, vol. 2, and in A. Fea, *The Flight of the King*, 1897.

6 'The Honour of Dying for the People'

1 Ludlow, *Memoirs*.

2 For complete document wording, see *Internet Modern History Sourcebook*: http://www.fordham.edu/halsall/mod/1653instrument-govt.asp

3 *The Instrument of Government*, Clause VI.

4 For a discussion of the evidence concerning the founding of the Sealed Knot, see David Underdown, *Royalist Conspiracy in England, 1649–1660*, Yale University Press, 1960.

5 Thurloe, *State Papers*, vol. 2.

6 Clarendon, *State Papers*, vol. 2.

7 *The Life of Edward, Earl of Clarendon, including a continuation of his History of the Grand Rebellion*, Oxford, 1857.

8 Thurloe, *State Papers*, vol. 2.

9 See S. R. Gardiner, *History of the Commonwealth*, vol. 3.

10 *A Treasonable Plot Discovered*, 1654, anon., BL.

11 Philip Aubrey, *Mr Secretary Thurloe*, Athlone Press, 1989.

12 *Weekly Intelligencer*, 1654, nos 243–4; *Mercurius Politicus*, nos 206–8.

13 Thurloe, *State Papers*.

14 *The Triall of Mr John Gerhard*. See: file:///Users/anonanon/Desktop/The%20Triall%20of%20Mr.%20John%20Gerhard%20 ... webarchive

15 Underdown, *Royalist Conspiracy in England*.

16 *Triall of Mr John Gerhard*.

17 Thurloe, *State Papers*.

18 *Life of Edward, Earl of Clarendon*, p. 25.

19 C. Durston, *Cromwell's Major-Generals*, Manchester University Press, 2001.

20 For the reasons transportation was often feared more than death, see Jordan and Walsh, *White Cargo*.

21 Perhaps the best telling of this episode is to be found in Peter Beresford Ellis, *Hell or Connaught, The Cromwellian Colonisation of Ireland, 1652–1660*, Hamish Hamilton, 1975.

22 Sir Henry Vane, *A Healing Question propounded and resolved, upon the late public and seasonable Call to Humiliation, in order to Love*

and Union amongst the Honest Party, London, 1656. Full text:
http://www.constitution.org/lev/healing.htm.

23 Cobbett, *State Trials*, vol. V, p. 841.

24 *Killing No Murder, Briefly Discussed in Three Questions, by William Allen*, 1657, BL, 100.f.41.

25 In later editions of *Killing No Murder*, Titus is named as the author – as in the edition of 1689, BL, RB.23.a.7072.

26 Charles II, letter to Lord Mordaunt, 17 April 1660, in *Letters of Charles II*, ed. Bryant.

27 Quoted in C. H. Firth, *Last Years of the Protectorate*, vol. II, 1909.

7 After Oliver

1 A *true and faithful narrative of Oliver Cromwell's compact with the Devil*.

2 *The Publick Intelligencer*, November 1658, BL.

3 Abraham Cowley, A *vision concerning his late pretended highness Cromwell the wicked*, 1658.

4 Thomas Burton, *Diary*.

5 Mark Noble, *Lives of the English Regicides*.

6 Abraham Cowley, A *Discourse on the Government of Oliver Cromwell*.

7 N. H. Keeble, *The Restoration*, Oxford: Blackwell, 2002

8 Clarendon, *History of the Rebellion*

9 Ronald Hutton, *The Restoration*, Oxford University Press, 1993.

10 Burton, *Diary*.

11 Clarendon, *State Papers*, vol. III.

12 Ludlow, *Voyce*.

13 M. Guizot, *The History of Richard Cromwell and the Restoration of Charles II*, Richard Bently, 1856.

14 Ibid.

15 Burton, *Diary*.

16 E. Budgell, *Memoirs of the Boyles*, 1737.

17 Burton, *Diary*

18 Masson, D., *The Life of John Milton*, Macmillan, 1873.

19 Woolrych, A., *Britain in Revolution*, Oxford University Press, 2001.

20 C. H. Firth, *Cromwell's Army*, Greenhill, 1992.

21 D. Underdown, *Royalist Conspiracy in England*.

22 Newsletter, Clarke Papers, 15 October 1659, PRO.

8 The Invader

1 Ludlow, *Voyce*.
2 Thurloe, *State Papers*, vol. 6.
3 François Guizot, *Memoirs of George Monck, Duke of Albermarle*, 1838.
4 Clarendon, *State Papers*, vol. III, PRO.
5 John Price, *The Mystery and the Method of His Majesty's Happy Restoration*.
6 Ibid.
7 Ibid.
8 Ibid.
9 Clarendon MSS, IXV, fol. 35, 15 October 1659.
10 Egerton MSS, fol. 457.
11 *The Parliamentary or Constitutional History of England From the Earliest Times to the Restoration of King Charles II* (MDCCLXIII), vol. 22.
12 Clarke Papers, vol. 4.
13 François Guizot, *Monck or the Fall of the Republic and the Restoration of the Monarchy in England*, Henry G. Bohn, 1851.
14 Clarke Papers.
15 Spalding (ed.), *The Diary of Sir Bulstrode Whitelocke*.
16 Price, *Mystery and Method*.
17 Masson.
18 Clarke Papers.
19 Pepys, *Diary*, 18 January 1660.
20 Clarendon, *History of the Rebellion*.
21 Spalding (ed.), *Diary*.
22 Clarke Papers.
23 William Dawson, *Cromwell's Understudy*, William Hodge & Co.
24 Pepys, *Diary*, 18 January 1660.
25 Clarke Papers.
26 John Aubrey, *Brief Lives*, 1626–95.
27 Ruth Mayers, *The Crisis of the Commonwealth*, University of Chicago Press, 2006.
28 Guizot, *Monck and the Fall of the Republic*.
29 T. Gumble, *Life of Monck*, 1672.
30 Thomas Skinner, *The Life of General Monck*, 1724.
31 Pepys, *Diary*, 7 February 1660.

32 Ludlow, *Voyce*.

33 Ludlow, *Memoirs*.

34 *House of Commons Journal* (hereafter *HCJ*), vol. 7, 13 February 1660.

35 Patrick Morrah, *1660: The Year of Restoration*, Chatto & Windus, 1907.

9 The Round-up Begins

1 Sir Arthur Forbes, letter to Marquis of Ormond, Clarendon, *State Papers*.

2 Geoffrey Robertson, *The Tyrannicide Brief*.

3 Ibid.

4 J. Cook, *A Sober Vindication of Colonel Ludlow*, 1660.

5 Pepys, *Diary*, 6 March 1660.

6 Thomas Rugge, *Diurnal*, Royal Historical Society.

7 John Price, *Mystery and Method*.

8 Ronald Hutton, *The Restoration*.

9 Clarendon, *State Papers*.

10 Pepys, *Diary*, 8 March 1660.

11 Samborn, letter to Hyde, 2 March 1660, Bodleian Library.

12 Clarendon, *State Papers*.

13 Pepys, *Diary*, 8 March 1660.

14 Anonymous correspondent to Hyde, 23 March 1660. *Life and Administration of England*, 1st Earl of Clarendon, vol. 2.

15 Clarke Papers.

16 Edmund Burke, *Dodsley's Annual Register*, 1774.

17 B. D. Henning, *History of the House of Commons 1660–1690*, Secker and Warburg, 1983.

18 Ludlow, *Memoirs*.

19 François Guizot, *Memoirs of George Monck, Duke of Albermarle*, 1838.

20 Ibid.

21 Ludlow, *Memoirs*.

22 Clarke Papers.

23 *Mercurius Politicus*, 19–26 April, *Mercurius Civicus*, 17–26 April.

10 Exodus

1 Mark Noble, *Lives of the English Regicides*.

2 William Howell, *Medulla Historiæ Anglicanæ. Being a comprehensive history of the lives and reigns of the monarchs of England*.

3   Henry Hallam, *The Constitutional History of England*, John Murray, 1850.
4   Gilbert Burnet, *History of My Own Time*, 1724.
5   William Cobbett, *Cobbett's Complete Collection of State Trials*, 1809.
6   Edmund Burke, *Letter to a Member of the National Assembly*, vol. 6 of his *Works*, octavo edition, 1808.
7   Letter from Charles II to George Monck, 10–20 May 1660.
8   *HCJ*, vol. 11, 29 August 1660.
9   Clarendon, letter endorsed by Edward Hyde, 23 March 1660.
10 Lemuel Aiken Welles, *The History of the Regicides in New England*, 1927.
11 *HCJ*, vol. 8, 12 May 1660.
12 David Masson, *The Life of John Milton*, Macmillan, 1874.
13 *DNB, Verulam MSS*, 58.
14 Clarendon, *History of the Rebellion*.
15 Ludlow, *Voyce*.
16 *Parliamentary Intelligencer*, 14 May 1660.
17 C. H. Firth, 'Thomas Smith's the guilt of blood as an intelligencer', *English Historical Review* XII, 1897.
18 Thomas Burton, *Diary*.
19 David Masson, *Life of John Milton*, 1873.

11 Death List

1   *HCJ*, 9 May 1660.
2   Ludlow, *Memoirs*.
3   Ludlow, *Voyce*.
4   *Confession of Richard Brandon, Hang-man*.
5   W. Lilly, *The last of the astrologers, Mr William Lilly*, Folklore Society, 1974.
6   Masson, *Life of John Milton*.
7   Ludlow, *Memoirs*.
8   *Life of Edward, Earl of Clarendon*, Oxford, 1857.
9   Spalding (ed.), *The Diary of Bulstrode Whitelocke*.
10 *HCJ*, 9 May 1660.
11 William Carlos Martin, *Life and Times of Milton*.
12 Fleetwood to Monck, Clarke Papers, vol. 4, 25 October 1659.
13 J. R. Jones, 'Political Groups and Tactics in the Convention of 1660', *Historical Journal*, 1 June 1963.

14 *HCJ*, vol. 8, 13–18 June 1660.
15 Masson, *Life of John Milton*.
16 John Price, *The Mystery and method of His Majesty's happy restaura-tion*, 1815.
17 *A true narrative in a letter written to Col B. R. of the apprehension of the grand traitor Thomas Scot*.
18 Lucy Hutchinson, *Memoirs of the Life of Col. John Hutchinson* (c. 1670).
19 C. H. Firth, 'Thomas Scot's account of his actions as an intelligencer during the Commonwealth', *English Historical Review*, 1897.
20 *The Diary of John Evelyn*, Routledge/Thoemmes, 1996.
21 *House of Lords Journal* (hereafter *HLJ*), vol. XI, p. 104.
22 Douglas C. Wilson, 'Whalley & Goffe', *New England Quarterly*, December 1987.
23 *Col. Papers*, vol. XV, no. 82.
24 *HLJ*, vol. XI, 7 September 1660.
25 Ludlow, *Memoirs*.
26 *Mercurius Publicus*, 30 August–6 September 1660.
27 Patrick Morragh, *1660: The Year of Restoration*, Chatto & Windus, 1960.

12 'The Guilt of Blood'

1 Cobbett, *State Trials*, vol. V.
2 *Letters of Charles II*, ed. Bryant.
3 Burnet, *History of My Own Times*.
4 Roger Sharrock, introduction to the Penguin edition of *The Pilgrim's Progress*, 1965.
5 Robertson, *Tyrannicide Brief*.
6 *An Exact and Most Impartial Account of the Indictment, Arraignment, Trial and Judgement (According to Law) of Nine and Twenty Regicides*, 1660; *Parliamentary Intelligencer*, nos 13 and 14, Thomason Tracts, BL; *The Speeches and Prayers of the Regicides*, 1660, Thomason Tracts, BL.
7 Regnal. 25, Edward 3, Statute 5, section 3, PRO: http://www.legislation.gov.uk/aep/Edw3Stat5/25/2/section/II.
8 Ludlow, *Voyce*.
9 Quoted in Cobbett, *State Trials*.
10 This is the version according to Cobbett. According to Kenyng, the

misspelling was Martyn.

11 *DNB.*

12 Pepys, *Diary*, vol. 1, 1660.

13 *Diary of John Evelyn*, ed. William Bray, vol. 1, 1901. The term 'oyer and terminer' is from Anglo-French, meaning 'hearing and determination'.

14 Cobbett, *State Trials.*

15 *HCJ*, 4 January 1642: http://www.parliament.uk/business/publications/-parliamentary-archives/archives-highlights/archives-speakerlenthall/.

16 *Dictionary of National Welsh Biography*, Honourable Society of Cymmrodorion, 2001.

13 Damned If You Do, Damned If You Don't

1 *DNB.*

2 *An Exact and Most Impartial Account* (see note 6 on p. 351).

3 *DNB.*

4 Cobbett, *State Trials.*

5 Cobbett, *State Trials.*

6 *DNB.*

7 Cobbett, *State Trials.*

8 Herbert, *Threnodia Carolina.*

9 *Speeches and Prayers of the Regicides* (see note 6 on p. 351).

10 Ibid.

11 Ibid.

12 *DNB.*

13 *An Exact and Most Impartial Account.*

14 Ludlow, *Memoirs.*

15 *An Exact and Most Impartial Account.*

16 Evelyn, *Diary*, Clarendon Press Association.

14 Disinterred

1 Burnet, *History of My Own Times.*

2 Clarendon, *State Papers.*

3 'Order for exhumation of Oliver Cromwell . . .' in Browning, *English Historical Documents 1660–1714.*

4 H. F. McMains, *The Death of Oliver Cromwell*, University Press of Kentucky, 1999.

5   Pepys, *Diary*, 4 December 1660.
6   *HCJ*.
7   Cobbett, *State Trials*.
8   R. L. Greaves and R. Zaller, eds, *Biographical Dictionary of British Radicals in the Seventeenth Century*, 1982.
9   Ibid.
10 *HLJ*.
11 Pepys, *Diary*.
12 Burnet, *History of My Own Times*.
13 Samuel Johnson, *Harleian Miscellany of Tracts*.
14 Thomas Rugg, *The Diurnal of Thomas Rugg*.
15 McMains, *The Death of Oliver Cromwell*.
16 James Heath, *The glories and magnificent triumphs of the restitution of King Charles II*, 1662.
17 John Howie, *The Life of the Honourable Archibald Campbell Marquis of Argyle*, Biographia Scoticana.

15 Bloodhounds

1   *Collections of the Massachusetts Historical Society*.
2   *Calendar of State Papers, Colonial* (hereafter *CSP Col*), vol. XV, 49–51.
3   Ibid.
4   Benjamin Brook, 'John Davenport', in *The Lives of the Puritans*, vol. 3.
5   Lemuel A. Welles, *The History of the Regicides in New England*, 1927.
6   William Emerson, *An Historical Sketch of the First Church in Boston*, Boston 1812.
7   Samuel Knapp, ed., *Library of American History* or The Hutchinson Papers, British Library.
8   *CSP Col*, vol. XV, 82.
9   John Beresford, *The Godfather of Downing Street*, R. Cobden-Sanderson, 1925.
10 Alan Marshall, *Intelligence and Espionage in the Reign of Charles II*, 1994.
11 R. J. Minney, 'No. 10 Downing Street, a house in history', 1963, quoting a contemporary manuscript.
12 G. Downing, letter to Thurloe, 19 August 1659, Thurloe, *State Papers* VII.
13 Downing, correspondence between Howard and the Marquis of

Ormond, March–April 1660, in 'A collection of original letters and papers concerning the affairs of England 1641–1660 by Thomas Carte', 1739.

14 Letter from Downing to the Earl of Clarendon, 6–16 June 1661. Lister, *Life of Clarendon*, vol. III.

15 S. R. Gardiner, *History of the Great Civil War*.

16 C. V. Wedgwood, *The Trial of Charles I*.

17 Letters from Downing to the Earl of Clarendon, June, July 1661. Lister, *Life of Clarendon*.

18 Ibid.

19 Ralph C. Catterail, 'Sir George Downing and the Regicides', *American Historical Review*, January 1913.

16 On the Word of a King

1 House of Commons Proceedings, vol. 1, 20 November 1661.

2 George Downing to the Earl of Clarendon, 9 December 1661.

3 Pepys, *Diary*, 27 January 1662.

4 *HLJ*, 5 September 1660.

5 *HLJ*, 8 September 1660.

6 *CSP*. Relating to English Affairs in the Archives of Venice, vol. 33, 1661–4.

7 *The Journal of William Schellincks' Travels in England 1661–3*, ed. Exwood and Lehmann, 1993.

8 Mark Noble, *Lives of the English Regicides*.

9 Pepys, *Diary*, 14 June 1666.

10 James Aikman, *Annals of the Persecution in Scotland from the Restoration to the Revolution*.

11 *The Crimes and Treason of Archibald Johnston, Lord Wariston*, 1663.

12 *Colonial State Papers, Domestic* (hereafter *CSP Dom*), 15–17 December 1662.

13 Marshall, *Intelligence and Espionage*.

14 *CSP Dom*, vol. LXV, 12, 24 January 1663.

15 Ibid.

16 Burnet, *History of My Own Times*.

17 Ibid.

18 Aikman, *Annals*.

17 The Tightening Net

1   For a glimpse of Elizabeth Ludlow in action in 1660 when her husband was in danger of being 'called in' and imprisoned, see his *Memoirs*, ed. Firth, vol. 2.

2   Ibid.

3   *Mercurius Politicus*, 3–10 September 1660.

4   Ludlow, *Memoirs*.

5   Ibid.

6   Clarendon, *State Papers*.

7   Unfortunately, we have no corroborating evidence for this plot. The sole source is Ludlow's heavily rewritten and edited diary as it appeared in 1698.

8   Ludlow, *Memoirs*.

9   *DNB*.

10 Ibid.

11 *The Apology of Algernon Sidney*, 1763.

12 Edmund Ludlow, *A Voyce from the Watchtower*, Bodleian MS, quoted in Jonathan Scott, *Algernon Sidney and the English Republic, 1623–1677*, 1988.

13 Algernon Sidney, *Court Maxims*, ed. H. W. Blom, E. H. Mulier, R. J. Janse, Cambridge University Press, 1996.

14 Blair Worden, ed, Edmund Ludlow, *A Voyce From the Watchtower*, 1978, and Sidney, *Court Maxims*.

15 Letter from William Cawley to J. H. Hummel, 26 November 1663.

16 Ludlow, *Memoirs*.

17 Letter from Riordane, appendix to Ludlow, *Memoirs*, 1894.

18 Ludlow, *Memoirs*.

19 Intercepted letter from the fugitives in Vevey. *CSP Dom*, 1663–4.

20 Ludlow, *Memoirs*.

21 *CSP Dom*, vol. LXXXVI. Riordane's statement is dated 19 December 1663, some weeks after the raid on Vevey, yet sets out what appears to be a blueprint for the raid. Either the dating is incorrect, or Riordane is simply reporting back and laying out a further plan, this time to abduct the regicides and take them to England. This seems the most likely conclusion as the raid in November appeared to be focused solely on Ludlow, while in the report in December, Riordane speaks of the regicides in the plural.

22 *CSP Dom*, vol. LXXXVI. 1663.

23 Ludlow, *Memoirs*.

24 Anthony à Wood, *Athenae Oxonienis*, 1721; ed. Bliss, 1813.

25 Ludlow, *Memoirs*; B. O'Cuiv, 'James Cotter, A seventeenth century agent of the Crown', *Journal of the Society of Antiquaries of Ireland*, 1959, vol. 80, no. 2.

26 Marshall, *Intelligence and Espionage*.

27 *Col. Papers*, folio XLII, No. 135.

18 Plans to Invade and Hopes Dashed

1 Ludlow, *Voyce*.

2 *CSP Dom*, vol. CLXXII, 1666.

3 Ludlow, *Voyce*.

4 Ibid.

5 Ibid.

6 *CSP Dom*, vol. CLXXII, 1666.

7 Ibid.

8 R. L. Greaves, *Enemies Under His Feet: Radicals and Nonconformists in Britain, 1664–77*, Stanford University Press, 1990.

9 Ludlow, *Memoirs*.

10 A. Boyer, *Memoirs of the Life and Negotiations of Sir W. Temple, 1665–1681*, 1714.

11 A. Sidney, *Discourses Concerning Government*, first published posthumously 1698.

12 *The Arraignment, Tryal and Condemnation of Algernon Sidney Esq., etc.*, London, 1684.

BIBLIOGRAPHY

As with any bibliography of works and sources relating to the seventeenth century, what follows hardly scratches the surface. It is intended by way of a general list of some works of scholarship the authors found helpful – and in many cases invaluable – and of a small number of key contemporary sources. For a fuller appreciation of the wide range of material consulted, the reader must refer to the references in the text or to the chapter notes. As for the body of seventeenth-century material itself, much of it is to be found in the British Library, with its wealth of data, including the Thomason Collection of Civil War tracts; at the Bodleian Library in Oxford with the Burney Collection of early newspapers and pamphlets; and the vast collections of the National Archives at Kew, where so much of British history resides, including Sir William Clarke's state papers; and at the Houses of Parliament at Westminster, where the Parliamentary Archives hold the records of proceedings, including the Death Warrant of Charles I.

Ashley, M., *Charles II, The Man and Statesman* (Weidenfeld & Nicolson, 1971)
—— *Cromwell's Generals* (Jonathan Cape, 1954)
Aubrey, J., *Brief Lives* (1626–95)
Aubrey, P., *Mr Secretary Thurloe* (Athlone Press, 1989)
Brandon, R., *The Confession of Richard Brandon, Hang-man* (1649)
Bryant, A., *King Charles II* (1931)

Budgell, E., *Memoirs of the Boyles* (1737)

Burnet, G., *Bishop Burnet's History of My Own Times* (1650)

Burton, T., *The Diary of Thomas Burton MP, 1656–1659* (1828)

Carlyle, T. B., *Cromwell, Oliver, Letters and Speeches* (1904)

Chapman, H., *The Tragedy of Charles II 1630–1660* (Jonathan Cape, 1964)

Charles I (posthumously in his name), *Eikon Basilike* (1649)

Cobbett, William, ed., *State Trials* (1809 and 1810)

Cook, J., *King Charles, His Case, an Appeal to All Rational Men, concerning His Tryall at the High Court of Justice* (1649)

Coward, B., 'Why Charles I was executed', *History Review* (1 December 1998)

Cowley, A., *A vision concerning his late pretended highness Cromwell the wicked* (1658)

Dictionary of National Biography (2004)

Falkus, C., *The Life and Times of Charles II* (Weidenfeld & Nicolson, 1992)

Firth, C. H., *The Last Years of the Protectorate* (1909)

—— *Oliver Cromwell and the Rule of the Puritans in England* (1900)

Gardiner, S. R., *History of the Commonwealth and Protectorate* (1897)

—— *History of the Great Civil War* (1893)

Greaves, R. L., and R. Zaller, eds, *Biographical Dictionary of British Radicals in the 17th Century* (Harvester Press, 1982)

Guizot, F., *Memoirs of George Monck, Duke of Albermarle* (1838)

Gumble, T., *La Vie du General Monk, Duc d'Albemarle* (1672)

Herbert, T., *Threnodia Carolina* (1678)

Hill, C., *Puritanism and Revolution* (Secker & Warburg, 1958)

—— *Milton and the English Revolution* (Faber & Faber, 1970)

—— *God's Englishman: Oliver Cromwell* (Penguin, 1970)

Holmes, C., *Why Was Charles I Executed?* (Hambledon Continuum, 2006)

—— 'The Trial and Execution of Charles I', *Historical Journal*, Vol. 53

Howell, W., *Medulla Historiæ Anglicanæ. Being a comprehensive history of the lives and reigns of the monarchs of England* (1679)

Hughes, A., 'The Causes of the English Civil War', in *Revolutions and the Revolutionary Tradition in the West*, ed. Parker (Routledge, 2000)

Hutchinson, L., *Memoirs of the Life of Col. John Hutchinson* (c. 1670)

Hutchinson, T., *The History of the Province of Massachusetts Bay* (1765)

James, J. R., 'Political Groups in the Convention of 1660', *Historical Journal*, June 1663

Keeble, N. H., *The Restoration* (Blackwell, 2002)

Lacey, A., *The Cult of King Charles the Martyr* (Boydell Press, 2003)

Ludlow, Edmund, *A Voyce from the Watchtower*, ed. B. Worden (1978)
—— *Memoirs*, ed. Firth (1794)

Mabbott, G., *Perfect Narrative of the High Court of Justice* (1649)

Marshall, A., *Intelligence and Espionage in the Reign of Charles II, 1660–1685* (Cambridge University Press, 1994)

Masson, D., *Life of John Milton* (Macmillan, 1873)

McIntosh, A. W., 'The Numbers of the English Regicides', *Journal of the Historical Association*, Vol. 67, issue 220, 1982.

McMains, H. F., *The Death of Oliver Cromwell* (University Press of Kentucky, 1999)

Muddiman, J. G., *The Trial of King Charles I* (1649)

Nalson, J., *A True Copy of the Journal of the High Court of Justice for the Tryal of Charles I* (1684; 1731)

Noble, M., *Lives of the English Regicides* (1798)

Ogg, David, *England in the Reign of Charles II* (Clarendon Press, 1955)

Peacey, J. T., 'Order and Disorder in Europe: Parliamentary Agents and Royalist Thugs, 1649–1650', in *The Historical Journal*, 40, 4, 1997
———— ed., *The Regicides and the Execution of Charles I* (Palgrave Macmillan, 2001)

Price, J., *The Mystery and the Method of His Majesty's Happy Restoration*, 1680

Roberts, Stephen, *Politics and People in Revolutionary England* (Blackwell, 1986).

Robertson, Geoffrey, *The Tyrannicide Brief* (Chatto & Windus, 2005)

Schellinks, W., *The journal of William Schellinks' travels in England 1661–3*, eds M. Exwood and H. L. Lehmann (Camden Society, 1993)

Skinner, T., *The Life of General Monck* (1724)

Sidney, Algernon, *Works* (1772)

Stevenson, G., ed., *Charles I in Captivity: From Contemporary Sources* (1927)

Underdown, D., *Pride's Purge, Politics in the Puritan Revolution* (Oxford University Press, 1971)

—— *Royalist Conspiracy in England* (Yale University Press, 1960)

Wedgwood, C. V., *The Trial of Charles I* (Collins, 1964)

Welles, L., *The History of the Regicides in New England* (1927)

Wheale, N., *Writing and Society: Literacy, Print and Politics in Britain, 1590–1660* (Routledge, 1999)

Whitelocke, B., *Memorials of the English Affairs* (1682)

Worden, B., *The Rump Parliament, 1648–53* (Oxford University Press, 1974)

—— *Roundhead Reputations* (Penguin, 2001)

ACKNOWLEDGEMENTS

We owe a huge debt to Tim Whiting of Little, Brown for his encouragement and belief in this project and to his brilliant team, especially the ever meticulous Vivien Redman, group managing editor, and Claudia Dyer, commissioning editor, who together did much more than weed out any dross from our prose. We are also indebted to Linda Silverman, picture editor, who discovered seventeenth-century images that we didn't know existed, and to Edward Vallance, who read the manuscript and suggested crucial improvements. Thanks also to copy-editor Steve Gove, proofreader Dan Balado-Lopez and indexer Mark Wells. Staff at the British Library and the National Archives are owed our gratitude too, as is John Goldsmith, curator of the Cromwell Museum in Huntingdon. We would also like to thank our agent Charlie Viney, but most of all we are indebted to our wives, Eithne MacMahon and Dian Proctor Walsh, our most stringent and supportive critics.

INDEX

To buy any of our books and to find out
more about Abacus and Little, Brown, our authors
and titles, as well as events and book clubs,
visit our website

www.littlebrown.co.uk

and follow us on Twitter

**@AbacusBooks
@LittleBrownUK**

To order any Abacus titles p & p free in the UK,
please contact our mail order supplier on:

+ 44 (0)1832 737525

Customers not based in the UK should contact
the same number for appropriate postage
and packing costs.